FREDERICK ASALS

Flannery O'Connor

The Imagination of Extremity

The University of Georgia Press
Athens, Georgia

Copyright © 1982 by the University of Georgia Press
Athens, Georgia 30602
All rights reserved

Designed by Sandra Strother
Woodcut by Michael McCurdy
Set in 10 on 13 Trump Medieval type
Printed in the United States of America

95 96 97 98 99   P   7 6 5 4 3

Library of Congress Cataloging in Publication Data

Asals, Frederick,
    Flannery O'Connor, the imagination of extremity.

    Bibliography: p.
    Includes index.
    1. O'Connor, Flannery—Criticism and
interpretation.   I. Title.
PS3565.C57Z52   813'.54   81-10513
ISBN 0-8203-0592-8   AACR2
ISBN 0-8203-0839-0 (pbk.)

FOR HEATHER

Contents

Acknowledgments

I wish to thank Robert Fitzgerald for allowing me to quote from unpublished material in the Flannery O'Connor Collection at Georgia College. In my use of that material, Gerald Becham, curator of the collection, was always most helpful, and Charles Beard and the staff of the Ina Dillard Russell Library gave me every assistance in my work there. Through their generous help and friendship, Mary Barbara and James Tate were in good measure responsible for making my visits to Milledgeville, Georgia, not only research trips but rich and pleasurable events.

My thanks to *Renascence* for permitting me to use in a different form parts of my essay "The Road to *Wise Blood*" (21 [1969]: 181–94); and to the *Flannery O'Connor Bulletin* for allowing me to reemploy the materials of "Flannery O'Connor as Novelist: A Defense" (3 [1974]: 23–39) and "The Double in Flannery O'Connor's Stories" (9 [1980]: 49–86).

I am very grateful to the Canada Council for a leave grant that assisted me in the writing of this book.

Hyatt Waggoner and George Monteiro gave me aid, advice, and encouragement when, long ago, I first began my inquiry into Flannery O'Connor's work. Lorine Getz and Peter Dyson managed to plow through the entire manuscript at a much later stage and offered valuable commentary on it. Ruth Reiffenstein, acting beyond the call of duty, patiently typed everything from the often messy pages I handed her. And, in an entirely different way, my children, Katharine, Sarah, and David, have helped to keep me within my own limits of extremity (while now and then sending me for a look at the borders thereof). My greatest debt is suggested in the dedication.

Note on Citations

Citations of Flannery O'Connor's works in the text refer to the following editions:

The Complete Stories. New York: Farrar, Straus and Giroux, 1971.
The Habit of Being. Edited by Sally Fitzgerald. New York: Farrar, Straus and Giroux, 1979.
Mystery and Manners. Edited by Sally Fitzgerald and Robert Fitzgerald. New York: Farrar, Straus and Giroux, 1969.
The Violent Bear It Away. New York: Farrar, Straus and Cudahy, 1960.
Wise Blood. New York: Farrar, Straus and Cudahy, 1962.

Introduction

Powerful is a word that seems to have become indispensable in speaking of Flannery O'Connor's fiction. Reviewers and critics have applied it repeatedly, and I have heard the term again and again from the lips of both inexperienced students and sophisticated readers. Not all, to be sure, have been admirers; but however outraged or repelled, very few, it appears, have emerged indifferent from an encounter with O'Connor's writing. Part of the impact of her work no doubt derives from some of its more obvious elements—strong narrative line, mordantly comic characters, violent action—but such isolated features seem insufficient to account fully for the effect so often remarked. Beyond any individual elements (yet of course including them), it appears to be the totality of her vision, the entire expression of her imagination, that creates a sense of Flannery O'Connor's literary power.

Now, however inarguable in the experience of individual readers, *power* is a little imprecise as a critical category, and the deepest springs of such power in the writer's imagination are probably (whatever psychologists and sociologists claim) finally hidden from us. Still, the expressions of that imagination are available, and the sources *within* the fiction that give rise to the impression of literary force can perhaps be indicated. It seems to me that central to the perceived power of O'Connor's writing is what Henry James called a "rich passion . . . for extremes,"[1] an attraction to polarities that reaches into every aspect of her work. That in itself may not be remarkable: one could point to a number of other writers, ancient and

I

modern, who might be so described. In O'Connor, however, extremes govern not only the matter of her fiction but the form as well, and while the antipodal perspectives introduced are played with and explored, characteristically they are not resolved. Rather than merging, blending, informing one another, they are sustained in a set of vibrant tensions that seem to open ever wider, to strain furiously toward a breaking point.

There are several ways these felt tensions, this "passion for extremes," might be approached, some suggested by O'Connor herself. One evident way would involve the venerable distinction to which James's phrase was in fact applied, that between novel and romance—or, in O'Connor's more characteristic language, between manners and mystery. She read and apparently took to heart Richard Chase's *The American Novel and Its Tradition*, sometimes speaking as if romance were not only the true American genre but her own as well. Her more considered views, however, took into account the importance of the convincing evocation of a southern locale for her work, the sharpness of eye and ear for regional patterns of behavior and cadences of speech that is the source of much of her most immediate fictional authority. Stories like her own, she remarked, were necessarily going to be wild precisely because of the tensions they embodied, and she was clearly groping for words as she tried to describe the process undergone by the creator of such fiction: "He's looking for one image that will connect or combine or embody two points; one is the point in the concrete, and the other is a point not visible to the naked eye, but believed in by him firmly, just as real to him, really, as the one that everybody sees" (*Mystery and Manners*, p. 42).

Yet romance and novel, useful as these generic categories can be and serviceable as O'Connor herself seems to have found them, do not seem quite flexible or deep enough to contain the polarities of her distinctive fiction. They are no help, for instance, in dealing with the tension between the affective qualities of laughter and terror evoked by her work, or that between the litotes of her "plain style" and the hyperbole of melodramatic action, or that between the powerful exercise of craft, with its implications of containment and control, and the extremity of the rendered experience, with its implications of wildness and release. They tell us nothing about the ironic detachment of narrative voice and the intensity and involving power of the action that voice contains, or about the violent tensions set up by the appearance again and again of the motif of the threatening "double" figure. The "passion for extremes" was, it seems, so native to the grain of Flannery O'Connor's imagination that it becomes refracted through whichever side of the critical prism is turned toward her fiction.

All of this, of course, ignores the manifest thematic concerns in her work, but a surface flashed in that direction reveals at once even more obvious expressions of the polarizing impulse. It appears negatively, for example, in the scorn with which she treats her compromising characters, the espousers of moderation, or positively in the apocalyptic and eschatological strain that runs throughout her fiction. The middle is always *mediocris* in O'Connor, a condition ultimately of illusion, for in the world she dramatizes only extremes have genuine existence. Camus's absurd man cried, "I want all or nothing." O'Connor both sympathized and went a step further, making all *and* nothing the determining perspectives of the realm her unsuspecting characters inhabit. Here it becomes evident that her lifelong Catholicism was a crucial—if finally indeterminate—factor in the shaping of her imagination.[2] Carl Jung has suggested that Catholicism seems to nourish extremes: while an apostate Protestant may gravitate toward a sectarian substitute, the lapsed Catholic tends toward atheism. "The absolutism of the Catholic Church," Jung observed, "seems to demand an equally absolute negation, whereas Protestant relativism permits of variations."[3] Moving from the other direction, Cardinal Newman had anticipated Jung's insight. In the *Apologia* he recalls his sudden discovery that "truth lay, not with the *Via Media*, but with what was called 'the extreme party.' . . . I came to the conclusion that there was no medium, in true philosophy, between Atheism and Catholicity, and that a perfectly consistent mind . . . must embrace either the one or the other."[4] In more than religious matters, O'Connor's mind seems as consistent as Newman's own, magnetized by the poles of acceptance and revolt, self-surrender and self-assertion, control and abandonment. It is the middle states—doubt, tentativeness, possibility, or harmonious integration, reconciliation, balanced merging—that seem rarely to appear in her work until very late in her career.

The following study is an attempt to sketch out and explore some of the principal polarities that inform O'Connor's fiction. In this effort I have of course much critical work on O'Connor behind me, some of it very illuminating indeed, and to all of which I am obligated. Some specific debts will be acknowledged below (in the notes, for the most part), others that no doubt should have been mentioned will have been inadvertently passed over, and still others are difficult to specify at all. How recognize the enlivening effect of Josephine Hendin's book when the main stimulus was to ferocious dissent? Much to my surprise, I found that my own exploration of O'Connor's work had led me closest to the views of one of her earliest critics, the late Stanley Edgar Hyman, whose little pamphlet on her writing has come under repeated attack. There is a good deal about which I too disagree with Hyman, but he grasped more firmly than has any critic since the principle of duality which pervades her fiction. However, this debt to Hyman was not, to paraphrase O'Connor, a premise I began with, but a discovery I made as my own study neared completion.

One of the first commentators on O'Connor was of course O'Connor herself. I have already cited some of her observations and at least partially separated my own views from them; I shall continue at different times to do both. The numerous comments bearing directly or obliquely on her own fiction can present the critic with the temptation to yet another set of extremes, and this pair I should like to disavow at once. At one pole, she can be taken as the final and definitive authority on her own writing; at the other, she can be viewed as so unaware of what she was up to as to be irrelevant if not positively misleading. Each of these stances has its attractions—the attractions of simplicity, if nothing else—and each has in fact been adopted by O'Connor's critics. In lectures, interviews, essays, and letters, her remarks are so unpretentious, wryly witty, and assured as to strike with the disarming force of the direct and clear-sighted; they can also seem—and sometimes simultaneously—either partial or even strangely wide of what one finds in the fiction. There is nothing very unusual in this, and it would be unnecessary even to raise the issue had it not come up, implicitly or explicitly, as a part of O'Connor criticism. Flannery O'Connor, it seems to me, was by no means completely unaware of what she was about; at the same time, she hardly intended her own comments to be received as definitive criticism of her work. She recognized that for her, total self-consciousness, full awareness of the sources and implications of her fiction, would have proved inhibiting, even paralyzing. "Perhaps," she wrote to a friend, "you are able to see things in these stories that I can't see because if I did see I would be too frightened to write them. I have always insisted that there is a fine grain of stupidity required in the fiction writer" (*The Habit of Being*, p. 149). No history of O'Connor's public utterances has yet been undertaken (nor do I propose to undertake it here), but such a study would, I suspect, show that the comments that reflect on her own work become generally less dogmatic and more suggestive as her career advanced. Nevertheless, "The Fiction Writer and His Country," one of the earliest, most defensive and simplistic essays, is still the text most frequently pointed to in defining the nature of her fiction.

That it makes sense to speak of Flannery O'Connor's "career," that in the two decades of her creative life her work shifted, changed, developed, has not usually been recognized. She is more often viewed, especially in studies of the entire corpus, as all of a piece, the elaborator (at least from *Wise Blood* on) of a vision which in itself remains static however her means of expression may have expanded and developed. This is by no means a completely unjustified position, and my own discussion, centering as it does on the tensions and extremities in her work, obviously posits these as permanent features of her imagination. But a given cast of the imagination does not necessarily result in a static vision, and a secondary aim of my study is to suggest that there is more change in O'Connor's fiction than has usually been allowed. *Wise Blood*, for instance, seems to me to stand alone: it could not have been predicted from the stories that precede it, nor does it have any real successors in her work. At the other end of her career, the final stories of the 1960s seem to show a shift in her writing, to suggest that had she lived longer the ensuing fiction might have been significantly different from what we have.

This aim of suggesting change and development in O'Connor (not, as she herself felt, to be confused with qualitative "progress") is, however, secondary to the more sustained attempt to plot out the central dimensions of her imagination. Perhaps it will help initiate further discussion of this neglected aspect of her writing; it is certainly not intended to end it. Nevertheless, these considerations have affected the organization of my study. I begin where O'Connor begins. The opening chapter takes up briefly some representative early stories before moving on to the achievement of *Wise Blood*. There is more talk here of sources, influences, analogues than in any of the ensuing chapters; unsurprisingly, these matters seem more important and more evident in the early stages of her career than later. The next three chapters focus on various features of O'Connor's practice as seen in her mature stories, moving in ever-widening arcs: from close attention to texture (Chapter 2) to examination of a crucial and recurrent pattern of character and action (Chapter 3) to exploration of some characteristic habits of mind and the fictional strategies that embody them (Chapter 4). Each chapter draws on a wide range of stories to illustrate its arguments, but examines one at some length to show how the tensions under discussion are developed in a single work. The penultimate chapter then looks at *The Violent Bear It Away* both as a culmination of trends in her fiction after *Wise Blood* and as a significant achievement in its own right. A final essay takes up the vexed matter of the "religious sense" of the fiction in the light provided by the extreme structures of her imagination.

Since my central contention is that despite shifts and developments the essential workings of that imagination remain recognizably characteristic, my approach to O'Connor's fiction is holistic. The overriding concern, in other words, is to plot out the most significant dimensions of the imagination. In this attempt the criterion of absolute literary worth, while hardly a matter of indifference, has not necessarily dictated the selection or emphasis of material at any given point. Thus a lesser work may provide a better (that is, balder, clearer) illustration of an important pattern than a greater one; conversely, prolonged attention to any particular work is not intended to bestow upon it an automatic seal of approval. This caveat seems advisable near the start of a study that will sometimes pause over works which received opinion on O'Connor does not rank highly. Here the most glaring examples are the two novels—which, I hasten to say, I do think better of than most O'Connor critics. But evaluations of their merits aside, *Wise Blood* and *The Violent Bear It Away* are necessary to my argument for demonstrating imaginative concerns at very different points in her career and for understanding certain of her characteristic preoccupations that simply do not get expressed in the stories. My own estimation of the aesthetic worth of works discussed at any length will usually be obvious enough (often explicitly so), but it was not primarily these considerations that dictated my use of the piece at that point in the argument.

My principal purpose, of course, has not been to rank Flannery O'Connor's stories and novels. The hope here is rather that the focus on her fascination with tensions and polarities creates a framework for the useful examining of her fiction that does not turn into a Procrustean bed—a structure firm enough to hold all of the work lightly within its grasp and to allow for the exploration of some essential matters without lashing her writing to a narrow thesis that ignores or squeezes out the vital complexities. As a method, it can only justify itself by the extent to which it fulfills one of O'Connor's own dicta: "What you have to do," she remarked, "is try to deepen your penetration of these things." [5]

CHAPTER ONE

Early Work and *Wise Blood*

Flannery O'Connor's first work of real importance is *Wise Blood* (1952). With that novel she truly launched her brief but brilliant career and staked an opening claim to lasting attention. But between 1945 and 1949 she wrote seven independent stories[1] (four of which she published during that period) that in light of her later fiction remain of some interest. They make up, in effect, her apprentice work, and if none of them is vintage O'Connor, neither is any without suggestiveness to someone interested in her career. O'Connor herself apparently thought little of them, at least in their original forms: the three she allowed to enter between hard covers did so only after extensive revision. The rest she simply abandoned.

It is not difficult to see why. Six of the seven stories[2] are quite early indeed: they make up her master's thesis for the University of Iowa and thus were all written before the late spring of 1947. Aside from their immaturity and general thinness, they show what we might well expect: the young writer casting about for her own distinctive voice and subject, trying out various modes, from psychological and sociological realism to the comic portrait to the foreboding "atmospheric" tale, testing her talents within recognized styles and subjects. If none of these in their conventional forms would precisely suit her gifts, elements of all would enter into the distinctive manner of her mature work. But seen as the fiction which somehow led up to *Wise Blood*, they are hardly a preparation for that novel. They seem too slight, often too derivative, too conventional to provide a context for that strange, exuberant, frightening book. Yet as well as revealing what for O'Connor would prove to be dead ends in both subject and technique, they also suggest some of the manner and the concerns that led toward and beyond *Wise Blood*.

There seems little point now in belaboring the obvious inadequacies of these early stories. Much more interesting is the discovery of hints, in however attenuated form, of what is to come, particularly of some of those characteristic tensions, those strains and sunderings, that govern the later fiction. For our purposes it will be enough to glance at four of the stories from the Iowa thesis—"The Geranium," "The Turkey," "The Crop," and "The Train"—although one of the remaining two might also claim some attention. "The Barber" is O'Connor's first treatment of a type which will become familiar much later in her fiction, the ineffective liberal intellectual. Like his descendant in *The Violent Bear It Away*, he is a teacher named Rayber who here takes up verbal political arms against the rednecks who cluster around the local barber shop. Both the setting and the quietly satirical point of view recall Ring Lardner, but the ending at least is genuine O'Connor. Enraged by the mockery his defense of his candidate receives, the "reasonable" Rayber knocks down the barber and rushes out of the shop like a mad dog, the lather beginning "to drip inside his collar and down the barber's bib, dangling to his knees" ("The Barber," p. 25). The context here is slight, the comedy has none of the bite of the later work, but this first attempt with the figure of the self-professed intellectual warrants at least mentioning.

"Wildcat," on the other hand, is a quite unconvincing piece about an old blind Negro's fear of being killed by a great cat that is loose in the neighborhood of his shack. Like Faulkner's "That Evening Sun," it is a story of fear and foreboding left narratively unresolved at the end—the fates of Faulkner's Nancy and O'Connor's Gabriel are not explicitly revealed to us, although *they* are certain that they are marked for violent death—and in its all-black setting it may also owe a debt to some of the early stories of Eudora Welty. But unlike either of her predecessors, O'Connor has here devised a work in which both situation and language seem contrived and literary. It was for her a venture into a setting and a kind of tale that would have no descendants, and its only interest now lies in the central character's fear of his helplessness in the face of a violent doom—a fear shared by several of her later protagonists and a fate visited upon more than a few.

As O'Connor's first published story, however, "The Geranium" (1946) holds a larger claim to interest. An elderly southerner, Old Dudley, is living out his last years in his daughter's New York apartment, and the story opens with him waiting for the geranium which is put daily in the window across the alley. Thinking of the flower releases in his mind a series of nostalgic memories of his old home, counterpointed against more recent and unsettling experiences in the unfamiliar city. Gradually the flashbacks narrow to juxtapose Dudley's relaxed friendship with the Negro Rabie, a friendship given form and even made possible by the southern social code, with his incomprehension of the northern "equality" of Negroes, a view accepted by his daughter: a Negro has moved into the next apartment and she merely shrugs as if she had "been raised that way" (p. 9). The central action of the story (indeed almost the only dramatized action) is Dudley's encounter with this Negro, whose behavior goes beyond "equality" to a kindly condescension toward the old man. At the end, back in the apartment, Dudley learns from the owner of the geranium that the plant has fallen from the window to the alley below, "smashed down six floors" (p. 14).

Aside from the evident debt to Caroline Gordon's "Old Red," what is most arresting about "The Geranium" is that it is conceived firmly in the mode of psychological and social realism. Extended interior monologues in the language and speech rhythms of Dudley himself; careful attention to manners, habits, and kinds of social relationships; the "ordinary" nature of characters, setting, and action—all these place the story squarely in the realistic tradition. O'Connor's later work, of course, would hardly scorn the rendering of manners or social relationships or the use of ordinary characters (although language and action will come to be handled with a sharp difference). But unlike those stories to come, "The Geranium" is exhausted in its psychosocial surface: it dramatizes the devastating effects of a sudden shift into an alien context. Had this been the only story O'Connor published before *Wise Blood*, we would have to call the novel almost a new start.

Almost—but not entirely. Nearly lost among the merging of narrative voice with the old man's consciousness and an often unconvincingly literal insistence on dialect is the counterpointed structure of "The Geranium," the attempt to create a tension between Dudley's recollections of life back home and his experiences in New York. That this never comes to much—the narrative voice does not establish enough independence to explore the ironies latent in both sides of the situation—should not obscure this mild first effort with a juxtaposition of opposites (past and present, country and city, home and exile), a tension between forces that prove irreconcilable. And there are other glimpses of what is to come. Near the end of the story Dudley goes into the hall with the intention of rescuing the geranium, and the writing rises to a frightening vision: "The steps dropped down like a deep wound in the floor. They opened up through a gap like a cavern and went down and down. . . . There'd probably be niggers with black flecks in their socks on every step, pulling down their mouths so as not to laugh" (p. 14). In a different way, the final exchange reveals O'Connor's inherent dramatic power:

> "I seen you before," the man said. "I seen you settin' in that old chair every day, starin' out the window, looking in my apartment. What I do in my apartment is my business, see? I don't like people looking at what I do."
> It was at the bottom of the alley with its roots in the air.
> "I only tell people once," the man said and left the window. [p. 14]

Released from the old man's consciousness into a rendered scene, the story acquires at the end the thrust that has been missing throughout.

The geranium itself has been gathering associations until in this final view of it, "with its roots in the air," it has come to imply the lost home, the impossibility of return, and the withering of the old man's life in a foreign environment. For the theme of the story is the loss of home—the "good place," as Dudley thinks of it—in a sense deeper than nostalgia: O'Connor means to suggest that profound estrangement from one's heritage that can produce a warping of the spirit. The subject was especially close to her in the late 1940s when she was in Iowa, New York, and Connecticut, for it is as central to

"The Train" and *Wise Blood* as it is to "The Geranium." As she matured, the persistent motif of home would itself become one source of tension: it appears crucially in both novels and in a variety of forms in story after story, often treated with deep emotional ambivalence. To this writer with a very firm sense of place, home seems to have meant some rather contrary things. In her hands it will evoke either the rich, and often stultifying, context of the southern locale or a place no longer of this world, the "true country" that lies beyond it. Not only are the claims of the two often incompatible, but each is typically viewed by her characters with a mixture of longing and denial. Home will become a resonant motif in O'Connor's fiction; "The Geranium" only begins to indicate what she would make of it.

If "The Geranium" turns on the home-exile polarity, "The Turkey" is most interesting as O'Connor's first initiation story. In this tale the twin impulses of rebellion against and acceptance of the divine are set within the larger tension between human notions of the ways of the world and the terrifying operations of Mystery. Discovering a wounded wild turkey while playing in the woods, eleven-year-old Ruller McFarney chases and almost captures it, but at the last moment he runs into a tree and the bird escapes. In his disappointment, he feels that God has played a "dirty trick" on him (p. 45), and in a childish revolt against Him he nervously begins to blaspheme. Suddenly, however, Ruller finds the turkey lying dead on the edge of a thicket. Now it seems to him he must be one of God's chosen. He parades into town with his trophy, but in the pride of his "election," he shows it to some country boys, who promptly walk off with it. The story ends this way: "He walked four blocks and then suddenly, noticing that it was dark, he began to run. He ran faster and faster, and as he turned up the road to his house, his heart was running as fast as his legs and he was certain that Something Awful was tearing behind him with its arms rigid and its fingers ready to clutch" (p. 53). The final image, echoing Ruller's chase of the turkey, suggests the movement from pursuer to pursued, from his childish fantasies of power to a frightened sense of the universe as mysteriously Other.

Like all the early stories, "The Turkey" is more compelling for what it prophesies than for what it achieves. Alone among the works before *Wise Blood*, this tale attempts to handle a specifically religious theme, and in exactly the form in which it will appear again and again—as a rebellion against what the protagonist takes to be the ways of God. Indeed, in an earlier manuscript version of the story lay the seeds of Hazel Motes, The Misfit, and young Tarwater. Here called, curiously enough, Manley,[3] the boy is given a Dostoyevskian reflection on injustice, the gap between the crime and punishment of his own destruction of a birthday gift (worth two dollars) and the ruin of his glasses and clothes (worth thirty-seven dollars) during the chase of the turkey. "The only way you could beat it [such injustice] would be by doing something that was so bad that being killed dead for it wouldn't be as bad as what you had done." Like Hazel Motes, he decides that such a sin is blasphemy: "The feeling of this evil was murky but cold. It was not like the feeling of his secret sins or the more open kind like smashing the bottle. Those made him tingle with a hot absence of thought. This was something entirely of the mind." How many of O'Connor's future protagonists are in that last sentence!

However, in this version when Manley finds the dead turkey and decides that "God must certainly feel that he was worth saving," suddenly "a very distinct and ugly voice inside him said, 'He must not be so hot if He has to bribe a jerk like you with a lousy turkey.'" The voice continues to mock the boy's new-found piety: "'God must be a real sucker to let you get away with this,' the familiar voice said."[4] All these passages disappeared from the final version of the story, but they seem worth reviving for their very specific anticipations of Haze's blasphemy, The Misfit's meditations on justice, and Tarwater's sardonic "voice." And the larger fascination with those sins "entirely of the mind" rather than of the flesh points unerringly the direction of the mature work.

But the finished story is itself a matrix of motifs and situations which will reappear, transformed, later: none of the other early pieces is so suggestive in this way. For instance, as a lonely child who feels neglected by his parents, Ruller serves as an early sketch for both Harry Ashfield of "The River" and Norton of "The Lame Shall Enter First." Like Harry, who thinks that "Jesus Christ" is a way of swearing and that pigs are "small fat pink animals with curly tails and round grinning faces and bow ties" ("The River," pp. 163, 161), Ruller has derived his childish notions of life from a secularized culture. "The Turkey" opens with the boy playing triumphant sheriff about to destroy an imaginary but wicked outlaw, thus easily ridding his small world of its threats and terrors. Later, after finding the dead turkey, he wonders, "Maybe finding the turkey was a sign. Maybe God wanted him to become a preacher. He thought of Bing Crosby and Spencer Tracy" (p. 49). The sheriff-and-outlaw metaphor reappears as Sally Virginia's way of dealing with experience in "A Circle in the Fire" and, as martyr-and-lions, in the child of "A Temple of the Holy Ghost." More generally, Ruller's inadequate notions of the ways of Providence look forward to the far more devastating treatment of this theme in the complacent "heroines" of several stories who assure themselves that Jesus "wouldn't shoot a lady" or that "we have a lot to be thankful for." And far more than "The Geranium," the ending here strikes the authentic O'Connor note: the sudden, ironic, terrifying revelation which in a flash focuses everything that precedes it, and the story is over.

"The Crop" is both the least ambitious and least successful of the four early stories we are considering, yet it is not without interest. For one thing, only two of these pieces (the other is "The Barber") are written in a comic mode that even faintly suggests the later manner, for while there are touches of muted humor in some of these works—in the treatment of Ruller's rebellion, for instance—O'Connor's comic genius is largely suppressed before *Wise Blood*. "The Crop" at least gives a hint, and in one passage more than a hint, of the mature manner. In essence, the story is a satiric portrait of a middle-aged would-be writer, one Miss Willerton, who in her banal boarding-house contemplates "subjects" for a story that will be both "arty" and "socially important" (the language is Miss Willerton's). She finally lights on sharecroppers (although she of course knows nothing about them) and provides herself with a handsome hero and his "woman." But before getting very far, she enters so fully into her imagined situation that the woman is replaced by none other than Miss Willerton herself, who then launches into a romantic daydream of helping "her man," Lot, on the farm and bearing his child—thus the double "crop" of the title. Interrupted to go on a domestic

errand, Miss Willerton fastidiously endures the vulgarities of the supermarket and emerges to encounter this couple:

> The woman was plump with yellow hair and fat ankles and muddy-col-
> ored eyes. She had on high-heel pumps and blue anklets, a too-short cot-
> ton dress, and a plaid jacket. Her skin was mottled and her neck thrust
> forward as if she were sticking it out to smell something that was always
> being drawn away. Her face was set in an inane grin. The man was long
> and wasted and shaggy. His shoulders were stooped and there were yellow
> knots along the side of his large, red neck. His hands fumbled stupidly
> with the girl's as they slumped along, and once or twice he smiled sickly
> at her and Miss Willerton could see that he had straight teeth and sad eyes
> and a rash over his forehead. [p. 41]

Miss Willerton's comment on this vision is "Ugh"; she does not recognize her own characters, Lot and his woman, stripped of their romantic aura and broken out in skin eruptions. Life defeats art, and
Miss Willerton returns home to contemplate a more "colorful" subject, the Irish.

I have quoted the description of the couple at length because it so
clearly bears the genuine O'Connor stamp. The passage might have
come from a mature work; in fact, the clause about the woman's for-
ward-thrusting neck will be appropriated entire and given to Hazel
Motes (*Wise Blood*, p. 37). This is the vein of the grotesque that she
would mine with such profit, and its appearance in these early stories is very rare indeed. The insistence on the literal, the sparely visual presentation, the sharp eye for the ugly detail—Miss Willerton
had imagined her Lot with "straight teeth" and "sad eyes" but not
with a dose of acne—all this is vintage O'Connor.

Unfortunately, the earlier sections of "The Crop" are less striking.
The self-evident tension the story exploits, between "art" and "life,"
is handled in a thoroughly conventional way. With her use of literature as fantasy-gratification and the inevitably awkward and absurd
figure she cuts in everyday life, Miss Willerton is no more than a
stock character. But however unconvincing, she may also be the first
of those comic authorial self-projections that would result in such
other failed writers as Asbury Fox of "The Enduring Chill" or such
frustrated intellectuals as Joy Hopewell of "Good Country People." If
so, the story casts an oblique light on O'Connor's dilemma at this

early stage of her career: How to realize that "delicate adjustment of the outer and inner worlds" (*Mystery and Manners*, p. 34), that interaction between reality and imagination, that would result in convincing and original fiction? Miss Willerton's pseudosolution—the arbitrary selection of fashionable "subjects," elaborated by free-floating fantasy—is of course held up to laughter, but the implied alternative—immersion in the banalities of everyday life, the sights of the supermarket, runny-nosed children, vulgar lovers—was already proving an inadequate medium for Flannery O'Connor. "The Crop" is, after all, contemporaneous with "The Geranium," and although she retained a keen sense for the sights and sounds of the ordinary, everyday life in Georgia (or elsewhere) would never be her subject. It is not only for Miss Willerton that the tension between outer and inner worlds remains unresolved in "The Crop."

Yet it is precisely that tension, here dramatized so conventionally in her aspiring author, that would become central to O'Connor's mature work: the disjunction between the mind's conceptions and a larger reality. As in "The Crop," that classic situation seemed to release her gift for comedy, and if in this story the confrontation with that greater "life"—Miss Willerton's encounter with the grotesque couple—produces no awareness in the protagonist, the bare bones of the essential O'Connor plot are nevertheless clearly visible. Later, of course, those climactic confrontations will come with much more devastating effect; it is one of the failures of "The Crop" that that powerful passage remains rather inert in the story, becoming nothing more than an obvious comment on Miss Willerton's silliness. The distinctive O'Connor eye for the grotesque is apparent, if only briefly, but its owner does not yet know what to do with what it so compellingly sees. Only with *Wise Blood* will she discover how to bring her own inner and outer worlds fruitfully together.

Read on its own, "The Train" could supply further hints of the later O'Connor, but the main interest of this work now is that it is the story out of which *Wise Blood* grew. Extensively rewritten, "The Train" became chapter 1 of the novel, and a juxtaposition of story and chapter reveals at once both the germ of *Wise Blood* and, more dramatically, the leap that occurred between all these immature stories and the novel. The plots of the two are almost identical and the protagonists share several crucial concerns, but in every other respect the differences are enormous. Like the novel, the story presents a country boy (here called Hazel Wickers) just out of the army and on his way to the big city. And like Hazel Motes, Wickers is obsessed with his lost home and, more explicitly even than his successor, with his dead mother: he too tries to make the porter confess his origins in Eastrod and undergoes a coffin fantasy in his upper berth. But here the significant similarities end.

Alone of these early stories, "The Train" is unquestionably in debt to Faulkner, particularly *As I Lay Dying*, both in conception and stylistically. The train journey, the loss of the mother, the central coffin image, the use of the name Cash are more than chance resemblances, and Hazel Wickers recalls both Darl and Vardaman in the nature of his fixation on his "unsatisfied" mother. The style is sometimes unmistakably Faulknerian: "For a minute he couldn't move for thinking it was Cash and he breathed, 'Cash,' and the porter pushed him off and got up and went down the aisle quick and Haze scrambled off the floor and went after him, saying he wanted to get in the berth now and thinking, this is Cash's kin, and then suddenly, like something thrown at him when he wasn't looking: this is Cash's son who ran away; and then: he knows about Eastrod and doesn't want it, he doesn't want to talk about it, he doesn't want to talk about Eastrod."[5]

All such traces of that telltale style—and there are others, like the occasional use of portmanteau words (*greyflying, black-spinning*)—have disappeared in *Wise Blood*, and the mother-fixation has been toned down so that the echoes of *As I Lay Dying* are no longer obtrusive in the novel. Moreover, the protagonist seems to have been almost turned inside out in the rewriting. Hazel Wickers has none of Hazel Motes's sharp and surly aggressiveness; he is a shy, confused country boy, given to blushes (!), wide-eyed at being on a train alone, stuttering incoherently to his fellow passengers. Most striking, in view of the novel, is the utter absence of religiosity in "The Train." There are no outbursts about redemption from Hazel Wickers, no preacher grandfather, no views on Jesus or sin or his soul: his thoughts are all of the dead mother and lost home. Yet just as startling as this overt use of religious obsession is the revolution in technique which accompanies it and seems to have made it possible.

The enormous differences are apparent from the start. Here is the way the two works begin:

Thinking about the porter, he had almost forgotten the berth. ["The Train"]

Hazel Motes sat at a forward angle on the green plush train seat, looking one minute at the window as if he might want to jump out of it, and the next down the aisle at the other end of the car. [*Wise Blood*]

The very opening word of the story reveals the narrative stance: as in most of the other early pieces, the approach is through a central consciousness, and diction and prose rhythms are designed to suggest its quality and state. In its own mode, the sentence is skillful enough. It presents at once the two key images (porter and berth) that will occupy Hazel Wickers precisely in the order in which they will concern him, and it hints at the relationship between the two. But the opening of *Wise Blood*, rather than suggesting a *consciousness*, dramatizes a *figure*. The distance and apparent objectivity of the narrator is almost clinical ("sat at a forward angle"); the removed voice is able to contain and heighten the character's potential violence ("he might want to jump") by virtue of its very detachment. Since the precise movements of a consciousness can hardly be rendered from such narrative distance, its restless obsessiveness can only be suggested through appearances, indirectly ("as if"). The result is at once comic and fierce. Both openings indicate that contradictory forces are at work in the protagonist, but (and perhaps this is the most important distinction) in *Wise Blood* we *see* him: physically located in space ("on the green plush train seat"), his very body is made to express his inner state. We may be on the same train, but we have entered a different fictional country.

More than any of the other early stories, "The Train" is thin in physical substance. O'Connor is so closely committed to her character's perceptions as to seem inhibited from rendering her material in concrete images, especially with a character as introspective as Hazel Wickers. Most of the figures lack defining physical presence, and setting remains nominal until Haze climbs into the berth. *Wise*

Blood, however, is an intensely visual book—like its hero, it seems almost a reversal of "The Train"—but visual in a very particular way. The imagery of the novel is sharp and spare, rendered with an acute eye to color and line but with almost no attention to shading and detail. People and objects seem to lose their third dimension as if, placed under klieg lights, their solidity and individuality were no longer visible. Here is Mrs. Wally Bee Hitchcock, also on the opening page of *Wise Blood*: "She was a fat woman with pink collars and cuffs and pear-shaped legs that slanted off the train seat and didn't reach the floor." The qualifying—and humanizing—questions (How fat? How far off the floor? What color dress? Material? Features?) have become irrelevant: in abandoning psychological realism, O'Connor has abandoned a closely mimetic technique altogether. The austere visual notation which is the description of Mrs. Hitchcock presents only enough to suggest the child-woman, vulgar, self-indulgent, and shallow, whom her grandchildren call "Mamadoll." There is, O'Connor would have us believe, nothing more to know about Mrs. Hitchcock. Further details, this technique implies, could only be redundant or inconsequential.

The stylized art O'Connor is practicing here is an art of distillation: only as much surface as will suggest essence is admitted. Comically distorting and simplifying appearances to reveal inner truths, these bright but bare images dominate the novel as they had none of the earlier stories. But if this intense visualization is new in *Wise Blood*, so are what seem almost necessary corollaries: plot and character handled dramatically and a taut, sharply economical style. The relationship between the distant narrative voice, the intensely visual image, and a highly dramatic effect has already been noted in the opening sentence of the novel, a sentence thoroughly characteristic of the book it begins. *Wise Blood* is centrally concerned with the psychological and religious conflict within Hazel Motes, but this internal drama is presented almost entirely from the outside, projected into various forms of action, image, and metaphor. Almost never do we see from Haze's point of view. Rarely, indeed, are we made privy to his conscious thoughts, and when they are given, they are merely reported, briefly and objectively. No longer are there any attempts to reproduce the diction and rhythms of the character's consciousness, and the stylistic change this brings is of crucial importance.

Faulknerian echoes aside, O'Connor's writing from the start had been relatively unadorned by rhetorical flourishes or "poetic" effects, but in the novel her style acquires a greater economy of notation, a flatter, sharper rhythm, and an expansion in suggestiveness. Precisely because the differences are superficially so minor, the following passages begin to show how the prose of "The Train," typical of the early stories, was wrought into that of *Wise Blood*:

> Going around the corner, he ran into something heavily pink; it gasped and muttered, "Clumsy!" It was Mrs. Hosen in a pink wrapper with her hair in knots around her head. He had forgotten about her. She was terrifying with her hair slicked back and the knobs like dark toadstools framing her face. ["The Train," pp. 59–60]

> Going around the corner he ran into something heavy and pink; it gasped and muttered, "Clumsy!" It was Mrs. Hitchcock in a pink wrapper, with her hair in knots around her head. She looked at him with her eyes squinted nearly shut. The knobs framed her face like dark toadstools. [*Wise Blood*, p. 18]

In "The Train" the narrative eye is primarily on the perceiving character. Mrs. Hosen is presented as she appears to Haze, and his explicit reaction ("He had forgotten about her. She was terrifying") absorbs and cushions our own. In *Wise Blood* all suggestion of Haze's response to this encounter is stripped away; even the impressionistic "heavily pink" becomes the more precise and objective "heavy and pink." The simple sentence which replaces the excisions—"She looked at him with her eyes squinted nearly shut"—is no less revealing: a single stark image that heightens the incongruity of the woman's appearance. And compared with its counterpart in the story, the final sentence from the novel is piercing, the soft falling effect of the three participles replaced by the abruptness of the decisive verb, and the neutral image of the slicked-back hair abandoned to throw into sharp relief the repellent knobs. In the flatness and simplicity of style which seems baldly to thrust the images at us, Mrs. Hitchcock is made to materialize through a power of language which renders her more terrifyingly present than in "The Train."

This excerpt from "The Train," like the description of the lovers from "The Crop," is in one respect misleading. Out of context, both passages may suggest that these early stories are more densely imagistic and more grotesque than in fact they are. What they do reveal is that the intense visualization and thoroughgoing grotesquerie of *Wise Blood* is less some newly acquired way of "seeing" than the throwing off of fictional modes that were alien to Flannery O'Connor's true gifts and interests.[6] Most startling in the novel after the early stories is the sudden discovery of a style, in the broadest sense, that could bring those distinctive gifts and interests together and turn them into original fiction. In this respect the movement to *Wise Blood*, from psychological realism and mild satiric comedy to the nonmimetic mode of the grotesque, made it at once imperative for O'Connor to create a language capable of giving fictional credibility to the outlandish materials of the novel. Thus the disciplined flat and simple sentences, which serve to counterweight the bizarre characters and events they convey and, as vehicles for the strikingly clear images, lend authority to the detached and ironic voice that mediates and controls *Wise Blood*. As she matured, this style, like other aspects of her technique, would become more flexible, capable of handling more varied aspects of experience, but it would not alter in its essence. By 1952 O'Connor had discovered her true medium.

Those early stories do, then, give us glimpses of what was to come—moments of dramatic power, flashes of grotesque perception, attempts at a comic perspective, sketches of some central character types—as well as false starts. And here too, in shadowy form, are versions of some of the significant tensions that would inform the later works: between home and exile, revolt and acceptance, the mind and reality. Nevertheless, in this context, *Wise Blood* remains a startling achievement. The early work is no preparation for the control and assurance of the novel. The stripped, disciplined writing, the carefully honed episodes, and the sustained vision of *Wise Blood* would have seemed beyond the reach of the author of the early pieces. Some literary catalyst was necessary to make that novel possible, and there is little doubt now what it was: the work of Nathanael West, and in particular *Miss Lonelyhearts*.

A number of critics have noted specific echoes of West in *Wise Blood*, but more important than any individual borrowings was the liberating example of West's fiction.[7] What O'Connor discovered in

Miss Lonelyhearts was the conjunction of an ironic voice, grotesque perception, and the theme of the religious quest. To the kindred sensibility of the younger writer, West showed the possibilities of indirection, the relationship between a nonrealistic approach to fiction and the explicit treatment of religious motifs, between serious intent and comic vision. The violence and comedy, the uncompromising satire of the contemporary world, the focus on the single figure and his search, the economical use of flat secondary characters, the episodic action, the careful structuring of the novel through image and motif rather than through a conventional plot—all these show O'Connor's debt to West, strikingly original in all the deeper ways as *Wise Blood* is.

Presumably she did not read West until the late 1940s, for while his impact is decisive for the novel, no trace of it appears in the early stories. And surely it is to the example of his fiction that O'Connor owed the sudden release of power that occurs in *Wise Blood*. Nothing is more central to her mature work than the tension between the distant, ironic narrative voice and the frightening materials that voice mediates. In showing her how to achieve a greater narrative distance from her materials, West seems paradoxically to have allowed her to tap a deep reservoir of psychic energy, a darker side of the imagination—perhaps even made it safe to do so. It is that quality that the reader of the later fiction immediately misses in the early pieces, for although they contain moments of intensity, none of them has it as a whole. The closeness between narrator and central consciousness in most of the stories tones them down, keeps them genteel, smothers less acceptable feelings and insights; and the two comic pieces are entirely without the sense of menace that is a part of the fabric of all, even the funniest, mature writings. Lacking the tension between comic bite and violent threat, none of these stories is likely to lodge ineradicably in our minds, whether we like it or not, as so many of the later ones do. Clearly she knew whereof she spoke when a number of years later she advised beginning writers to get some distance from themselves, to judge themselves "with a stranger's eye and a stranger's severity."[8] Only through a comparable detachment did Flannery O'Connor discover her own individual power as a writer.

Crucial as Nathanael West was to the achievement of *Wise Blood*, two other influences—again unheralded by the early stories—seem important in the shaping of that book. One of these was literary, the other more broadly intellectual; one a century old, the other fashionably up to date; one specifically southern, the other international. Opened by West to a sense of its own possibilities, O'Connor's imagination lost no time in seizing on material from Edgar Allan Poe and the existentialists.

II

"It's like one of them gory stories, it's something that people have quit doing—like boiling in oil or being a saint or walling up cats," she said. "There's no reason for it. People have quit doing it."

"They ain't quit doing it as long as I'm doing it," he said. [*Wise Blood*, p. 224]

So, near the end of *Wise Blood*, did Flannery O'Connor anticipate her critics by putting into the mouth of her hero a laconic defense of her novel's unreasonableness. Not surprisingly, however, many of them, like Haze's landlady, have found it a gory story indeed: "grisly," "gruesome," "horror upon horror" are some of the typical epithets bestowed on the book by earlier readers.[9] If such language seems to ignore O'Connor's sustained comic perspective, it is fair enough as directed at the materials of *Wise Blood*. What has passed almost unnoticed is how close many of those materials are to the American master of gory stories.[10] It is Poe, after all, who holds the patent on walling up cats.

Wise Blood is such an odd, angular book that perhaps it is understandable that the debt to Poe has gone unappreciated. It was some years before the more obvious influence of West was recognized, yet critical as his example was for this novel, and for O'Connor's development, the less overt but strongly felt presence of Poe may finally be more useful in defining the uniqueness of *Wise Blood*. Although there are, as everyone has noticed, distinct resemblances between O'Connor's first novel and her second, *The Violent Bear It Away*, there are also fundamental differences that constitute almost a reversal in her imaginative thinking. A glance at the Poe element in

Wise Blood should prove helpful in exploring more precisely the vision of that book.

O'Connor herself did not, of course, encourage such an investigation. By the time she began speaking out on her writing, *Wise Blood* was several years behind her, the first collection of stories had appeared, and some uncongenial labels were already being attached to her work. Her early essay "The Fiction Writer and His Country" was a clarification and an apologia, an attempt to remove some of those labels. One was the vague designation "the southern school," a term, O'Connor noted, that usually "conjures up an image of Gothic monstrosities and the idea of a preoccupation with everything deformed and grotesque." Most of the members of the so-called southern school, she sardonically went on, "are considered, I believe, to be unhappy combinations of Poe and Erskine Caldwell" (*Mystery and Manners*, p. 28).

There is a defensiveness behind the wry tone here, for although she always bristled at the term *Gothic*, later she would happily embrace *grotesque*. But in this essay O'Connor is determined to assert not only the seriousness of her concerns as a writer, but the grounding of her fiction in Christian orthodoxy. In that undertaking Poe (to say nothing of Erskine Caldwell) was a dubious ally indeed. Better to claim Hawthorne as one's literary ancestor, as she would repeatedly, than the shady Poe, whose seriousness is still a matter for debate. She was willing to admit privately that she had had an "Edgar Allan Poe period" when young which had in fact "lasted for years," and she was capable at the age of thirty of summarizing accurately a number of his tales (including "The Man Who Was Used Up"[11]) that she had encountered in a collection of his humorous writings. Privately or publicly, however, she never spoke of Poe without a note of deprecation: "This is an influence I would rather not think about" (*The Habit of Being*, p. 98), or "Sometimes the most profound books are not the ones that bestir you most."[12]

But in *Wise Blood*, at least, O'Connor was more deeply bestirred by Poe than she was willing (or able) to say. Nor is it primarily his comic tales that resonate in the novel, although Poe's practice of treating his horrific materials humorously may have contributed to that blend of nightmare and ironic comedy which is characteristic of

Wise Blood. Yet a reader who spoke of encountering such matters as the corpse of a murdered girl stuffed up a chimney; a hysterical terror at being shut up in coffinlike enclosures or a sense of being buried alive; a fascinated fear of and attraction to sudden drops, lowered places, "the abyss"; the sudden appearance of a look-alike, dress-alike figure identified as one's conscience whom the protagonist proceeds to murder—such a reader might recently have come from a collection of Poe's better-known arabesques *or* from *Wise Blood*. For it is on Poe's tales of entrapment, suffocation, premature burial, and paralyzing rift in personality that O'Connor has most heavily drawn in dramatizing the strange existence of Hazel Motes.

The parallels are at times so close that it becomes difficult to believe Flannery O'Connor was unaware of them. Such specific echoes as walling up cats ("The Black Cat") and the story of the body in the chimney ("The Murders in the Rue Morgue") would seem open (if tongue-in-cheek) allusions. Other and less overt borrowings, however, have greater significance. Hazel Motes's recurrent fear of being "not dead but only buried" (*Wise Blood*, p. 160) has of course a number of possible sources in Poe's tales, but the action toward the end of the first chapter of *Wise Blood* parallels remarkably that of "The Premature Burial." The narrator of that tale, a victim of catalepsy and the consequent fear that during one of his attacks he will be mistaken for dead and so buried, dreams obsessively that others have met that horrifying fate. At the end of the story he seems to awaken to find his terrors realized: opening his eyes to darkness, feeling the "coffin" surrounding him, he screams out for help, only to discover that he is the occupant of a narrow berth in a ship. In *Wise Blood* the ship's berth has become a train berth where Hazel Motes, dozing, recalls the funerals of various members of his family and his own vivid sense of coffin lids closing over figures still alive. As doze becomes dream, Haze, like Poe's narrator, becomes the creature in the coffin-berth, and he too cries out for release. *Wise Blood* thus begins where "The Premature Burial" ends, for while Poe's narrator claims that his experience has broken his obsession with death, Hazel Motes will suffer this defining terror again and again in the course of the novel.

Much later we discover him preaching (contradictorily) the unreality of conscience: " 'Your conscience is a trick,' he said, 'it don't exist though you may think it does, and if you think it does, you had best get it out in the open and hunt it down and kill it, because it's no more than your face in the mirror is or your shadow behind you.'" With comic inevitability, a rival preacher, dressed exactly like Haze, arrives on the scene at precisely this moment. Discovering even more than his "face in the mirror," Haze is "so struck with how gaunt and thin he looked in the illusion that he stopped preaching." "Him and you twins?" a listening woman asks. "If you don't hunt it down and kill it, it'll hunt you down and kill you," Haze mutters. "He's nuts," the woman responds. "I never seen no twins that hunted each other down" (pp. 166–68). Clearly she has never read Poe's "William Wilson." "What say of it? what say of CONSCIENCE grim, / That spectre in my path?" asks the epigraph. The tale's narrator has of course a good deal to say of his bothersome namesake. Although he tries to disclaim any real relationship between them, he admits that others' impression that they are brothers is not wholly inapt. Indeed, "if we *had* been brothers we must have been twins," for they share the same birthdate, and as he furiously observes, the other Wilson manages to "perfect an imitation of myself" in word, action, and dress. Dogged for years by this meddlesomely moral shadow, the narrator finally turns on the "imposter" and murders him. As he does, he seems suddenly to gaze into "a large mirror" to discover "mine own image, but with features all pale and dabbled with blood." Thus the act is ultimately suicidal: "*See by this image,*" the double concludes, "*which is thine own, how utterly thou hast murdered thyself.*"[13]

The identification of both antagonists as conscience and the closeness in language suggests that Poe and O'Connor share more here than a vaguely similar use of the *Doppelgänger* motif. Like William Wilson, Hazel Motes does hunt down and kill this mocking mirror image, but unlike Wilson, whose charge of "imposter" is a desperate wish, Haze discovers that his double is a deliberately constructed replica, an impersonator named Solace Layfield. At the moment of Solace's death, Haze looks not at "mine own image," but at a more devious mirror, a man who no longer "look[s] so much like Haze" yet whose conscious impersonation reflects Haze's unconscious attempt to create a *false* self. "Two things I can't stand," Haze says, "—a man that ain't true and one that mocks what is" (p. 204), but the charges ironically rebound to himself. In, as it were, doubling the double motif, in using Solace Layfield's duplicity to reflect Haze's unacknowledged internal split, O'Connor manages to use Poe's situation both comically and seriously. Although both works treat us to a grisly murder, *Wise Blood* leaves us not with the awe of "William Wilson" but with the absurdity of an uncomprehending protagonist. If Solace Layfield functions as Haze's conscience, it is not, as in Poe, by being that essential alter ego without which existence itself becomes impossible, but by being an exact reflection, a duplicate so comically precise that the very externals of his appearance create a judgment. Haze is indeed mocked, but not in the way he thinks.

These distinctions may suggest why, for all the echoes of Poe, O'Connor's indebtedness in *Wise Blood* has passed unnoticed, for in its astringent comedy the novel *feels* so different from his fiction. We are returned, for ironic laughter, to that other powerful literary influence on the book, Nathanael West. If it is a bit too glib to say that *Wise Blood* reads as if it were Poe rewritten by the author of *Miss Lonelyhearts*—other things aside, West himself is not wholly innocent of a debt to Poe—such a formulation perhaps begins to suggest the quality of the book and to distinguish it from the work of both predecessors. For if Flannery O'Connor learned much from West's example, the emotional core of *Wise Blood*, the forces that drive its protagonist, owe nothing whatever to *Miss Lonelyhearts*. West's columnist is haunted by anguish and frustration, his own pain and revulsion at the spectacle of irremediable human suffering. These are far from the concerns of Hazel Motes. What Haze feels and guiltily masks from himself is a deep sense of dread, a psychological and metaphysical terror so overwhelming it usurps his entire being. So fierce and undeviating is Haze's obsessiveness that by comparison Miss Lonelyhearts, hardly a flexible figure, looks almost dilettantish.

It is of course in that dread, in the terror and obsessiveness of its hero, that *Wise Blood* most obviously touches on the realm of Poe's tales. But if these had been given classic literary expression by another southerner a century before O'Connor started her novel, they were receiving contemporary confirmation at the very moment she was writing *Wise Blood*. Walled-up cats, premature burials, and murdered doubles are peculiarly Poesque images, but the metaphysical angst that lay behind them was by the 1940s being discovered anew.

"A catchword when Flannery O'Connor began to write was the German *angst*," Robert Fitzgerald has recalled. "The last word in attitudes was the Existentialist one."[14] Existentialism was both in the air and in print. From late in World War II on into the 1950s the influential literary journals—such journals as *Partisan Review*, *Kenyon Review*, and *Sewanee Review*, to which Flannery O'Connor herself would be contributing by the late 1940s and early 1950s— poured forth a stream of translations, interpretations, and reviews which delivered to their audiences word of this newest mode of thought. Sartre and Camus had just been discovered by the English-speaking world, and several years before such key books as *L'être et le néant* and *Le mythe de Sisyphe* were available in American editions, even a browser in the journals could hardly escape some familiarity with their contents. Sartre's essays and two chapters of *The Myth of Sisyphus* appeared in *Partisan Review*; reviews of and extended essays about both writers sprouted everywhere.

But existentialism is not limited to those two influential Frenchmen. As one commentator of the time was noting, "existentialism is more an attitude toward life than the somewhat restricted mode of thinking proper to any group within a specific philosophical climate. . . . Man stands at the rock of division between the two poles of existential thought. On the one hand he is drawn by the polarity of the Absolute whose focus is God; on the other, by the polarity of Nothingness whose focus is the Absurd." Both poles, he went on, can be traced back to the "coincidence of opposites" in the writings of Søren Kierkegaard.[15] And indeed, although Heidegger, Jaspers, and Marcel received attention in the intellectual journals, the real rival there of Sartre and Camus was Kierkegaard, whose works were being translated throughout the 1940s. By 1947 another writer could say, "A friend, returning from a recent philosophical convention reported to me that everyone there seemed to be talking about Kierkegaard and no one there seemed to know what Kierkegaard was all about."[16] Certainly it was from no lack of essays attempting to explain precisely what Kierkegaard was "all about," essays that to the reader of

Wise Blood often produce small shocks of recognition. Their suggestiveness for O'Connor lies not simply in their summaries of the ideas of Christian existentialism, but in their very choice of language and imagery.

For instance, in the 1947 *Kenyon Review* one might read this description of Kierkegaard's "subjectivity": "Not the understanding of any general relation of man to God, not the building of any elaborate theological edifice, but the way to eternal blessedness for 'my own little I' is every Christian's whole concern. . . . It means, in a word, turning from tautology to paradox." Thus there was the need to live "constantly in the face of death, in the awareness that here and now may be the last moment." "Only to find God could one relinquish the brightness of things seen for the dark despair of the mind turned in upon itself; only to find God could one renounce the splendid dream-palaces of speculative fancy for the cramped quarters of one's tortured solitary self." The religious life for Kierkegaard "is the life of what he himself calls 'an intensive point'. . . . Only before God is a man really himself," but "before God the finite individual is as nothing; and it is the bitter realization of that nothingness that marks the religious stage of existence." In sum: "For the intellect, pure paradox; for the spirit, pure suffering. This is indeed the life of the intensive point."[17]

Two years later an essay in *Thought* stressed "the tension of opposites" in Kierkegaard: "The result was paradox. Fear and hope, doubt and faith, apostasy and orthodoxy," only emphasized "the impossible distance between finite man and infinite God. Contradiction, sin, guilt feeling—these necessarily demand God as the fulfillment of individual experience." But since there exists "no rational bridge between the Absolute and the contingent," the "void can be crossed only by a blind irrational leap which is faith. . . . Because the leap of freedom and the leap of faith are blind and irrational, man reels with a spiritual vertigo as he stands constantly on the brink of nothingness, the null, the absurd. . . . The anguish produced by the nothingness, the *nihilum* which envelops the individual, leads him to God. God, on the other hand, becomes at once a necessity and an absurdity." In Karl Jaspers's modern extension of Kierkegaard, "Man moves from within, but yet—and this is the tiny light of hope—he is aware that he cannot achieve fulfillment by himself alone. By this negative awareness, man grasps more or less vaguely some notion of transcendence which may or may not be God."[18]

Such articles—and there were many others like them in the post-war years—of course draw heavily on Kierkegaard's (and Jaspers's) own language, language which sometimes seems to have been put to typically literal use in *Wise Blood*.[19] The concern with one's own salvation versus the construction of an "elaborate theological edifice"; the void, the abyss of nothingness; the foregoing of the "brightness of things seen" for the "darkness" of the self; the "blind" leap of faith; the "intensive point" and the "tiny light"; the paradox, that "tension of opposites"—all of this might have come from O'Connor's novel. For Hazel Motes is indeed a walking paradox, torn by opposing impulses, who attempts to construct a new theological edifice, a "Church Without Christ," but finds himself only hanging over empty, abysslike drops. And when he finally gives up all "things seen" by literally blinding himself, he becomes the novel's "pin point of light."

Perhaps, then, we need to modify Fitzgerald's contention that "in *Wise Blood* she did parody the Existentialist point of view," for he is speaking of the atheistic variety, the notion "that beyond any immediate situation there is possibly nothing—nothing beyond, nothing behind, nada."[20] Who can doubt that through the backwoods rhetoric of Hazel Motes there does seep the relativistic nihilism of a Camus or a Sartre? "I preach there are all kinds of truth, your truth and somebody else's, but behind all of them, there's only one truth and that is that there's no truth," Haze cries from the hood of his Essex (p. 165). But Haze's preaching presents only one pole of the paradox of his existence, the tension of opposites that he is. Atheistic existentialism is not, after all, the only brand, and Kierkegaardian views seem more deeply important for the novel than the overt satire of the unbelievers. As W. H. Auden was saying in a symposium called "Religion and the Intellectuals"—another sign of the times— "no religion is credible today which lacks an existentialist aspect."[21] At least one young writer with religion on her mind seems to have agreed.

The existentialist aspect of *Wise Blood* apparently developed rather late in the novel's composition, which suggests that its author was indeed responsive to the current intellectual climate. Several "plans for work" survive, and although they are undated, all seem to have been written before 1949. Juxtaposing these synopses with the published novel reveals the radical modifications that took place in the conception of the central figure. For instance, all three summaries stress Hazel Motes's "search for a home": "Home, in this instance, stands not only for the place and family, but for some absolute belief which could give him sanctuary in the modern world."[22] The potent motif of home survives in *Wise Blood*, but Haze himself fiercely denies its connection with absolute belief. "The misery he had was a longing for home; it had nothing to do with Jesus" (p. 24), we read in the novel's opening chapter. Similarly, all the synopses insist not only on Haze's sense of sin, but on his overwhelming and quite conscious feelings of guilt. In "The Heart of the Park," published early in 1949, the most striking difference from the corresponding fifth chapter of the novel is that the earlier Haze is made to tell the waitress and the caged owl, "I ain't clean" ("The Heart of the Park," pp. 89, 90), rather than to insist truculently, "I AM clean" (*Wise Blood*, pp. 91, 95). Clearly at this point the key conception of Haze as a walking tension of opposites, a conscious rebel against and unconscious seeker after Jesus, has not taken form. Yet it is precisely the brilliant stroke of turning Haze into an ambulatory paradox, driven through blasphemy to Sartrean nihilism and then blindly and desperately beyond both, that most compellingly contains the existentialist aspect of the novel.

If the immediate postwar period introduced America to existentialism, it was also the time when in Catholic circles the revival of interest in Thomism got well under way, and the most influential of the neo-Thomists, Jacques Maritain, was keenly aware of the threat of this latest form of infidelity to Christian orthodoxy. In 1948 his book defending Thomism against the "newer existentialism" appeared in English as *Existence and the Existent*. Slightly earlier, two chapters had been published in the *Sewanee Review*, including the conclusion, there entitled "From Existential Existentialism to Academic Existentialism." It appeared in the same issue as Flannery O'Connor's story "The Train."

In that essay Maritain contends that the original existentialists inevitably delivered their work into the hands of the atheist academicians because they confused "two fundamentally different positions of the spirit." These tensions Maritain distinguishes as the posture of "detachment from oneself in order to know" and "the attitude of dramatic singularity or of supreme combat for the salvation of myself." Confusion of the two is for Maritain literally non-sense: "One does not philosophize in the attitude of dramatic singularity. One does not save his soul in the attitude of theoretical universality and of detachment from oneself in the interest of knowledge."[23] But the tension Maritain describes here is precisely what we see, rendered as comic non-sense, in *Wise Blood*. Hazel Motes's deepest unadmitted desire is to be saved ("the clamor from the depths of the abyss . . . 'Who will deliver me from the body of this death?'" as Maritain says), but his overt posture is that of the seeker and proclaimer of universal insights. One exchange in the novel epitomizes the inversion of attitudes. Sabbath Hawks resentfully tells him, "I knew when I first seen you . . . you didn't want nothing but Jesus!"; Haze replies, "I don't want nothing but the truth!" Yet as he says this, he begins to cough. "It sounded like a little yell for help at the bottom of a canyon" (pp. 188–89).

The confusion Maritain charges against the existentialists he traces back to Descartes, whose rationalism, he argues, "raised a wall of insuperable enmity between intellect and mystery." That argument had been more fully developed in an earlier book, *The Dream of Descartes* (1944). There Maritain identifies the thought of Descartes as the villain in modern life, the source of various splits— of science from religion, knowledge from faith, soul from body, thought from feeling—that, opened wider rather than healed, continue to haunt us. Like T. S. Eliot's claim that a cultural "dissociation of sensibility" occurred at about the same time, Maritain's contention is that Cartesian thought is everywhere a force which "separates and dissociates, isolates." Most centrally, Descartes draws a firm line between soul and body, reduces the individual to the soul, and further reduces the soul to thought. The result for Maritain is that "Cartesian dualism breaks man up into two complete substances, joined to one another no one knows how: on the one hand, the body which is only geometric extension; on the other, the soul which is only thought—an angel inhabiting a machine and directing it by means of the pineal gland." The cultural ramifications of this split are thus double: on the thought side is the "theorist's illusion" of contempt for the body and the world of the senses, and an ignoring of the affective life to the point that feeling becomes only "a confused idea" (although, Maritain warns, "affectivity will have its revenge"). The body, on the other hand, has been delivered over "to the universal mechanism, to the energies of matter regarded as forming a closed world" and thereby becomes viewed as "an automaton," no longer "human by essence." The forces man has unleashed, Maritain concludes, "split him asunder."[24]

Maritain's analysis of the plight of modern man provides a striking gloss on the dualisms dramatized in the two major characters of *Wise Blood*. With his attenuated "gaunt" body and the theoretical assurance that "he didn't have any soul" (p. 24), Hazel Motes attempts to turn himself into a machine for pure thought, a thought so abstract that he is literally unable to see the world around him. Thus, the soul subsumed under a compulsive intellectualism and the body programmatically reduced to a mechanism for "sinning"— "He felt that he should have a woman, not for the sake of the pleasure in her, but to prove that he didn't believe in sin since he practised what was called it" (p. 110)—Haze becomes a dangling man, presented from the opening of the novel in the imagery of explosive tension, pulled helplessly in opposed directions.

If Haze is surrounded by images suggesting mechanicalness (of which his broken-down car is only the most developed), his complementary counterpart, Enoch Emery, is everywhere associated with animals. It is Enoch who claims the wise blood of the book's title, an instinctivism as rending for him as is Haze's intellectualism. Feeling is indeed a confused idea for Enoch. "Enoch's brain was divided into two parts. The part in communication with his blood did the figuring but it never said anything in words. The other part was stocked up with all kinds of words and phrases" (p. 87). And in Enoch such affectivity does have its revenge. Driven by his blood and vague about his distinction from the animal world, Enoch's body literally ceases being human by essence as he happily transforms himself into a gorilla. In Enoch the closed world of matter is resoundingly triumphant.

It is Hazel Motes, however, who most compellingly illustrates Maritain's notion of post-Cartesian man as "an angel inhabiting a machine." In insisting on the abstract clarity of his thought—"I've seen the only truth there is!" he shouts in triumphant despair (p. 189)—and in the concomitant inability to perceive the sense world, Haze comes to the center of his pseudointellectuality with the conception of the "new jesus," "one that's all man, without blood to waste" (p. 140). But this is exposed as the most hypothetical of abstractions. "There's no such thing as any new jesus," Haze confesses. "That ain't anything but a way to say something." To which his listener's response is pertinent: "That's the trouble with you innerleckchuls . . . you don't never have nothing to show for what you're saying" (pp. 158–59). If the logic of Haze's thought forces him beyond the verbal fiction of the "new jesus" to Sartrean nihilism, his final self-blinding and mortification of the flesh seem admissions both that he has seen nothing all along and that his intellectualism was only "a theorist's illusion." At the end of *Wise Blood* he appears to know, with Maritain, that "only the ascetics have the means of scorning the body."[25]

Yet useful as Maritain is as a gloss on the dualisms of the novel, its resolution moves not toward that healing of splits that he deems desirable but to an even more marked sundering; for as Enoch becomes all body, Haze moves toward pure spirit. In impelling her hero toward the desperate embrace of one pole of his being, O'Connor comes closer to existential thinking than to Maritain's Thomism. Despite their opposition to one another, what the existentialists share with neo-Thomists such as Maritain—and what corresponds so remarkably to the grain of Flannery O'Connor's imagination—is the language of extremity, an insistence on duality, dissociation, splits, paradox, the tension of opposites. This cast of thought was particularly influential in the late 1940s, but we should not forget that with its terrifying drops, premature burials, and accounts of murderous doubles, the fiction of Poe had made it visible much earlier.

III

The area where Poe meets the existentialists has been pinpointed by David H. Hirsch in a brilliant reading of "The Pit and the Pendulum." Examining the language of that story, he notes: " 'Sick unto death,' 'long agony,' 'dread sentence,' 'a most deadly nausea over my spirit,' 'nothingness,' 'silence, and stillness, and night were the universe,' 'shuddering terror,' the 'pit,' the 'abyss,' 'unmeaning despair,' 'the keen collected calmness of despair,' 'groped my way to the wall': it is almost as if 'The Pit and the Pendulum' could have been written out of a glossary of existential jargon. When Poe said that terror was 'of the soul' he was not merely defending himself with a bit of typical effrontery but was expressing a literal truth that he discovered about the same time Kierkegaard was discovering it— that the quintessence of terror is not man's fear of death; it is the dread ensuing from a confrontation with the possibility of his own immortality."[26]

That claustrophobic language of dread is not likely to recall the diction of *Wise Blood*, for unlike Poe, O'Connor does not allow her haunted protagonist to tell his own tale, does not draw us into the terrified confines of his mind—treats him, in fact, with a comic detachment cooler even than that she had found in Nathanael West. Her technique in this novel is one of indirection, the rendering of emotion through image, metaphor, and action rather than through direct expression. Nevertheless, the *nature* of Hazel Motes's obsessiveness is hard to mistake. For instance, when at the end of the first chapter he springs up from dreams of closing coffins and cries out from the berth, "I'm sick! . . . I can't be locked up in this thing. Get me out!" (p. 27), that sick terror is clearly, like Poe's, of the soul, a frightened dreaming his own death that also closely relates it to Kierkegaard's "sickness unto death." "It is in this . . . sense that despair is the sickness unto death," writes Kierkegaard, ". . . everlastingly to die, to die and yet not to die, to die the death. For dying means that it is all over, but dying the death means to live to experience death; and if for a single instant this experience is possible, it is tantamount to experiencing it forever." With his recurrent coffin dreams, Haze is Kierkegaard's man of despair who cannot die out of fear of some "more dreadful danger," and his reversal takes the form of genuinely learning how to die.[27] In one sense *Wise Blood* is a novel of education for death.

Nor is that potent term *abyss* a part of the vocabulary of *Wise Blood*. The image, however, is everywhere. Lowered places in the earlier parts of the novel—the carnival tent floor where young Haze looks down on a sight that brings sex and death together in his mind, the swimming pool in the park that confirms that association, the valley of the museum that contains the dead emblem of his new church—these deepen into the sudden drop outside his room and finally move inside Haze himself, where his sickness and the abyss become clearly identified. He feels "as if he were about to be caught by a complete consumption in his chest; it had seemed to be growing hollow all night and yawning beneath him, and he had kept hearing his coughs as if they came from a distance" (p. 186), a distance that becomes "the bottom of a canyon." "Converted to nothing" (p. 24), Haze's course takes him deeper and deeper into the pit of despair.

Tension of opposites that he is, however, Haze is less converted than he thinks, and he peeks at those many abysses with the helplessness of terrified fascination. For they seem hints in the world outside the self, in space, that support his nihilistic theories, and Haze proudly marshals his physical mobility to confirm his denials. "I come a long way," he boasts, "since I would believe anything. I come halfway around the world" (p. 51). At the same time, he repeatedly flees from the terrors of unconfined space, from a genuine confrontation with the unknown. Like those many figures in Poe who escape open spaces by immuring themselves in vaults, catacombs, caves, ships' holds, and strange chambers, Haze rushes to surround himself with one narrow box after another, from the train berth to a lavatory stall to his narrow room to his car—and then in dread bursts forth once more. For space in *Wise Blood* is again and again presented as blank or empty, and Haze both hopes and fears that it will produce some sign to rescue him from the nothingness it seems to proclaim. Only when he stands on the edge of the final abyss in the novel, the precipice over which a patrolman pushes his car, is he saved from the pit by at last being forced to face that dimension he has so long avoided.

If, then, O'Connor reverses those priorities Hirsch points to in Poe and Kierkegaard—"that the quintessence of terror is not man's fear of death; it is the dread ensuing from a confrontation with the possibility of his own immortality"—she nevertheless confirms their analysis, for these *are* the rending terrors that pull Hazel Motes in hopelessly opposed directions. So torn, his posture throughout the novel is self-contradictory and self-defeating, and he is surrounded by images defining his helpless and comic immobility. For despite his energetic efforts, despite his angry assertions that he is "going places," he absurdly gets nowhere. As we have seen, the opening sentence of the novel immediately establishes the double pull. Later in that chapter he is described as hanging: "He looked as if he were held by a rope caught in the middle of his back and attached to the train ceiling" (p. 12). Chapter 2 opens with him trying simultaneously to catch his hat and the train and so being left stranded; chapter 3 with his "neck . . . thrust forward" but his shadow "walking backward" (p. 37); and variations are rung on the image until, late in the novel, as he drives out of the city he feels that "the road was really slipping back under him" (p. 207). At this moment the patrolman appears who will force him to resolve his dilemma by leaving him naked to that "blank gray sky that went on, depth after depth, into space" (p. 209).

Haze's twin obsessions are introduced in the opening chapter of *Wise Blood* and there given a local habitation in his family past. It is the imagined figure of Jesus, of course, who confronts the boy with the ambiguous possibility of his own immortality. Hearing his grandfather preach that Jesus "would chase him over the waters of sin," Haze's guilty and terrified young mind inverts the metaphor. Jesus becomes imagined not as pursuing Redeemer but as dangerous Tempter, luring the boy "off into the dark where he was not sure of his footing, where he might be walking on the water and not know it and then suddenly know it and drown." The risk of Jesus, it seems, lies in the terrible possibility that the saving miracle of an *imitatio* may at any moment collapse, subverted by self-consciousness— Haze's personal version of the deadliest of sins, pride—that would sink him into everlasting damnation. Far better to avoid Jesus altogether, to refuse the dark threatening extremes He offers, to remain safely at home "with his two eyes open, and his hands always handling the familiar thing, his feet on the known track, and his tongue not too loose" (p. 22). Haze's resolution is destroyed when he is drafted into the army, but even earlier it had been deeply undermined by his imaginings of death.

The series of recollections and dreams presented in chapter 1 of *Wise Blood* dramatizes an ambivalence in Haze towards coffins quite as profound as that which he feels towards Jesus. He remembers his fascination as members of his family were placed one by one into their enclosing boxes. Dream-distortion shows them not as dead but as still alive, struggling to emerge from mortal confinement. As grandfather, father, brother all pass in funereal procession before Haze, what both mesmerizes and horrifies him is the action of the lid closing, an image of the ineluctable finality of death. But as the dream reaches Haze's mother, looking in her coffin "as if she wasn't any more satisfied dead than alive," something further happens. Even as the top closes, "she might have been going to fly out of there, she might have been going to spring. He saw her in his sleep, terrible, like a huge bat, dart from the closing, fly out of there, but it was falling dark on top of her, closing down all the time" (p. 27). Terrified, Haze in his dream becomes the dead mother, experiences the closing down, and leaps up crying for release.

Buried alive—we are back of course with Poe again, but, in the dream of the mother, with a difference. The female who returns from the dead vampirishly ("like a huge bat") to threaten the living makes several appearances in Poe's tales, but the passage in *Wise Blood* perhaps most recalls the best known of these, "The Fall of the House of Usher." There, in an atmosphere heavy with overtones of incest, Madeline Usher, literally buried alive, emerges from her tomb to destroy her brother and herself, thus unifying the divided house of Usher in a moment of apocalyptic catastrophe. For the post-Freudian O'Connor, however, drawing on both the Oedipus complex and its Sophoclean source, the duality succinctly implied in Haze's dream images—the mixture of guilty desire and fear, identification with the mother and projection of her as devouring monster, attraction to the closing of the coffin and terror at its claustrophobic finality—will characteristically be solved not in a coming together, but in a splitting apart. Different as their final images are—the deadly embrace and the mortified body—both Poe's tale and O'Connor's novel end by pointing beyond themselves, dissolving the material realms they have presented in suggestions of otherworldliness.

The full importance of Haze's mother emerges only later in the novel, for as well as focusing his ambivalence toward death, she is also the most important source of his ambivalence toward Jesus and thus the psychological nexus of the conflict that rends her son. Reared under her fundamentalist piety, Haze has been made overwhelmingly aware of sin, a state from which only Jesus can deliver him but which is given meaning only by the existence of that same Jesus. When young Haze sees at the carnival a naked woman in a coffin, his Oedipal imagination substitutes the figure of his mother, thereby fusing sex, death, and his own sense of sinfulness. "Jesus died to redeem you," she tells the guilty boy, and his muttered reply, "I never ast him" (p. 63), is the beginning of that rebellion which in the present of the novel produces such obsessively comic non sequiturs as, "If you've been redeemed, . . . I wouldn't want to be" (p. 16). Little wonder, then, that the vision of the mother emerging from her coffin—a dark version of redemption out of Gothic and backcountry lore—has such power to terrify Haze, or that he later preaches the creed that "what's dead stays that way" (p. 105). Determined to create a new life for himself, free of those influences out of his past, Haze at the opening of *Wise Blood* believes himself in full revolt against his Protestant upbringing.

That he proves a remarkably ineffectual, and thus comic, rebel is attributable partly to his own self-contradictions and partly to the ironic tensions O'Connor creates between Haze and his context. Ostensibly preaching a new religion, he adopts a posture that is actually designed to offend, to shock and scandalize, and thus to provoke a response, to elicit some sign that might save him. But in the modern city of this novel, Haze is a mere anachronism. The rejection of Jesus, the secularist creed he advocates from the hood of his car, has long since been adopted by the inhabitants of Taulkinham. Ironically, he is also too spiritual for such a society: he preaches materialism with an austere intellectuality incomprehensible to his audiences. Indeed, they see no real difference between this founder of the Church Without Christ and a conventional Christian evangelist. Haze can shout blasphemies from the nose of the Essex, but his listeners draw no subtle distinctions. " 'He's a preacher,' one of the women said. 'Let's go'" (p. 105). Hearing seems short-circuited and human reactions harden into a mechanical tic. When Haze tells his landlady the name of his church, " 'Protestant?' she asked suspiciously, 'or something foreign?'" (p. 106). Haze's inner struggle is thus enacted in a vacuum, for the city will not provide the battle he implicitly demands. Projected as an exterior action, the real conflict of values in the novel remains within.

Nevertheless, Haze's career is, as he assures his landlady, distinctly Protestant rather than "something foreign." With a theology no more elaborate than the concepts of sin and redemption, with his relentless subjectivity, his urge to be a preacher of some creed or other, indeed to found his own church (which is literally a protest against Christianity!), Haze's experience almost inevitably shapes itself into a journey—the modern pilgrim's progress of a blaspheming believer. If the physical journey, the journey through space, keeps breaking down like the ancient Essex in which so much of it is taken, Haze is nevertheless constantly in motion. Contrary to his own declared faith in bodily mobility, the real journey he takes is both interior and backward. At the start of the novel his eyes look "like passages leading somewhere" (p. 10); in the final paragraph of *Wise Blood* his "deep burned eye sockets seemed to lead into the dark tunnel where he had disappeared" (p. 231). Haze's desperate unacknowledged search for Jesus, that dark figure "in the back of his mind" (p. 22), gives his paradoxical journey meaning only on the spiritual level, for the forward physical movement takes him, in every sense, nowhere. "Was you going anywheres?" asks the patrolman who destroys his car. "No," Haze replies (pp. 209–10). It is the backward quest which finally confers on him the image of light, pinpoint though it is.

Like everything else in his story, then, Haze's journey is caught up in that tension of opposites that defines his being. Unable to acknowledge the division within, he attempts to suppress one side of the self—the side that feels sinful, that dreads death, that longs for Jesus. It is, of course, precisely his denials that lead him, with poetic and psychological justice, to coffin after coffin, deeper and deeper into the experience of a living death. But, as in Poe, the buried self will have its revenge: it bursts forth again and again to mock Haze in the form of the "double" motif. Indeed, the entire world of *Wise Blood* is one of ironic duality. The woman's question to Haze, "Him and you twins?" points to the recurrent appearance of two figures who mirror one another in absurd detail—little boys at the swimming pool, attendants at the lot where he buys his car, listeners to his sidewalk preaching, the policemen who find him dying—nameless grotesques who drift in and out of the pages of the novel and give to Taulkinham the air of a sinister funhouse where distorting mirrors send mocking images of man back at himself. But the specific reflectors of Hazel Motes are not anonymous, and if Solace Layfield is the only one the myopic hero himself can recognize, he is actually the climax of a series.[28]

Soon after his arrival in the city, Haze encounters Asa Hawks, the onetime preacher who has apparently blinded himself to witness his faith in Jesus. Entering the novel with a comically garbled mutter to a crowd, Hawks is a transparent confidence man: "Help a blind preacher. If you won't repent, give up a nickel. I can use it as good as you. . . . Wouldn't you rather have me beg than preach? " (p. 40). Haze, however, sees only what he wishes to see: in the preacher's supposed witness to his belief is perhaps a sign, a pinpoint of light that may indicate the reality of the Redemption. Hawks is thus a kind of objective correlative for Haze, the apparent embodiment of that desire for total commitment to Jesus that he has denied in himself. It is the example of Hawks that leads directly to the founding of the Church Without Christ, an act which is at once a challenge and a plea. As a result, "Haze couldn't understand why the preacher didn't . . . act like a preacher should when he sees what he believes is a lost soul" (p. 145).

In *Wise Blood*, however, all characters are masked, and superficial impressions are sometimes truer than a closer look. The initial distant image of Asa Hawks, cadaverous, dressed in black, his expression that of "a grinning mandrill," the lines on his face seemingly "painted on" (p. 39), faithfully suggests the nature of the man, whereas the subsequent view, which shows the scars to be real, turns out to be the deception. Haze's belated discovery of the preacher's falseness is thus shattering to him, for the unmasking seems another nail in the coffin of his hopes for rescue: his eyes seem "to open onto a deeper blankness" (p. 162). What Haze never does recognize is that Hawks's hypocrisy mirrors, in reverse, his own, that the pseudo-Christian and the pseudoatheist are merely upside-down reflectors of one another.

Much later Haze encounters a very different double, another masked figure, but this time one who openly espouses the secular humanism Haze so desperately preaches. "Onnie Jay Holy," as he calls himself, is as consciously duplicitous as Haze is unconsciously so. Under his oily "Soulsease" manner he echoes the doctrines of

Hazel Motes as well as his name, for his true patronym, he admits, is Hoover Shoats. Unlike Hawks, Shoats's obvious phoniness is immediately and outrageously apparent to Haze, but he utterly fails to see that this confidence man's saccharine language does not in essence falsify his own creed. The "new jesus," for both of them, is to be man himself. When Haze objects that his church is the Church Without Christ and not the Holy Church of Christ Without Christ that Hoover has called it, Shoats replies, with justice, "It don't make any difference how many Christs you add to the name if you don't add none to the meaning, friend" (p. 157). Nor does it matter, finally, how you package the product for the Taulkinham market: the "religion" is the same, however preached. Aside from affording O'Connor some sharp satire on the strain of decadent Protestantism that issues into self-help and ethical culture movements, "Onnie Jay Holy," with his huckster's language, parodies Haze's doctrines to expose their essential falseness. It is he who will produce Solace Layfield as a deliberate replica of Haze, a double that even he cannot miss, but although infuriated by the mockery of both these figures, Haze cannot see the implications for himself.

The most extensively developed reflector of Haze in *Wise Blood* is of course Enoch Emery, who occupies a subplot parallel to the main action. When they first meet early in the novel, O'Connor carefully establishes the situation they share. Both are country boys new to the city and friendless there, and both long for their respective homes. As Haze in chapter 1 insists to the porter that they both come from the lost Eastrod, so Enoch is sure that he and Haze share a common past. Both are denied. Enoch sums it up: admitting that he has "nobody nor nothing," he tells Haze, "You don't know nobody neither. . . . I knew when I first seen you you didn't have nobody nor nothing"—and then the crucial distinction—"but Jesus" (p. 58). The two encounter each other only twice again, but the true interaction between them is symbolic rather than narrative, for the career of Enoch is both an expansion of and a commentary on Haze's experience. Enoch's role in the novel is that of antihero, an inverted mirror of the protagonist. He is the comic embodiment of all that Haze claims he wishes to be, and his function in *Wise Blood* is not to preach a secular humanism but to act out its *reductio ad absurdum*. If Hoover Shoats parodies Haze's doctrines through his preposterous language, Enoch burlesques them through his moronic actions.

Enoch's "divided brain" is the comic counterpart of the rending split within Haze, but whereas Haze's fierce Protestant energy shapes his experience into the traditional form of the questing journey, Enoch is a kind of ur-Catholic, driven by his "blood" into obscure rituals which, on closer look, turn out to be parodies of biblical or Christian ceremonies.[29] If Haze preaches values that Taulkinham has already adopted, Enoch eagerly lives them. Country boy though he is, there is an inner truth in his boast to a policeman that he was "born and raised here," and he congratulates himself on having found a job at the zoo, "the heart of the city." In this he no more than fulfills his name: Cain was the founder of cities, but he "called the name of the city, after the name of his son, Enoch" (Genesis 4:17). It is to his "daddy," after all, that Enoch traces his wise blood.[30]

Like Haze, Enoch declares his freedom from "Jesus business," but he is far from irreligious. He places his faith—not always willingly—in the mystique of the blood, sign of the god within. But if his daddy is founder of this religion, Enoch is its high priest. Sensitized by his blood to a kind of mystery, he soon discovers it in the center of the park, but this mystery is so awesome (just to think about it makes him sweat) that Enoch cannot approach it without proper preparatory reverence. Chapter 5 of *Wise Blood* presents Enoch, with Haze as unwilling attendant, performing a comic inversion of the Mass. His established ritual demands not purification from sin but a formalized indulgence of instinct which leads from lust (leering at the women at the swimming pool) to gluttony ("gassing" a malted milk at the Frosty Bottle) to envy (a furious review of the zoo animals who "don't do nothing" yet receive lavish attention). Properly sanctified, Enoch can then mount the steps of the mausoleumlike MVSEVM as if approaching an altar and, inside, commune with the central mystery his faith has revealed to him: a shrunken mummy who was "once as tall as you or me" (p. 98). When Haze makes a noise, "it might have come from the man inside the case. In a second Enoch knew it had." Transported by the sense that the object of his devotions is a living mystery, Enoch undergoes a moment of mystical communion: unable to stand, he collapses outside the museum "with an exalted look on his face." When Haze hits him on the forehead with a rock, Enoch, filled with wonder, discovers the still deeper mystery of his blood. "He turned his head and saw a drop of blood on the ground and as he looked at it, he thought it widened like a little spring. He sat straight up, frozen-skinned, and put his finger in it, and very faintly he could hear his blood beating, his secret blood, in the center of the city" (pp. 99–100). This bloodletting is a form of both baptism and marriage, as the ambiguity of the final sentence suggests: the secret blood that pulses through Enoch also seems to spring from the very center of the city itself, and henceforth his fate is bound to the values of Taulkinham.

For Flannery O'Connor, Enoch's brainless devotion of course parodies the true purposes of worship. At the heart of the city, and at the heart of the world depicted in *Wise Blood*, is (in every sense) nature, and its appropriate temple is the museum, emblem of an existence bound to time and death. There is no transcendence in Enoch's mock Mass: instead he literally descends (the museum is in one of the novel's many abysses) to embrace the mystery of enduring death. Washed in his own blood, Enoch's regeneration can only be in another form of himself. But marked though he is, he must first prove himself worthy of his final reward: he must "justify his daddy's blood" (p. 129).

The chapters in which Enoch is driven to do the bidding of his importunate blood contain some of the most effortlessly comic passages in the novel. Enoch himself has only a very dim notion of what he is doing, for his moronic version of the dissociation of sensibility leaves his consciousness dark to the deeper purposes of his being: "his tongue, which edged out every few seconds to test his fever blister, knew more than he did" (pp. 129–30). The first task demanded of him is a ritualistic cleansing and refurbishing of his room beginning with "the least important thing and work[ing] around and in toward the center where the meaning was" (p. 132). A disastrous washing of the furniture is thus followed by a more successful struggle with the pictures, but only when he reaches his washstand, center and end of this ceremonial, does the purpose of his activity become apparent. For the washstand is Enoch's Holy of Holies, O'Connor's parody of the Ark of the Covenant, and his formal cleanup is the purification of the tabernacle preparatory to the entrance of his god.[31] In keeping with the tenor of his religion, the washstand is adorned with images drawn from nature and surmounted with the wings of eagles rather than cherubim. Instead of a mercy seat there is a place for a slop-jar—a sly comment on the value of Enoch's worship—and it is here, he vaguely imagines, that "rites and mysteries" will be performed.

But as the demands of his daddy's blood intensify, Enoch attempts to escape his mission. Such rebellion brings a fitting punishment: he is driven to undergo a Jonah-like ordeal in a dark movie house. There he experiences a fearsome revelation of the cosmology of his universe as heaven, hell and earth pass before his eyes in a triple-feature show. The first picture is "about a scientist named The Eye who performed operations by remote control," the second about "life at Devil's Island Penitentiary," and the third about a heroic baboon who is rewarded with a medal by a pretty girl. All three are terrifying to Enoch, but the last, focusing as it does on his own sphere, is the most personally threatening. When he emerges from the theater, "his resignation [is] perfect," and he is prepared to recognize the meaning of Hazel Motes's overheard plea that someone "bring us a new jesus" (pp. 138–41). What else but the mummy?

Having stolen it from the museum, however, Enoch is twice disappointed in the reward he feels is his due. What he expects, in his burlesque Christianity, is that he will become a "new man," which to Enoch means "with an even better personality than he had now" (p. 175). But a communion with the new Jesus produces not a shower of grace but a "loud liquid" sneeze, and the opportunity to "insult a successful ape" outside a movie house backfires when the star gorilla, one Gonga, tells him to go to hell. Still, he retains "the virtue of Hope, which was made up, in Enoch, of two parts suspicion and one part lust" (p. 191), and his third attempt produces the reward he has desired. Inspired by the comic strips that he reads daily "like an office," he overpowers Gonga, steals the ape suit, and happily becomes the gorilla himself.[32]

Thus, in a fierce travesty of Christian Redemption, Enoch is metamorphosed into the new man he has longed to be. His internal division is resolved simply by discarding his human dimension and turning himself into an ape. As O'Connor writes in an over-explicit sentence, "Burying his clothes was not a symbol to him of burying

46

his former self; he only knew he wouldn't need them any more" (p. 196). If the ceremonies and rituals his blood drives him to suggest a natural human impulse to worship, that worship is finally bestial, for in his brainless inversion of the relationship between matter and spirit, Enoch has embraced the purely physical in man. No wonder, then, that he envies the animals: in his thoroughgoing materialism he is indeed in competition with them. Now, having become an ape, he stretches out a hand to the world around him, but the hand "clutched nothing." Enoch's story ends here. For Flannery O'Connor, having pursued the logic of his commitments to their inevitable extremity, there is literally nothing more to be said. And so as the happy gorilla "whose god had finally rewarded it" (p. 198), the first biblical Enoch, who named his father's city, is ironically merged with the second, exemplary Enoch of Genesis 5: "By faith Enoch was translated that he should not see death; and was not found, because God had translated him: for before his translation he had this testimony, that he pleased God" (Hebrews 11:5).[33] In the translation of Enoch Emery, nature and the city are revealed as one. The final tableau of chapter 12 shows the gorilla alone, staring at "the black uneven wall against the lighter sky" (p. 198) which is both the silhouette of Taulkinham and the cage of man caught in matter. The human milieu of the novel has become indistinguishable from the zoo.

The parallels between Enoch and Haze are deliberate and extensive.[34] What Haze in rebellion preaches, Enoch in submission to the demands of his blood (*his* rebellion squelched) lives. It is Haze who articulates the spiel of this new religion: " 'Look at me!' Hazel Motes cried . . . 'and you look at a peaceful man! Peaceful because my blood has set me free. Take counsel from your blood and come into the Church Without Christ and maybe somebody will bring us a new jesus and we'll all be saved by the sight of him!' " (p. 141). But it is Enoch who knows where to find precisely the "new jesus" such a creed demands. If Haze is the prophet of the blood-religion, Enoch is its high priest, and his fate demonstrates more clearly than anything else in *Wise Blood* the consequences of Haze's professed values.

But Haze, of course, does not practice what he preaches. Paradoxical figure that he is, his professed values are deeply opposed by his unacknowledged longings, and nowhere is Enoch's role as inverted reflector more significant than at the resolutions of their respective stories. Both of these split figures at last achieve oneness by violently shedding one part of the self as inessential. Enoch, falling into the law of the jungle, destroys the original Gonga, buries the clothes that have proclaimed him human, and thereby emerges in his true identity. Haze gains self-unification only when that part of the self projected into his remarkable car, the broken-down machine that embodies his apostasy, is destroyed. Enoch puts on the gorilla suit; Haze takes off his means of physical vision. As Enoch turns outward to the world, a new star, hand extended in greeting, Haze turns wholly inward, taking, his landlady imagines, "the whole black world in his head" (p. 218). As Enoch plunges downward into bestiality, Haze rises upward into a desperate spirituality.

These, then, are the concluding polarities that *Wise Blood* confronts us with. Yet the extremes symbolized in the final state of the two central figures should come as no surprise, for the novel has by other means been confronting us with them from the start.

IV

The principle of duality dramatized in Hazel Motes and Enoch Emery and in the roles they play—hero and antihero—is one that informs every level of *Wise Blood*. If O'Connor's debts to West and to Poe produced her own distinctive blending of the disparate modes of comedy and terror, it is the peculiar way in which they come together in *Wise Blood* that sets that novel apart from the rest of her work. The comic sense in this first book, ranging from poker-faced farce to astringent satire, is not significantly different from that to be found throughout O'Connor's mature fiction, but *Wise Blood* is, in a precise sense, nightmarish in a way found nowhere else in her work. It is not only that the novel deals in frightening, Poesque materials—doubles, self-torture, obsession with death, murder, and so on—but that the entire treatment of action and landscape denies the daylight world. As in a terrifying dream, characters assume strange and distorted shapes, appearing and disappearing in defiance of waking probability; the familiar landscape of the modern city turns foreign and forbidding; and objects and gestures shimmer with symbolic resonance. Yet the narrator, having summoned up this dark and dangerous material, relates it to us in the voice of ironic comedy.

There is, then, a powerful tension, a deep doubleness, at the very heart of *Wise Blood*. One way of expressing this might be to say that the novel seems to strain toward two poles at once, toward the comic rationality of satire and toward the terrifying irrationality of dream. A somewhat different way would be to suggest that in *Wise Blood* there is a profound tension between the prevailing tone, one of poised and detached irony, and the texture, the very density of images that reveals a revulsion at the physical, a horror not only of the human body but of the world of matter altogether.

Nowhere is this tension more blatant than in O'Connor's handling of the pervasive motif of the dissolution of categories. Animal and human, mechanical and organic, inanimate and animate merge almost indistinguishably in *Wise Blood*. Enoch enters a drug store: "The fountain counter was pink and green marble linoleum and behind it there was a red-headed waitress in a lime-colored uniform and a pink apron. She had green eyes set in pink and they resembled a picture behind her of a Lime-Cherry Surprise" (p. 136). The peculiar combination of the comic and the frightening in such a passage stems from an awareness of the potential separateness of the elements, the implied conception of a possible order in which counter, waitress, eyes, and fountain concoction might be distinguishable from one another, yet which denies the imagined alternative even in the act of evoking it. To observe a picture of "a cow dressed up as a housewife" (p. 88) is to see literally a part of the commercial American scene. It is also to suggest that the categories *cow* and *housewife* might, in some other order—or some other world—be clearly distinct.

But in the world of *Wise Blood* there is no such distinction. Human figures are well on their way to being absorbed into the lower orders of animals and things. Haze's nose resembles "a shrike's bill," Asa Hawks wears the expression of "a grinning mandrill," Sabbath Hawks's eyes glitter "like two chips of green bottle glass," and Haze's landlady is hardly to be distinguished from her mop (pp. 10, 39, 42, 106). *Mutatis mutandis*, animals and objects take on the qualities of each other and of the human. A hot dog stand sprouts seats "like toad stools," bears in the zoo look like "matrons having tea," trees are painted to look "as if they had on ankle-socks," and for several pages Enoch is humiliated by a malevolent umbrella (pp. 88, 93, 96, 173, 176–77).

Examples of such metaphoric activity might be piled up almost endlessly, and its very density makes *Wise Blood* often read like a naturalistic novel gone berserk. In adopting the stock naturalistic device of applying animal and mechanical metaphors to her characters and investing natural and manufactured objects with human traits, O'Connor has pushed it to an extremity of comic horror. The novel achieves its pervasive terror precisely from the totality of the interchange, for here matter in its most bestial and mechanistic forms is triumphant: human figures are reduced to animals, puppets, or things in a landscape whose central symbols are a successful gorilla, a shrivelled mummy, and a broken-down car. Inevitably, the comedy that animates this dehumanized scene is often Bergsonian. Dialogues between characters are repeatedly at absurd cross-purposes, and Haze's ferocious anti-Christianity is greeted with the indifference usually reserved in the modern world for orthodoxy. An automatism of speech seems to afflict almost all of the characters, from Haze's obsessive "Sweet Jesus" to Enoch's bemused "I got to go now," to Hoover Shoats's tic of tagging "friend" onto all his sentences, to the indirect discourse of "she said" which reduces Mrs. Hitchcock to a talking doll. Action similarly becomes mechanical. Haze "jerk[s] his hands in and out of his pockets as if he were trying to move forward and backward at the same time" (p. 43). Puppetlike, Solace Layfield spouts his prophecy whenever Hoover Shoats raises his hand. Haze throws a bundle of tracts at Enoch: "It hit Enoch in the chest and knocked his mouth open" (p. 59).

This kind of comedy is always unsettling in its implications, but beyond it—and reinforcing it—runs the strong current of the imagery of repulsion, a repulsion at the physical deeper than anything required by the novel's motif of reverse evolution or the satire of a secularized society. Leora Watts, the whore Haze visits on his arrival in Taulkinham, has "white skin that glistened with a greasy preparation" and teeth that are "small and pointed and speckled with green" (pp. 33–34). Enoch is presented as a "damp-haired pimpled boy" with a "fox-shaped face"; he resembles "a friendly hound dog with light mange" and later acquires a purple fever blister (pp. 38, 44). A woman at the swimming pool with a "stained" bathing suit and "bandage-like" cap has a "cadaverous" face and "sharp teeth protruding from her mouth." She emerges from the pool this way: "She rose on her hands until a large foot and leg came up from behind her and another on the other side and she was out, squatting there, panting" (pp. 81, 84–85). A boy at the car lot where Haze acquires his Essex has a sour face and scratches at a scab on his ankle that "stuck up out of a pulp of yellow sock." He curses "as if he were trying to get up phlegm" (pp. 71, 69). One waitress resembles a man and wears a uniform "clotted" with stains; another has "a big yellow dental plate and hair the same color" (pp. 88, 192). A woman appears with blue hair and "two bright flea eyes"; another has hair "stacked in sausages" around her head; and still another has hair "like ham gravy trickling over her skull" (pp. 55, 105, 47).

The imagery of revulsion is by no means confined to the presentation of the human body. On the train Haze eats "something spotted with eggs and livers" which later returns as "something in his throat like a sponge with an egg taste" (pp. 17, 19). A machine "belch[es] popcorn," a leather pouch resembles "a hawg bladder," houses have "ugly dog face[s]" (pp. 136, 74). Even the color gray is not merely neutral in this novel: Haze's car is repeatedly called "rat-colored," the museum is "soot-colored," a cloudy sky is "surly gray like the back of an old goat" and soon lets out "putty-colored drops" (pp. 83, 139, 201, 96, 173). At other times that same sky sports "a dark sour-looking sun," or it "leaks" all over the landscape (pp. 68, 74). The winter wind "slashe[s]" at houses, "making a sound like sharp knives swirling in the air" (p. 255). Nothing is more revealing of the general tenor of the imagery in *Wise Blood* than the descriptive adjective that appears most often: *ugly*, a word followed at some distance by *sour*.

Sour and ugly—key terms to characterize the world of the novel, not merely its human inhabitants or urban scene, but the physical landscape altogether, the varied forms of matter. On one of the few occasions in *Wise Blood* when the action moves outside of the city, Haze drives along the highway past fragmentary "patches" of field and "string[s]" of pigs, the sky "leak[ing]" over the entire scene: "He had the feeling that everything he saw was a broken-off piece of some giant blank thing that he had forgotten had happened to him" (p. 74). The "giant blank thing" that Haze has forgotten is presumably Original Sin, the no-thing that is the absence of Grace, but if it has indeed "happened to him," it has also, as the sentence's double reference makes clear, happened to the entire landscape of *Wise Blood*. Matter here is repellent, without value, a "giant blank"—and finally unredeemable. Beneath the novel's sometimes exuberant comedy lurks a horror of earthly existence not unlike that expressed by the mummy: "There was just a trace of a grin covering his terrified look" (p. 185).

That the body ties us to matter, to the world of animals and things, indeed immerses us in it, and when it dies becomes *nothing but* a part of that world—these implications are manifested not only in the complementary careers of Haze and Enoch, but in the very texture of *Wise Blood*. The "blood" of the book's ironic title is no source of wisdom but the very substance that immures the self in the horror of the physical, a deadly cage and a coffin. In *Wise Blood* the self is buried alive in matter. The texture of the novel thus confirms its hero's deepest convictions, while its tone treats as ironic comedy his attempts to deny them. Hazel Motes may preach the primacy of the physical, of the body and the blood, and (ever more despairingly) a nihilistic hedonism of the here and now. He may doggedly engage in sex because he believes it sinful, but the spirit in which he does so gives the game away: "Don't you want to learn to like it?" asks Sabbath as she finally succeeds in seducing him. "'Yeah,' he said with no change in his stony expression, 'I want to'" (p. 169). For Haze is essentially profoundly ascetic, and his *contemptus mundi* is a thoroughgoing rejection not only of sex, but of all levels of physical existence, of life in the body altogether.

Enoch cherishes his blood, indeed absurdly lives by its dictates. Haze finally sheds his blood, as if trying to empty himself of it as quickly as possible. Yet why he does so, what precisely accounts for his final conversion (and conversion to what?) has been a matter of some perplexity.[35] The moment occurs, as we have noted, when a patrolman pushes his car over a cliff. That remarkable vehicle has been for Haze the means of his physical journey, his home, his church, the comic symbol of his creed ("Nobody with a good car," he claims, "needs to be justified" [p. 113]), his shelter from the terrors of space, and, ironically, his coffin-prison. With its destruction he is forced to encounter unprotected that dimension of existence he has so long avoided. The crucial paragraph reads this way: "Haze stood for a few minutes, looking over at the scene. His face seemed to reflect the entire distance across the clearing and on beyond, the entire distance that extended from his eyes to the blank gray sky that went on, depth after depth, into space. His knees bent under him and he sat down on the edge of the embankment with his feet hanging over" (p. 209).

Informing this pivotal paragraph are echoes of two quite different passages earlier in the novel. The first occurs soon after Haze's arrival in Taulkinham: "The black sky was underpinned with long silver streaks that looked like scaffolding and depth on depth behind it were thousands of stars that all seemed to be moving very slowly as if they were about some vast construction work that involved the whole order of the universe and would take all time to complete" (p. 37). The other is that already-cited episode in which Haze feels that the bleak countryside scene reflects some "giant blank thing" that has happened to him. Now, the protective car gone, Haze comes face to face with the blank, the emptiness that is both in him and in the landscape ("the entire distance that extended from his eyes to the . . . sky"). But the faint impingement of the earlier passage ("depth after depth") with its suggestion of a transcendent order introduces a note of ambiguity into this critical paragraph. Given the indirectness of O'Connor's method in the entire final movement of the novel, one must proceed with caution, but among uncertainties, one thing at least seems clear: unlike a number of her later protagonists, Hazel Motes receives no revelation. What he had earlier preached—"You needn't to look at the sky because it's not going to open up and show no place behind it" (p. 165)—is both ironic (Haze does need to look at the sky) and valid (it doesn't open up) in this novel. *Wise Blood* is a book of many nightmares but no visions. In fact, the upshot of this experience is that Haze abandons the expectation of any sign from this world, the world of overwhelming matter and the blank, turns wholly inward in blindness, and seeks out death. Why?

The doubleness of the crucial passage suggests that, finally stripped of defenses, forced at last to confront the reality of the nothing that has been only an intellectual abstraction to him, Haze overpoweringly discovers it both in himself and in the world beyond the self. At the same time, he also finds just the faintest hint—and the delicacy of O'Connor's echo is very much to the point here— that there *may* be something more, that the universe might contain a dimension beyond matter, that transcending the blank, depth on depth, may be another order altogether. It is here, it would seem, at the climax of Haze's story, that O'Connor most reveals her debt to the Christian existentialists. For the horror of this world, the blank, is when really confronted so devastating—"his knees bent under him" in terror and supplication—that Haze risks everything in a Kierkegaardian leap, a leap which at once acknowledges the blank of the self and places everything on the wager that there may be something more. Akin to Karl Jaspers's "negative awareness"—"that man cannot achieve fulfillment by himself alone"—Haze grasps "more or less vaguely some notion of transcendence" and thus becomes "the tiny light of hope" (what O'Connor calls "the pin point of light").[36] Haze's violent rejection of this world is thus a desperate attempt to validate within himself the existence of another order.

From the time he was a guilty child, Haze has been looking for some evidence of Jesus. Once he had lined his shoes with rocks and then walked for a mile, but "nothing happened. If a stone had fallen he would have taken it as a sign" (p. 64). Asa Hawks's self-blinding had seemed a clue, but when Haze discovers he is only a petty fraud, the unmasking leaves him with "a deeper blankness." Now, however, in fulfillment of Hawks's broken vow to blind himself in witness to Jesus, Haze *becomes* the sign that in hope and dread he so long looked for. As Kierkegaard had maintained, Haze's dread is a nothing, a blank, that exists in dialectical relation to his guilt. "The relation, as it always is with dread, is sympathetic and antipathetic. . . . for though dread is afraid, yet it maintains a sly intercourse with its object, cannot look away from it, indeed will not, for if the individual wills this, then repentance sets in."[37] This is the dialectic, the tension of opposites, that has defined his existence, but when he finally stares directly at the nothing that he has so long evaded not only does repentance set in, but Hazel Motes becomes a wholly otherworldly figure.

There can be little doubt of Haze's otherworldliness in the final chapter of *Wise Blood*. His landlady observes that his face has a "dead look"; when they sit on the porch together, she feels she must look as if "she was being courted by a corpse" (pp. 219, 227). And indeed he is dead to this world, so much so that O'Connor is forced to introduce the landlady as an intermediary between Haze and the narrator in this last chapter. The exterior point of view of the novel cannot directly present a character whose real existence has suddenly turned all interior, and the highly ironic tone would be inappropriate in view of what Haze has become. Thus the sudden prominence of Mrs. Flood as a reflecting device whose obtuseness both makes her an appropriate target of narrative irony and allows O'Connor to suggest the significance of Haze's final phase by comic indirection. Yet if she is a necessary narrative device, the landlady is made to serve a crucial thematic function as well. For as Haze has become wholly otherworldly, Mrs. Flood is (as Henry James wrote of a very different female) "the great round world itself." In the final chapter of *Wise Blood* Flannery O'Connor poses these two against one another in a way she never would again, for in this novel their claims prove antithetical and irreconcilable.

Mrs. Flood might be called a recapitulatory figure, for she summarizes the secularized worldliness Haze has encountered everywhere and gives final ironic expression to the matters that have so obsessed him. Although she is given a name, O'Connor insists on the term *landlady* to emphasize her earthliness, and with her "switchbox" mind she is as empty and absurd as the other grotesques of the novel. She is also, however, potentially threatening. Like all the women in Haze's life, from his mother to Sabbath Hawks, she would imprison him, and his final flight is from her devouring proposal: "'I got a place for you in my heart, Mr. Motes,' she said and felt it shaking like a bird cage" (p. 227). As she recalls the earlier female characters, she recapitulates Haze's male doubles as well by mouthing back at him parodies of the doctrines he has preached. She does not, of course, believe in Jesus. "I believe that what's right today is wrong tomorrow and that the time to enjoy yourself is now so long as you let others do the same," she tells him. "There's nothing, Mr. Motes . . . and time goes forward, it don't go backward. . . . It's you that can't see, Mr. Motes" (pp. 221, 228, 223).

But Haze is beyond such taunts and temptations. With his life turned wholly inward—the landlady, in wondering "what would be inside his head and what out," can "only imagine the outside in"— the preoccupations that have held him from the start of the novel are suddenly transformed. The physical journey that ends with the destruction of the car becomes the penitential spiritual journey. Whereas the outer movement had been marked by the cul-de-sacs of the coffin and the abyss, the inner quest is seen by Mrs. Flood as "walking in a tunnel and all you could see was a pin point of light" (p. 218). Space too is internalized: Mrs. Flood imagines "the whole black world in his head and his head bigger than the world, his head big enough to include the sky and the planets and whatever was or had been or would be" (p. 218). The lost home that he had tried so desperately to replace is no longer a matter of this world at all. When this landlady tells him he has "no other place to be but mine!" (p. 228) he simply leaves her. It is she who pronounces with unwitting appropriateness the end of his search for "a place to be": "Well, Mr. Motes," she says, "I see you've come home!" (p. 231). But she is greeting a corpse.

Haze's last words in *Wise Blood* are, "I want to go on where I'm going," but we can follow him only through Mrs. Flood, who imagines him disappearing into "the dark tunnel" and moving "farther and farther into the darkness until he was the pin point of light" (pp. 230, 232). Haze acquires the image of light precisely because he has immersed himself in the destructive darkness that he had so dreaded. As his fiercely penitential practices show, he hopes his journey is not to end in the grave—although he may find annihilation preferable to the empty and repugnant world of the novel. Even before she finds the glass and rocks in his shoes, the bloody nightshirt, and the barbed wire, Mrs. Flood is made to reflect, "He might as well be one of them monks . . . he might as well be in a monkery" (p. 218). But Haze is beyond even a modern "monkery." The violent asceticism of his end is a thoroughgoing rejection not only of a secularized age but of life taken in through the senses at all—life in a world of matter. The grisly comic victory of Hazel Motes is exactly to escape from this world, to mortify his body and seek out death.

By the end of *Wise Blood* the chasm between inner and outer, spirit and matter, is absurdly and terrifyingly absolute. Between Haze and the total milieu of the novel there has been from the beginning no genuine point of contact. Like his status in Mrs. Flood's house, he is a boarder in this world, never truly of it, and his obsessiveness is as grotesque in its final phase as it has been throughout. He is consistently ridiculous and offensive; his overstated Protestant guilt, his warped sexuality, his perverse refusal to live as if he has real physical existence, his comic lack of self-knowledge, his gruesome mutilations—all make him an easy object of revolted laughter. He is repressed, masochistic, monomaniacal, but in a context wholly immersed in the contrary excess of repugnant and debasing matter, he has the single saving grace of spiritual integrity that confers on him the image of light, "pin point" though it is. Twisted and private as his strange martyrdom may be, perhaps only a guilt-laden fundamentalist would even hazard a *via negativa* in the modern world.

Yet however one responds to Haze's final otherworldliness, the novel dramatizes no acceptable alternative in this world, nor does the narrative imply any other source of value. *Wise Blood* presents complementary extremes: there is Enoch or Haze, the monkey or the monkery, the immersion in the repellent world of matter or the grotesque search for God. The desperate violence of Haze's self-abnegation in the final chapter may seem so medieval as to surround him with the traditional aura of sainthood, but in the loneliness and privacy of his commitment, in a landscape which offers no real support for his actions, nothing to sustain his leap, he is a thoroughly modern, even existentialist, saint. If we try to evade the full implications of his terrible comic journey, his name reaches out of the novel to remind us that whatever the motes we have found in his obsessive life, we might look to the beams in our own.

V

The temptation to evade the implications of *Wise Blood* has been very strong, a temptation made more seductive by the apparent ease of "reading back"—viewing the novel through Flannery O'Connor's later fiction or, even better, through her pronouncements about her aims and commitments in writing. If—so the argument runs—she was an orthodox Catholic, surely she must not quite have approved of Hazel Motes in his final phase, or if she did at all approve, surely it must have been because, like several of her later protagonists, Haze has received a blinding vision that has revealed to him the reality of the Christian universe. Surely the thoroughgoing grotesquerie of the novel was purely satirical, a matter of drawing "large and startling figures" (*Mystery and Manners*, p. 34) of the perversions of man and nature at the hands of a secularized society. What else, after all, could a self-described Christian sacramentalist have meant? [38]

The "Catholic sacramental view of life," as O'Connor called it, is at the core of the question of *Wise Blood*. For our purposes, her most useful reference to it is also her most orthodox: "St. Augustine wrote that the things of the world pour forth from God in a double way: intellectually into the minds of the angels and physically into the world of things. To the person who believes this . . . this physical, sensible world is good because it proceeds from a divine source." The function of the artist who shares this conviction is thus to "penetrate the concrete world in order to find at its depths the image of its source, the image of ultimate reality" (*Mystery and Manners*, p. 157). However such a statement may illuminate O'Connor's later fiction, it is an odd description indeed of what one finds in *Wise Blood*. As we have seen, the imagination that informs the novel does not perceive the "physical, sensible world [as] good," nor does it present clearly "the image at its source, the image of ultimate reality," that is, the Christian God. What it does show on page after page is a world of matter so overwhelming that its hero can only seek out "the image at its source" by turning away from that world, denying the physical and sensible in blindness, asceticism, and the pursuit of death. In short, rather than being pervaded by the "Catholic sacramental view of life," *Wise Blood* is in its deepest implications a "Manichean" book. [39]

Now of course the standard view of the novel as essentially satirical, attacking the distortions that secularized man has inflicted both upon himself and on the world of things in his pursuit of a barren humanism, is a response to genuine elements in the text. Such a reading is less wrong than partial. No orthodox religious theme, after all, will account either for the thoroughgoing revulsion at the human body that is everywhere in *Wise Blood*—pimples, fever blisters, scabs, protruding teeth, dental plates, and so on can hardly be attributed to godlessness—nor for the treatment of the natural landscape in the novel. The opening paragraph, for instance, presents this passage: "The train was racing through tree tops that fell away at intervals and showed the sun standing, very red, on the edge of the farthest woods. Nearer, the plowed fields curved and faded and the few hogs nosing in the furrows looked like large spotted stones" (p. 9). Anyone familiar with O'Connor's later fiction and its fiercely symbolic suns might well anticipate in the contrast of the stillness of the sun and the motion of the train that pattern of suggestion she so frequently developed in subsequent works (and skim over the second of those sentences, with the "nosing" hogs being absorbed to "spotted" inanimacy). But the sun appears only once more in *Wise Blood*, and when it does there are no sacramental overtones to be discerned: "The sky was like a piece of thin polished silver with a dark sour-looking sun in one corner of it" (p. 68).

Hard as one may search for the informing sacramental vision in this novel, no such sustained perspective emerges. When the narrator's eye shifts from the sky to an earthly landscape, it finds it drowning in matter; when it looks more generally at space, it discovers again and again that it is blank or empty. Furthermore, like the sun, even the sky is not handled in any consistently symbolic way. Only in the early passage already discussed, in which the stars seem to be about "some vast construction work," is it clearly so presented—and that passage, it is worth noting, was a late insertion: when chapter 3 was originally published as "The Peeler," it contained nothing about the stars.[40] But in *Wise Blood* the sky is just as likely to appear as "a surly gray like the back of an old goat" or to "leak" all over the earth like faulty plumbing (pp. 173, 74). Or it may be treated ambiguously. In chapter 7, Haze drives out into the country. In the sky is a large white cloud "with curls and a beard" which at the end of the chapter has turned into "a bird with long thin wings" (pp. 117, 127). The First and Third Persons of the Trinity, no doubt. But surely the "curls and a beard" are more than a little absurd, the neat metamorphosis deflatingly comic, the tone here a humorous mocking of the hero's obsessions? Or is it?

However such a passage might be read, examination of the imagery of *Wise Blood* leads to one inescapable conclusion. If the only sacramental overtones are carried by the sky rather than the earth, and if even the sky only occasionally holds them, the novel can hardly be said to be deeply informed by the "Catholic sacramental view of life." Throughout Flannery O'Connor's mature fiction, the skies that carry supernatural suggestion do so in a very traditional way: they point toward the otherworldly. And in her later work those skies are always supported by resonant symbolic objects embedded in the earthly landscape: by artificial niggers, scrub bulls, shimmering fountains, burning trees, mysterious hogs, bloody woods, glittering peacocks. It is entirely characteristic that a decade after her first novel O'Connor would praise Teilhard de Chardin for a "sight" that can "penetrate matter until spirit is revealed in it. Teilhard's vision sweeps forward without detaching itself at any point from the earth."[41] But in *Wise Blood* Hazel Motes's moment of recognition comes from staring at the sky, not from any earthly source, and he further must blind himself in a desperate attempt to see anything at all. Haze's creator shares in his plight, for the narrative eye of the novel too can discover no spirit in the earthly matter at which it stares. It is little wonder that Haze's end can only be otherworldly.

In the ordinary sense of the term, *Wise Blood* is a radically symbolic novel, but the forms of its symbolic utterance are limited. Naturalistic symbolism—the imagery of animals, objects, and machines that inundates the landscape of the book—epitomizes without transcending: it defines a world wholly given over to mechanistic laws and a primitive evolutionary ethic. At the same time, the Christian motifs of the novel are presented with a kind of negative indirection—in the elaborate parodies of Catholic or biblical ritual stumbled through by the unconscious Enoch and in Haze's backward journey marked by his compulsive blasphemies, rickety counterchurch, and insistent stance as a yokel antichrist. Neither of these forms of symbolic expression is sacramental. The human action of the novel depicts a world that is, to use O'Connor's later coinage, "Christ-haunted," but even at its best only conducting an obsessive search for Him; while its metaphoric action suggests that His image is too deeply buried in repellent matter to be discovered. Rather than embodying the sacramental vision, *Wise Blood* far more convincingly presents what O'Connor herself said the modern believing novelist might achieve: "instead of reflecting the image at the heart of things, he has only reflected our broken condition" (*Mystery and Manners*, p. 168).

60

The broken universe depicted in *Wise Blood* is thus fittingly haunted by Poe in a way no other work by O'Connor is. Murderous doubles, devouring females, the suffocation of matter, the abyss threaten Haze at every turn and proclaim their engulfing inescapability in this life. Yet if the world dramatized by the novel moves toward nightmare, the treatment of that world is everywhere comic; if one pole of the sustained tension of *Wise Blood* seems to validate its hero's deepest fears, the other pole mocks him with ironic laughter. Haze and his creator may share a revulsion from matter that amounts to a rejection of the physical world, but they do *not* share a sense of comedy. Hazel Motes is a character entirely lacking in humor. As Enoch observes early in their first meeting, "You don't never laugh" (p. 48). Yet it is precisely the zest of this novel, its comic exuberance, its unerring eye for the absurd human gesture, its unflagging mockery of the shabby, the base, even the loathsome, that makes the vision presented in *Wise Blood* bearable. The world is indeed "a empty place" (p. 227) in this novel, and for Hazel Motes there seems no alternative to getting out of it just as quickly as he can. But the sustained ironic tone of the book gives O'Connor distance from her own perception of the repellent and the frightening; laughter, however edged, becomes a means of survival.

To argue that *Wise Blood* is not the sacramental work it is usually said to be is not of course to pass adverse judgment on the novel, but simply to try to define the nature of O'Connor's achievement here and to begin to distinguish this first book from her later work. *Wise Blood*, after all, has had more than enough adverse critics. It seems to have become the whipping-boy of the O'Connor canon, a mass of faults that reveals the greater expertise of *The Violent Bear It Away* or the superiority of the stories to both novels. The supposedly rickety structure of the book is taken to task, or its highly stylized mode is condemned ("life is not like that").[42] Indeed, *Wise Blood* is the most thoroughly grotesque and estranging work O'Connor ever wrote. The bizarre figures, the weird and terrifying and comic presentation of action and landscape immediately shatters our expectations that whatever the real subject of a modern novel, it will at least provide the outer semblance of plausibility, a mimetic treatment of experience, however outlandish the experience itself may be. But if the materials of *Wise Blood* suggest those of a frightening dream, they are nonetheless also strangely familiar, and the unmistakable vein of satire that runs throughout prevents our turning away from the book as simply a gruesome fantasy, unrelated to the world we inhabit in our saner moments. However violently that world has been refracted into the novel, its essential shape is all too disturbingly recognizable: if *Wise Blood* suggests nightmare, it is waking nightmare. And adding still further to the disorienting powers of the novel is the coolly ironic authorial voice which presents all the grisly absurdity of her vision with such disconcertingly detached poise. *Wise Blood* is not an easy novel to feel comfortable with. Even after a quarter of a century it presents an affront to our sensibilities, a sharp challenge to conventional notions of what makes up novels—and life.

There is, finally, no real answer to those who demand that all fiction be realistic, writers from Poe to Borges notwithstanding.[43] Critics who complain about the book's faulty architecture, however—and one early commentator went so far as to cite the blank pages between chapters as proof that what we have here is a series of "short stories . . . strung together" rather than a proper novel[44]—would seem to have been definitively answered long ago. Jonathan Baumbach, in the first sustained close reading of the novel (1963) discovered a pattern and structure so severe that he reached the disapproving conclusion that the novel is "all very neatly worked out" and that "this very neatness" is its "besetting limitation."[45] But if Baumbach's essay seems a sufficient reply to those who complained that "the theme dribbles away through the holes in the structure" or that "the [secondary] characters fade off,"[46] his counterobjection that the book is excessively patterned, overdetermined, does not do sufficient justice to the texture of *Wise Blood*. What he overlooks is the sense of creative playfulness in the novel, the sheer joyousness of an imagination first discovering its full powers, spinning off minor figures and episodes, comically elaborating its own inventions—all of this held loosely within the larger design of the book, but with a whirling energy that is clearly its own justification. This sense of release, this aesthetic exuberance, exercised as that exuberance is on the frightening and the repellent, is not to be found elsewhere in O'Connor's fiction. It is one of the marks of the uniqueness of *Wise Blood*.

In short, *Wise Blood* does seem to me a successful novel, though not, certainly, a perfect one. At moments (although not as a whole) it is, as Baumbach claims, overly schematic, the parallels between characters and the use of such symbols as the mummy and the gorilla a bit too pat.[47] The only sign of inexperience in the writing itself is the unsureness with which the significance of the material is sometimes handled: the narrator is occasionally too explicit, as if afraid that the action and imagery by itself has not conveyed meaning. We need not be told, for instance, that Solace is Haze's double or that when Enoch buries his clothes he is "burying his former self" (p. 196). Perhaps the problem is most succinctly apparent in the revision of the sentence describing Enoch's response on donning the gorilla suit. When that chapter first appeared as "Enoch and the Gorilla," the sentence read, "No gorilla anywhere, Africa or California or New York, was happier than he" (p. 115). In *Wise Blood* this becomes, "No gorilla in existence, whether in the jungles of Africa or California, or in New York City in the finest apartment in the world, was happier at that moment than this one, whose god had finally rewarded it" (pp. 197–98). Certainly the phrasing here is more polished, and the addition of the plain final clause could be considered an improvement, but "in New York City in the finest apartment in the world" is not only overly explicit but redundant, "the jungles of . . . California" having already and more subtly made the point. This occasional uncertainty of handling is not a major flaw, but it does sometimes inhibit one's response to the imaginative world of the novel itself.

Surely the strongest objection that can be lodged against *Wise Blood* is not a matter of faults at all, but of limitation: O'Connor's first novel simply does not have the richness and depth that she achieved in her later work. But even here there is a compensation in the creative exuberance mentioned above. One manifestation of this is the often brilliant use of the comic simile, a technique she employed only sparingly after this book. Not all are equally successful, and at their weakest they seem strained, but the best of these tropes are superbly witty, as in the unforgettable presentation of Hoover Shoats, who "was not handsome, but under his smile there was an honest look that fitted into his face like a set of false teeth" (p. 148).

Whatever the shortcomings of *Wise Blood*, they seem to me far from disabling. The novel remains a remarkable book, brilliantly conceived and written with precision and insight. Despite the episodic nature of the action and the dreamlike appearances and disappearances of secondary characters, *Wise Blood* is a genuinely sustained performance, its unity gained from the images, symbols, and motifs that flow outward from its hero rather than from a conventionally well made plot. Critics who have faulted the book for its supposed lack of control or structure or coherence or verisimilitude seem actually to be disappointed that O'Connor had not written another kind of novel altogether and to damn the existing one on grounds it never set out to hold. What is in *Wise Blood* is a stunning grasp of the possibilities of paradox, a mordantly humorous view of some of the darkest obsessions of the human psyche, the creative use of insights derived from sources as diverse as Edgar Allan Poe and traditional Christianity, Nathanael West and the existentialists, and the ability to imagine for these a fable that powerfully embodies a vision of existence both repellent and comic. In a prefatory note written ten years after the book was first published, Flannery O'Connor modestly pronounced *Wise Blood* "still alive." It seems likely to remain so.

CHAPTER TWO

The Duality of Images

Wise Blood seems an anomaly in Flannery O'Connor's fiction, for although its antimaterialism is clearly as much an intensely personal response as it is a philosophical position, everything she published after 1952 reflects an opposed conception of existence. These later works appear to mirror a profound need to come to terms with the physical, to accept corporeal life, however abhorrent or painful, as the given from which there is no escape. The blood that is so relentlessly mocked in that first novel as the pulse of a bestial determinism continues to flow through the fiction, but no longer ironically. Instead it becomes a terrifying force of inexorable limitation, revealing to her appalled characters their unarguable kinship with despised animals and hated ancestors. For the hero of her second novel the blood literally becomes the bearer of his feared prophetic summons, but the doom of physical existence, whether in the form of an undesired pregnancy, a stray bull, a mindless nymphomaniac, or "the enduring chill" of a long and unwanted life, crashes down on all those figures who so assiduously try to evade it.

But that early repugnance toward matter is not simply reversed in O'Connor's later writing; instead, it becomes absorbed into the larger imaginative dialectic of her fiction. As one might expect, the clearest traces appear in the stories published immediately after *Wise Blood*, but even there it no longer pervades the texture of the work. The Misfit of "A Good Man Is Hard to Find" searches the sky for a sign as desperately and as futilely as Hazel Motes had, but the focus of that story is elsewhere. "The World Is Almost Rotten" was an early working title for "The Life You Save May Be Your Own,"[1] but the line belongs to Mr. Shiftlet, not the narrator. Little Harry Ashfield of "The River" is as determined to "go on where [he's] going" (*Wise Blood*, p. 230) in seeking out death as was Haze, but the emptiness that impels him is localized in his immediate environment, not diffused throughout the landscape of the story. Yet beyond these traces, the impulse persists through O'Connor's career in her almost obsessive projection of it into her characters, who comically and confidently divest the world of its materiality. One after another, they turn away from the "threatened intimacy of creation" (*The Violent Bear It Away*, p. 22), attempting to manipulate the physical (including their own bodies) until it conforms to the snug confines of their minds. Sex hardly seems to exist for them except as an embarrassment or an outrage, yet they avoid close contact, reacting furiously to the touch of another. The world of matter beyond the body is treated with a similar violence: the intellectuals abstract it into laws and theories, and the intensely practical farm types labor until they can discern nothing more than "the reflection of [their] own character[s]" ("Greenleaf," p. 321) in the landscape around them. They take a grim satisfaction in making themselves two-dimensional figures in a two-dimensional world, in denying that sex, time, pain, love, death—the inevitable corollaries of life in a physical universe—have any meaning for them.

The central thrust in all of Flannery O'Connor's later fiction is to explode this complacent escapism or pseudotranscendence by insisting again and again that existence can only be *in* the body, *in* matter, whatever horrors that may entail. To recall that in its deepest implications *Wise Blood* moved precisely in the opposite direction is to point to the profundity of the shift that occurred in her imaginative thinking. For if the narrative eye of the novel can discover no spirit in the matter at which it gazes, the author of the later work firmly suggests that there is no point in looking for it anywhere else.

Yet it is not only in her characters that the terror of matter persists, for O'Connor herself never simply abandoned the methods of *Wise Blood*. The reductive naturalistic imagery, parodies of familiar rituals, deflationary metaphors, blank and threatening landscapes continue to appear throughout her fiction. What happens after that first novel is not a sudden or radical change in technique and vision, but the gradual extension of her resources. As the things of this world come to convey her religious preoccupations, the larger sense of those preoccupations undergoes a shift. Alongside the blasphemers and deniers begin to appear outrageous figures of affirmation; mixed with the ubiquitous cars, trains, and bulldozers come those mysterious artificial niggers and visions of the woods. The reductive and comically threatening animals of *Wise Blood* reappear as the peacocks, scrub bulls, and hogs of the later stories, emblems still of man's absurd entrapment in nature but also bearers, now, of divine revelation.

Thus the tendency of the metaphoric activity in Flannery O'Connor's later fiction is to move toward two poles at once, to strain away from the vision of a distinctively humanistic center. One impulse in her writing is downward, an absorption of the human to the realm of things, of animals and objects; the contrary drive is upward, a touching of the human with the grotesque luminosity of the divine. If one of her characters is "as real as several grain sacks thrown on top of each other" ("Good Country People," p. 271), another has a face "shaped like a rough chalice" ("Greenleaf," p. 314); if one cares for her wooden leg "as someone else would his soul" ("Good Country People," p. 288), another finds his "spider web soul" transfigured into "a perfect arabesque of colors, a garden of trees and birds and beasts" ("Parker's Back," p. 528). If old Lucynell Crater of "The Life You Save May Be Your Own" is "about the size of a cedar fence post," her idiot daughter and namesake looks, according to one character, "like an angel of Gawd" (pp. 146, 154). These two perspectives might be called the hylic and the numinous,[2] the first suggesting a lack, the second an excess of spirit. But the reductive imagery of thinghood in O'Connor's later work often verges on or is transformed into the demonic, and those figures sunk in matter frequently give off a whiff of sulphur. Their revealing eyes become like those of "a tree toad that has sighted its prey" ("The Partridge Festival," p. 442) or "like two steel spikes" ("Good Country People," p. 289). With such motion, the hylic perspective is bent round to form the dark underside of the numinous, as if for O'Connor the very sinking of the human into matter is simultaneously a movement toward the pit. Her outraged characters begin to discover that

67

they inhabit a world which, without ceasing to be corporeal, has taken on eschatological dimensions. The radical tension of this double perspective pervades O'Connor's later work, and Mrs. Turpin's cry in "Revelation," "How am I a hog and me both? How am I saved and from hell too?" (p. 506) articulates the duality that underlies all the stories.[3]

Similarly, O'Connor's treatment of landscape after *Wise Blood* suggests her expansion beyond the resources of that novel. If her urban scenes remain ugly to the point of revulsion—from the presentation in "The River" of the distant city "like a cluster of warts on the side of the mountain" (p. 165) to the view of city houses in "Everything That Rises Must Converge" as "bulbous liver-colored monstrosities of a uniform ugliness" (p. 406)—the natural landscape often comes to possess a spare beauty. The sentence in "The River" preceding the view of the wartlike city, for instance, quietly notes "a low red and gold grove of sassafras with hills of dark blue trees behind it." In the most lyrical of these passages in O'Connor's fiction, a "profusion of azaleas" in "The Partridge Festival" "seemed to wash in tides of color across the lawns until they surged against the white house-fronts, crests of pink and crimson, crests of white and a mysterious shade that was not yet lavender, wild crests of yellow-red. The profusion of color almost stopped his breath with insidious pleasure" (p. 426). But the natural scene may also present a face of terror. In "A Good Man Is Hard to Find," the early sentence "The trees were full of silver-white sunlight and the meanest of them sparkled" (p. 119) has been cited as an instance of O'Connor's swift notation of beauty,[4] but far more striking in that story is the way in which, after the car accident, the landscape becomes an ominous and ever more animated witness to the grim actions. The grandmother and her family suddenly discover themselves surrounded by woods that are "tall and dark and deep" and that after The Misfit's appearance "gaped like a dark open mouth." When the first pistol shots are fired from those woods, the grandmother "could hear the wind move through the tree tops like a long satisfied insuck of breath" (pp. 125, 127, 129).

This extension of emotional range in O'Connor's response to the physical world is itself a development beyond *Wise Blood*, for there the landscape possessed neither beauty nor terror, unless it was the terror of emptiness, the blank. But at least as important is her increasing use of setting to create symbolic resonance. Metaphoric gradually begins to glow through literal, intimations of the true country to appear through the recognizable face of the countryside. The fiercely animistic suns that are featured in story after story (and that have no precedent, as we have seen, in her first novel) are only the most obvious of these symbolic devices,[5] yet those suns are often accompanied by the complementary setting of a fortress line of trees beyond a field. As Robert Fitzgerald has said, this image reappears frequently enough to be termed a signature, immediately stamping the story a Flannery O'Connor work.[6] But it also holds a fairly constant significance as the objective correlative in landscape of the protagonist's resistance to the devastating revelations portended by those angry suns. Mrs. Cope in "A Circle in the Fire," Asbury in "The Enduring Chill," Mrs. May in "Greenleaf" all gaze at that wall of trees as the final line of their ego's defense against the mysterious force that threatens to burst in upon them. For Hazel Motes too an interior condition had been mirrored in the setting, the blank within reflected in the exterior world, but in *Wise Blood* matter had remained impenetrable and no revelation had come. To the protagonists of the later work, however, the terrifying awakenings to the dimension embodied in those suns prove ultimately irresistible.

Two related rural settings will help to illustrate how O'Connor learned to move smoothly from a landscape presented as convincingly literal to the same scene pregnant with symbolic overtones. "A View of the Woods" is another tale containing a field with woods beyond it, slightly but significantly differing from the settings just mentioned. This scene is first described as a "lot where there was nothing but a profusion of pink and yellow and purple weeds, and on across the red road . . . the sullen line of black pine woods fringed on the top with green. Behind that line was a narrow gray-blue line of more distant woods and beyond that nothing but the sky, entirely blank except for one or two threadbare clouds" (p. 347). In its apparent blankness, such a setting might almost have come from *Wise Blood*. Consequently, the story's protagonist, old Mr. Fortune, is bewildered by his granddaughter's violent resistance to his scheme to have a gas station erected on the field. Several times he gets up from his bed to look at this view, and "every time he saw the same thing:

woods," mere woods, where the sun makes the trunks of the trees stand out in all the nakedness of their seemingly empty actuality. However:

> The third time he got up to look at the woods, it was almost six o'clock and the gaunt trunks appeared to be raised in a pool of red light that gushed from the almost hidden sun setting behind them. The old man stared for some time, as if for a prolonged instant he were caught up out of the rattle of everything that led to the future and were held there in the midst of an uncomfortable mystery that he had not apprehended before. He saw it, in his hallucination, as if someone were wounded behind the woods and the trees were bathed in blood. . . . He returned to his bed and shut his eyes and against the closed lids hellish red trunks rose up in a black wood. [p. 348]

View has become *vision*, the literal the metaphoric, and the rest of the story exploits the symbolic overtones of the old man's sudden (and temporary) revelation: the archetypal dark wood, the suffering body of the earth itself, the "bloody wood" of primitive sacrificial ritual—and its New Testament analogue.

In a significant development of the methods of *Wise Blood*, "Good Country People" presents an ironic counterpoint to the use of landscape in "A View of the Woods." Here too a setting that at first seems simply a literal backdrop takes on metaphorical implications, but rather than opening up on a suggested added dimension, it provides mocking commentary on the pretensions of the protagonist. Near the end of the story, as Joy-Hulga Hopewell and the Bible salesman head for their tryst in the barn, they cross a landscape that seems merely noted in passing: "they came out on a sunlit hillside, sloping softly into another one a little smaller. . . . The hill was sprinkled with small pink weeds" (p. 286). From the barn loft, at the moment that Joy-Hulga "*lay back against* a bale," this landscape reappears as "two pink-speckled hillsides [that] *lay back against* a dark ridge of woods" (p. 287; italics added), and the echoing language identifies girl and scene. A minute later, her glasses in the Bible salesman's pocket, "She looked away from him . . . down at a black ridge and then down farther into what appeared to be two green swelling lakes" (p. 287). It is at this moment that the girl believes she is succeeding in her plan to seduce the naïve country boy, and the unmistakable mammary suggestions of the landscape provide an apt commentary on the action—but not in the way she thinks. For the roles the two have fallen into are not, as she had anticipated, temptress and sexual innocent, but rather mother and child: "His breath was clear and sweet like a child's and the kisses were sticky like a child's . . . [his] mumbling was like the sleepy fretting of a child being put to sleep by his mother . . . 'You poor baby,' she murmured" (pp. 287–88). But without her glasses, the landscape appears "shifty" to the girl's blurred vision, and at the story's close O'Connor gives it yet another ironic turn. As he leaves her, the wooden leg that she has treated like her soul safely in his suitcase, the man she has identified as her secular savior ("surrendering to him . . . was like losing her own life and finding it again, miraculously, in his" [p. 289]) seems to walk on water: "When she turned her churning face toward the opening, she saw his blue figure struggling successfully over the green speckled lake" (p. 291). The pseudomiracle is admirably fitted to the nature of this "Christ."

The movement in "Good Country People" from a neutrally observed landscape to the same scene presented as mock biblical symbol is a characteristic one in O'Connor's later fiction, but no more so than its counterpart in "A View of the Woods," the blank setting which opens onto a terrifying numinous reality. The perspectives are complementary, each employing a form of that double vision she attributed to the writer of grotesque fiction: "He's looking for one image that will connect or combine or embody two points; one is a point in the concrete, and the other is a point not visible to the naked eye, but believed in by him firmly" (Mystery and Manners, p. 42). O'Connor's literary and theological concerns merge here, for the process she discusses under the rubric "grotesque" she elsewhere calls "sacramental," and the double vision she describes is that classic Christian one.

O'Connor's declared sacramentalism would seem to rest more easily on the passage from "A View of the Woods" than on the mock miracle of "Good Country People," for if the former endows the created world with a genuine sense of mystery, the latter would appear at best to parody such a vision. Yet like those metaphors that undercut the full humanity of her characters, that drag them toward the world of matter, these ironic images in O'Connor's later work are

pressed into double service. Their mockery becomes a form of purgation, and the ironic demolishing of secularist assumptions simultaneously unveils the dark side of the sacramental landscape. Joy-
Hulga Hopewell's discovery of the true nature of her pseudosavior is
also a discovery of the reality of evil. In thus retaining and extending
the ironic and reductive perspectives of *Wise Blood*, O'Connor
comes to make them testify to an absence that is paradoxically also
a presence, to the felt reality of an evil that is theologically a priva-
tion of good. And if hell is the final negation, the hypostatic state of
the absence of God, the diminishing drag of matter opens up on a
still deeper abyss. The bleak nay-saying trees remain as much a feature of her landscapes as the fierce suns, and the deep current in her
fiction flows across the tension between them.

O'Connor's interchangeable use of *sacramental* and *grotesque* is a
reminder that both of these notions rest on irresolvable tensions.
The Catholic concept of sacramentalism insists on both the material and the spiritual, the specific and the universal, the outer and
the inner. Focusing as it does on the Incarnation, the sacramental
view stresses both the existential and the transcendental significance of the Creation: the Word made flesh has returned to the
world its full dimensions, to things and persons their uniqueness
and value, while at the same time raising them to participation in a
higher reality. The sacrament is thus not only the sign pointing to
the mystery, it contains and bestows the mystery itself; and as this
view extends beyond the specific liturgical act, it implies a physical
world pregnant with spiritual presence. If this concept hardly describes the vision that informs *Wise Blood*, it becomes more and
more appropriate as one reads through O'Connor's later work.[7]

The inevitable technique that would embody such sacramentalism is of course the symbolic, and indeed the suns and fortress lines
of trees, the visions of the woods and ironic walkings on water
are instances of symbolic images in the familiar sense that appear
throughout the later fiction. But the tension between outer and inner, the seen and the unseen, is so radical in her work that a pervasive doubleness reaches into almost every corner. For instance,
consider the description of the grandmother in "A Good Man Is Hard
to Find": "She said she thought it was going to be a good day for driving, neither too hot nor too cold, and she cautioned Bailey that the

speed limit was fifty-five miles an hour and that the patrolmen hid themselves behind billboards and small clumps of trees and sped out after you before you had a chance to slow down" (pp. 118–19). In context, the sentence is part of O'Connor's satiric portrait of this woman, epitomizing her garrulousness, triviality, and banality. But in retrospect it reaches beyond social satire to capture her moderation, worldly prudence, or "balance"—that very balance which, The Misfit says, Jesus has forever destroyed. The sentence, in short, reverberates on two levels, but if this is symbolism at all, it is symbolism in the broadest and most concrete sense.

At the fringes of her work, the tension of this duality can occasionally slacken. The tractors that figure in such stories as "The Displaced Person" and "Parker's Back," for instance, seem merely the workaday implements of the literal countryside; on the other hand, such names as Head or Hopewell, or such images as the "Jesus-seeing" hats her fundamentalists invariably wear appear an overt employment of allegory. But to isolate these elements falsifies the larger shape of her fiction which at its center resonates with a doubleness that is the genuine embodiment of her vision. In her best work the key images are firmly lodged in a convincing actuality before they are asked to function symbolically, and her artificial niggers, club feet, wooden legs, and tattoos are persuasively part of a physical landscape as well as the means to a larger revelation. Of course she is not everywhere equally successful. The peacock in "The Displaced Person," for example, seems intended as a plausible part of the farm scene in that story, but from the first it too insistently "means"; it never acquires sufficient actuality to convince us of its presence, it seems dragged in. But this is one of O'Connor's rare confusions between life and literature, between her all too well known fascination with peacocks and her sense of the viable symbol. Her intense devotion to the local as the raw material of her fiction usually assured the persuasive concreteness of the weighted imagery it bears.

Similarly, the roles her characters play out begin to reverberate on a double frequency, for while pursuing their quite individual concerns, they act their personal dramas on a stage which acquires a second level of reference. Here O'Connor's sacramentalism often appropriates the related assumptions and methods of typology, whereby a figure retains its particular historicity while also metaphorically participating in the larger patterns of Christian myth. The Misfit, for instance, remains a frighteningly lucid psychopath, a criminal anti-hero who attempts to define himself in existentialist terms. But to the grandmother, he takes the form of her final earthly destiny, death ("His face was as familiar to her as if she had known him all her life" [p. 126]), and at the moment he shoots her he becomes a type of the Antichrist. The three boys of "A Circle in the Fire" are unruly city-bred juveniles; they also become, rather abruptly at the story's end, types of the prophets in the fiery furnace. In her ironic mode, O'Connor had no need for the resources of typology. She creates of course no genuine Christ-figures, but pseudosaviors like the Bible salesman abound, and Mr. Shiftlet of "The Life You Save May Be Your Own," swinging "both his whole and his short arm up slowly so that they indicated an expanse of sky and his figure formed a crooked cross" (p. 146) is in part a sardonic parody of the fashionable literary device of appropriating Christ's attributes to purely human creatures. Her grasp of the typological method is, however, vital to what she makes of the scrub bull that is the center of "Greenleaf." That scrawny beast could hardly be called a Christ-figure, but O'Connor's sacramentalism enables her to cast him in a role that makes him, among other things, a type of Christ. Without ever ceasing to be a plausible farm animal, the bull takes on the burden of another dimension.

That creature moves through "Greenleaf" with an aspect that is alternately comic and frightening. Appearing first as he munches on Mrs. May's hedge, a piece of the shrubbery caught in his horns, "chewing calmly like an uncouth country suitor," he soon "lowered his head and shook it and the wreath slipped down to the base of his horns where it looked like a menacing prickly crown" (p. 312). At the story's climax his comic reentry with "a gay almost rocking gait as if he were overjoyed to find her again" is suddenly transformed terrifyingly into a "violent black streak bounding toward her," and as he "buried his head in her lap, like a wild tormented lover," the double vision coalesces in the action of the bull's horns which at once embrace and destroy Mrs. May: "One of his horns sank until it pierced her heart and the other curved around her side and held her in an unbreakable grip" (p. 333). Here O'Connor's typical meta-phoric action reverses itself, and the hylic world becomes both ab-surdly human and terrifyingly numinous. But the upshot is that this embodiment of the distant in the local, of the true country in the countryside, emerges as yet another of her grotesques, as fully es-tranging as any of her human figures.

The treatment of that bull is a reminder that there is nothing in the tradition of Christian humanism that demands that it be presented in the mode of the grotesque. Quite the contrary. If for O'Connor that literary term became a synonym for *sacramental*, it was precisely because she was not a humanist. In her work the per-spectives trained on the distinctively human cause it to become un-stable, to begin to dissolve, to seem to be invaded by the extremes of matter and spirit embodied in the landscapes that menace from every side. In those landscapes, we watch the "familiar and natural" world turn into the "strange and ominous,"[8] as the leading modern theoretician of the grotesque has said, but in O'Connor there is a hidden theological cause: a creation which has both fallen and been redeemed. She would have agreed that the grotesque is "the expres-sion of our failure to orient ourselves in the physical universe," but she would have added that, given the eschatological dimensions of reality, we never *can* do so. As a result, she laconically remarked, "We're all grotesque."[9] In such characters "it is as if an impersonal force, an alien and inhuman spirit, had entered the soul," but in O'Connor's fiction, as we have seen, the alien and inhuman can seem to come either from below or from above, to press her figures downward toward the level of animals and things or upward toward the mania of numinous possession.

The merging of the sacramental, committed to both matter and spirit, and the grotesque, uniting the comic with the terrifying, cre-ates a set of radical tensions that receives striking expression in the intensely literal cast of O'Connor's imagination. Although "A Good Man Is Hard to Find" had been called grotesque, she remarked to one audience, "I prefer to call it literal. A good story is literal in the same sense that a child's drawing is literal. When a child draws, he doesn't intend to distort but to set down exactly what he sees" (*Mystery and Manners*, p. 113). In this view the literal seems almost effortlessly to

75

give rise to the grotesque. But it is not only children who see literally: the affinities between this approach to the materials of fiction and the fundamentalism of the Protestant South would seem unmistakable. It is thus hardly surprising that this essential quality of her imagination receives its clearest incarnation not in the stories but in *The Violent Bear It Away*. The literalism of those backwoods prophets the Tarwaters is a source of comedy throughout the novel. Old Mason Tarwater's intimate relationship with God reaches into the most minute corners of his existence. When, for instance, the truant officer had come after his schoolless nephew, "the Lord had told the old man to expect it and what to do and old Tarwater had instructed the boy in his part against the day when, as the devil's emissary, the officer would appear." Following the divine instructions as passed on by his uncle, Tarwater escapes the official clutch by appearing with his eyes "open but not well focused. His head rolled uncontrollably on his slack shoulders and his tongue lolled in his open mouth" (pp. 17–18). Although young Tarwater believes that "escaping school was the surest sign of his [prophetic] election," he is usually not so certain about his dealings with the Lord. Nevertheless, his imagination is fully as concrete as his great-uncle's: a lake, for example, looks to him "so unused it might only the moment before have been set down by four strapping angels" (p. 167).

Here as elsewhere in the novel, comic literalism edges toward grotesque revelation, but when the Tarwaters confront Rayber, their literal imaginations produce the reductively grotesque. The boy's first view of this uncle's hearing aid gives rise to "the thought that his head ran by electricity" (p. 87), and he later defies his deaf relative with, "Why don't you pull that plug out of your ear and turn yourself off?" (p. 175). Rayber's intellectualism leaves him insensitive to all but the tritest metaphors, and when he produces such a pearl as "My guts are in my head," Tarwater's concrete mind immediately responds to his uncle's bizarre confusion: "The boy only stared at him, his eyes filmed with a dull cast of nausea" (p. 172). At other moments, Tarwater uses the particularity of his perception as a means of sardonic assault on Rayber. "What you wired for?" he asks with reference to the hearing aid. "Does your head light up?" And a bit later, "Do you think in the box or do you think in your head?" (pp. 103, 105). In such passages as these the very literalness of the boy's mind transforms the familiar into the estranged, and Rayber begins to be absorbed into the machine he wears.

Capable of the vision of the grotesque, Tarwater is inevitably also capable of the doubleness of sacramental vision in a way that Rayber will not allow himself to be. The basic opposition dramatized in uncle and nephew is not that between the literal and the symbolic, but that between the literal and the abstract, for Tarwater's grasp of the concrete itself leads into the symbolizing process while Rayber's intellectualizing dissolves the specific image in a vague mental landscape that hovers blurrily above the actual one. But the literal vision that O'Connor projects through the Tarwaters can also reverse itself, drawing its imagery not from a material world where "everything looked like exactly what it was" ("The Artificial Nigger," p. 264), but from the central source of the world of myth and mystery. With the startling clarity of her "fundamentalist" imagination, she seizes again and again on biblical metaphors or familiar pious texts and fixes them in her fictional landscape, a literalizing process in which metaphor becomes actualized, but without in the least surrendering its symbolic extensions. For instance, Paul explains (Romans 6) that in baptism we all die with Christ so that we may live with Him; O'Connor's baptisms in "The River" and *The Violent Bear It Away* thus become literal deaths, but they continue to carry distinct overtones of redemption. With the advent of Christ, "a man's foes shall be they of his own household" (Matthew 10:36), and the hero of "Parker's Back" is violently ejected from his house by his pious wife when he assumes the Byzantine tattoo which, as Stanley Edgar Hyman has pointed out, makes him "literally *chistophoros*, Christ-bearing."[10] At the end of *Wise Blood* Haze's landlady meditates on his mysterious blindness and on the darkness of death: "If she was going to be blind when she was dead, who better to guide her than a blind man? Who better to lead the blind than the blind, who knew what it was like?" (p. 229) and indeed within two paragraphs Haze falls into a ditch in ironic fulfillment of Matthew 15:14. If the great beast rising out of the sea in Revelation 13 is traditionally identified with the Antichrist, O'Connor will rediscover his features in Mr. Paradise of "The River"—blasphemies, head wound, and all—and have him end the story surfacing emptyhanded from the river "like some ancient water monster" (p. 174). If the last of this world shall be the first of the next (Matthew 20:16), she will present Mrs. Turpin of "Revelation" with a vision that is shocking precisely in its unmistakable literalness.

Indeed, the entire central action of "A View of the Woods" appears to be a complex, expansive, but nonetheless literal embodiment of Habakkuk 2:5–7, a prophecy against the proud and greedy man ("he is never satisfied") who oppresses all people to his purpose but in the end manages only to burden himself with the "thick clay" of worldly things. "Shall they not rise up suddenly that shall bite thee?" the passage asks. For old Mark Fortune, whose oppression of his family is intimately related to an insatiable pursuit of worldly progress designed to perpetuate his own name, the answer comes in a furious battle with the granddaughter on whom he has doted. "Then with horror he saw her face *rise up* in front of his, teeth exposed, and he roared like a bull as she bit the side of his jaw. He seemed to see his own face *coming to bite him* from several sides at once" (p. 335; italics added). At the end of the story the old man seems to sit helplessly in the diggings for his latest project gazing at a mirror image, a machine "as stationary as he was, gorging itself on clay" (p. 356).

The literalism of O'Connor's imagination is finally more extreme than the fundamentalism with which it has such evident affinities. After all, even the most rabid evangelists recognize the metaphorical sense of Paul's words and tend not to drown their converts while baptizing them. But in O'Connor's work, the incarnation of biblical language in fictional action reverses the relation between literal and metaphorical: as the Bible's metaphors become her literal actions, so their underlying actuality is made part of her metaphorical implications. This form of foreshortening collapses into a single perspective two levels conventionally held separate and thus becomes the most compressed expression of her sacramentalism.[11] At the same time, it is the technical analogue of that literal child's vision of which she spoke, a vision which reveals itself in the instinctual desire of her baptized children to seek "the Kingdom of Christ in the river" ("The River," p. 173). That desire is only apparently confused, for the actual river meets the transcendent "Kingdom of Christ" exactly at the horizon line of death. What is shocking in such actions as these desired drownings is not their confusion, but, on the contrary, their literal precision.

Whether in these embodiments of the timeless Word in modern action or in the discovery in the local and contemporary—in a tattoo, a scrub bull, or a view of the woods— of new sacramental metaphors, Flannery O'Connor's dualistic imagination produces the grotesque vision of a universe in which the disquieting conjunction of matter and spirit, of the eternal and the present, is perhaps best evoked by the "guffawing peal of thunder" ("The Life You Save May Be Your Own," p. 156) that bursts over the end of one of her stories. Caught in a landscape that teems with animals, machines, and inanimate objects, that sometimes seems almost to overwhelm them with thinghood, her characters increasingly find the familiar scene opening onto the pain and terror of a numinous dimension that threatens to absorb them as completely, to warp—if not destroy—them as fully as the world of matter. A few seem to achieve a precarious tension, to discover how they can be "a hog and me both," but for most the center will not hold, and the mechanical and the mad stalk through O'Connor's fiction. It is a world of extremities, a world off balance, and there is no *via media*.

II

"The Artificial Nigger" is not one of Flannery O'Connor's more extreme stories, and its major protagonist, Mr. Head, is precisely one of those few figures in her fiction to achieve a saving awareness which permits life to continue. This narrative of a rural grandfather and grandson's trip to the big city, a tale of initiation, betrayal, and reconciliation, is milder and more tender than most of her shorter works. For that very reason, an examination of the story provides an appropriate test of the general arguments advanced above.

First published in 1955, "The Artificial Nigger" comes almost exactly at the middle of O'Connor's career and fully exhibits her mature sacramentalism, that double vision which seeks to use imagery both literally and symbolically. As it now stands it is a polished and accomplished story, both comic and painful, local and archetypal, convincing as experience and resonant in its metaphorical suggestions. Yet the surviving manuscripts of this work suggest not only that such achievement was anything but automatic for her, but that in this story, at least, her initial commitment was to the local, the literal, and the actual. What they reveal is the central action virtually accomplished, the incidents and much of the dialogue almost fully in place, while their maker gropes for those images and metaphors that will convey the larger significance of that action.

Although several manuscripts pertaining to "The Artificial Nigger" have survived, they are clearly far from the complete record. The story initially seems to have spun out of the episode in *The Violent Bear It Away* in which young Tarwater and his great-uncle visit the city. In an early draft of that novel (and in much briefer compass than in the story), the old man denies his kinship with the boy and the two observe the little plaster statue. Tarwater is infuriated by his great-uncle's betrayal, but the act seems to affect this old man much less than it will Mr. Head, and the statue itself is simply observed in passing rather than becoming the focus of the episode. There would then appear to be a gap in the manuscript record, for in all the others which remain, we seem in most ways to be near the finished story. The relationship between the two Heads, the various incidents of their trip to the city, even much of the final dialogue, all appear essentially as they do in the version eventually published. It is what is not there that, from our present perspective, is most revealing.[12]

Immediately striking to the reader familiar with "The Artificial Nigger" is O'Connor's fumbling for the significance of the Heads' climactic encounter with the title figure. In two somewhat different manuscript versions, she knows (as she had not in that early draft for *The Violent Bear It Away*) that the discovery of the little statue will bring the old man and the boy together once more, but she is uncertain of the meaning of that reconciliation, and thus of the resonance of the story's central symbol. Both versions introduce the climactic episode in a similar way: "Neither Mr. Head nor Nelson ever knew how they were actually reconciled and neither suspected that it was the plaster negro that did it."[13] Nelson in both manuscripts "did not like to think about it," but Mr. Head is given two quite different reactions. In one version he thinks it is attributable to "the mercy of God," in the other he "continued to suppose that the fat man had saved them." Both these notions are presented as clearly erroneous. As in the finished story, the statue unites the Heads by presenting them with an image of black suffering which both reflects their own misery and differs from it. Yet in neither manuscript has that suffering anything to do with "the mercy of God" as it does in the final version. As a result, O'Connor here winds the story up very quickly, treating the Heads' return home in one brief and perfunctory paragraph.

In its published form, of course, the ending bears the explicit theological burden of "The Artificial Nigger," and its full resonance is established by the images that surround the return to the country. But those images, in turn, acquire their reverberations by echoing earlier passages in the story, particularly the complex opening sequence. It is not surprising, then, that the beginning of the manuscript versions is much flatter than that of the finished story. In the drafts the tale focuses at once on the rivalry of Mr. Head and Nelson. Mr. Head is given no pretensions to being "one of the great guides of men," and the key allusions to Dante and Tobit do not appear. Far less is made of the moonlight, which seems simply functional, serving to pick out the slop jar, the alarm clock, and Mr. Head's features for description. It bears few (if any) symbolic overtones, and the body of the moon itself, of which a good deal is made in the final version, does not appear at all. With none of the irony and mystery of the fully developed opening, this is a much more utilitarian start.

The manuscripts for "The Artificial Nigger" thus reveal O'Connor's primary commitment to the literal and the actual and her struggles to penetrate that world of matter, to discover within it the metaphorical resonance that would create the double vision. That she succeeded is of course attested by the finished story itself. In its final version "The Artificial Nigger" is a characteristic O'Connor work, everywhere informed by sharply dualistic extremes. Yet what makes it unique in her fiction is that in this story the polarities do not seem to move ever further apart to create a violent rupture, but bend in on each other, interpenetrate and mingle, and thus make possible that unparalleled reconciliation of characters with which "The Artificial Nigger" ends. And in this singular play of opposites, the key images that define the final perspectives are precisely those that did not appear or were left undeveloped in the earlier manuscripts: the moon of the opening and closing scenes of the story and the bright, transforming sun of its central action.[14]

The moonlit vision with which "The Artificial Nigger" begins creates for Mr. Head a silvery world of faërie, a land of heart's desire.

Awakening on the night before the trip to the city, he discovers that there is "a dignifying light on everything": his pillow ticking "might have been brocade," his trousers on the chair seem "almost noble . . . like the garment some great man had just flung to his servant." The moon itself he observes in his shaving mirror "as if it were waiting for his permission to enter" (p. 249). But the inflated imagery and carefully qualified language, the subjunctives and simile constructions ("*might have been* brocade," "*like* the garment," "*as if it were* waiting") work quietly here to detach the narrative point of view from Mr. Head's vision. Further, the moon, itself a reflecting body, is perceived by Mr. Head only at one reflective remove in the illusion-producing surface of his mirror, a surface which intensifies the "dignifying" effect of the light but also implies its narcissistic base in his own fantasy. But this doubled moon has another and less comforting aspect, one which Mr. Head wants no part of: "The face on the moon was a grave one. It gazed across the room and out the window where it floated over the horse stall and appeared to contemplate itself with the look of a young man who sees his old age before him." Mr. Head, however, prefers to believe that age is a "choice blessing," bringing him wisdom, fitting him, perhaps, for "one of the great guides of men" (pp. 249–50).

The tension between the light of the moon and its face, between the dream of human grandeur and the inevitable subjection to time, change, suffering, and death, adumbrates the central conflict of the story. Although Mr. Head responds only to the miraculous light, the one dark spot in his room, in which the sleeping Nelson lies, points quite literally to the old man's blind spot. And by the time the two leave for the city early the next morning, this sphere has been reduced to "a gray transparent moon, hardly stronger than a thumbprint and completely without light." Instead, a "coarse-looking" sun is beginning to dominate the sky of the story (p. 252). The influence of the moon continues to be felt in the "gray transparencies," ghostly reflections the Heads glimpse in the train windows like spiritual selves unwillingly dragged through the Dantean landscape; but the actual trip itself takes place in the burning heat of the sun. Under its pitiless light, the old man discovers what he really is.

Disoriented, hungry, and exhausted, apparently trapped in a threateningly alien black section of town, Mr. Head is gradually stripped of his pretensions to being a wise Vergilian guide. Since "it was for the most part in moral terms that he conceived" this excursion, his vague knowledge of the actual city as a geographical and social reality soon gets them lost. And since his vaunted role has been reared on this base of ignorance, he is about to betray altogether his moral superiority by denying Nelson. At this critical moment—in a sentence that appears in no previous manuscript—O'Connor briefly and firmly places the scene: "The sun shed a dull dry light on the narrow street; everything looked like exactly what it was" (p. 264). This is naked actuality. Unlike the romantic moonlight, the sun allows no fanciful self-aggrandizement. The simile form collapses into itself ("like exactly what it was"), achieving no illusory transcendence. When in this context the next sentence presents Mr. Head "hunched *like* an old monkey on the garbage can lid" (italics added), the simile strikes with the force of literal description. In "a dull dry light" that is all this old man is, an apelike clown who passes off his "garbage" as moral wisdom.

Only through the desolating aftermath of his betrayal of the boy, in which he experiences a bitter foretaste of hell, does Mr. Head begin to see himself as this absurd and reductive figure, recognizing at last his "true depravity." But he comes to this realization through the "action of mercy" which the encounter with the little statue seems to release and which recurs in the story's final scene, a scene again dominated by the moon. It comically "sprang from a cloud" as the Heads themselves prepare to spring from the train at their home junction, "restored to its full splendor," producing once more its "silver" effects on the sage grass of the clearing, but also causing "the clinkers under their feet" to glitter "with a fresh black light" (p. 269). Like the opening, this landscape presents a scene of beauty, but now without personal inflation. Here the moon sheds a light which is not only silver but also black—the transfigured image of pain and death, of the suffering, passion, and abasement that has been associated with the blacks of the city and, through their encounter with the statue, in a measure with the Heads themselves. The deliberate Edenic overtones of this final scene (the disappearance of the train "like a frightened serpent," for instance) stand in contrast to the excessive fantasies of the story's opening precisely because they include the black light of the experience under the sun. This is not the reflected moon, but the unmirrored thing itself, and if it creates a sense of paradise regained, it is a New Testament version, not a return to primal innocence. Sun and moon, then, define the literal and symbolic perspectives of the story, for while the moon is given multiple metaphoric extensions, the sun, unlike the numinous dimension it suggests in most of O'Connor's work, here reveals the bareness of the world of actuality, the nakedness of the human condition cast out to discover a hell of its own devising. Mr. Head's pilgrimage from complacent self-inflation to the emptiness of his "true depravity" to intimations of paradise is rendered imagistically in his movement from the illusions of the mirrored moon to the reductive sun of the barren actual to the moon purged, as it were, by contact with the sun.

If sun and moon, the literal light of day and the metaphor-inducing rays of night, seem at first to represent antithetical extremes in "The Artificial Nigger," they are revealed by the story's ending to be complementary perspectives: had Mr. Head not tasted hell under the sun, the moon would have brought him no glimpse of paradise. But although the sun and moon embody in its largest dimension the double vision that governs the story, all of "The Artificial Nigger" is built on similar antitheses of image and motif, antitheses that as the story proceeds keep breaking down under the pressure of a complicating and enlarging experience.

One of the first antitheses the story presents is that of youth and age, trailing along with them the traditional corollaries of ignorance and wisdom. Mr. Head firmly believes that "only with years does a man enter into that calm understanding of life that makes him a suitable guide for the young" (p. 249), the young here being of course Nelson, of whom the old man later says, "He's never seen anything before. . . . Ignorant as the day he was born" (p. 254). And in that early moonlight, we are told, Mr. Head's eyes "had a look of composure and ancient wisdom." But this polarity turns unstable when we discover that Nelson looks almost exactly like the old man: "They were grandfather and grandson but they looked enough alike to be brothers and brothers not too far apart in age, for Mr. Head had a youthful expression by daylight, while the boy's look was ancient, as if he knew everything already and would be pleased to forget it" (p. 251). As the action unfolds, Mr. Head's experience and wisdom

84

are both unmasked as fraudulent; he knows neither the city nor himself, and his cry "Oh hep me Gawd I'm lost!" reveals more than a geographical displacement. At this point the encounter with the plaster statue absorbs the antithesis into a different dimension altogether.

"It was not possible to tell if the artificial Negro were meant to be young or old," and as the two confront this mysterious image, "they could both feel it dissolving their differences," differences that cut deeper than the estrangement that has arisen from the old man's denial of the boy. Facing the little statue, they become mirrors of it—and of each other. "The two of them stood there with their necks forward at almost the same angle and their shoulders curved in almost exactly the same way and their hands trembling identically in their pockets. Mr. Head looked like an ancient child and Nelson like a little old man." From the perspective opened by the statue, a perspective that ultimately reaches beyond time altogether, the ordinary human measurements of youth and age and of such pretensions as wisdom collapse: Mr. Head comes to realize that he has been "forgiven for sins from the beginning of time . . . until the present." Although both of them feel the common human need to reestablish the old man's wisdom, Mr. Head's attempt to make a lofty statement brings him to full self-awareness: he *"heard himself say,* 'They ain't got enough real ones here. They got to have an artificial one'" (italics added). "Judging himself with the thoroughness of God," Mr. Head acquires genuine wisdom only at the end of the story, but it is the wisdom of his own humility (pp. 267–70).

One of the story's central antitheses is the racial one of black and white, a dichotomy established immediately by the use of the loaded term *nigger* in the title. O'Connor makes no pretense of exploring racial relationships here—the Heads themselves are the sole white characters of any importance, and only two Negro figures are at all individualized—but the use of conventional southern attitudes is essential to the shaping of her tale. It is Mr. Head of course who so insists on the black-white antithesis, but that dichotomy begins to break down with the appearance on the train of a "coffee-colored" man. Although Nelson fails his grandfather's catechism to see whether the boy knows a "nigger" when he sees one—a series of questions and answers that in itself reveals the values of an entire society—his protest points to the complexities that Mr. Head's racial pigeonholing conveniently ignores: " 'You said they were black,' he said in an angry voice. 'You never said they were tan' " (p. 255). Yet despite his ambiguous color, his elegant dress, his "majestic" bearing, despite the fact that he and his two women create a "procession" down the train aisle, this imposing figure is reduced by Mr. Head to the traditional contemptuous epithet: "That was a nigger."

Deciding that "the Negro had deliberately walked down the aisle in order to make a fool of him," Nelson now believes he hates all of his race. But when, lost in the black section of town, they stop to ask directions of a Negro woman, he experiences a very different reaction. The woman is large and wears a dress "that showed her exact shape," and the boy, "drinking in every detail of her," is "paralyzed." From deep inside him comes a response he has never had before, feelings of abandon he did not know he possessed: "He suddenly wanted her to reach down and pick him up and draw him against her and then he wanted to feel her breath on his face. He wanted to look down and down into her eyes while she held him tighter and tighter" (p. 262). She is, of course the archetypal dark lady, the black temptress—"Beware of dark women," his fortune from the weighing machine had warned—and the boy immediately feels intense shame at his involuntary reaction. Yet what she tempts him to is hardly simply evil, nor is it merely to sexual experience—this ten-year-old orphan's responses are as much to a maternal as to an erotic figure (*The Habit of Being*, p. 78)—but to the abandonment of everything implied in the name *Head* for the sake of deeper, stronger feelings. Like grandfather, like grandson—the name they share reflects their fiercely comic competitiveness based on common characteristics: their pride and independence, their willfullness, their quick minds, their self-control. Mr. Head has nothing but disdain for this display of Nelson's—"standing there grinning like a chim-pan-zee" (p. 263), he sneers—but, "an old monkey" himself, he is about to reveal an even more shameful lapse of control, for which disgrace the boy, a true Head, will show the loftiest contempt.

Once, in denying that "the South has a guilt complex on account of the Negro," O'Connor commented, "In Southern literature the Negro, without losing his individuality, is a figure for our darker selves, our shadow side."[15] It is precisely on this psychological level, with the emergence of the dark unacknowledged self, that the racial black-white antithesis of "The Artificial Nigger" finally collapses. Soon after his encounter with the Negro woman, as he dozes on the city sidewalk Nelson becomes "half conscious of vague noises and black forms moving up from some dark part of him into the light" (p. 264). Those impulses and feelings his head has never recognized become ever more active when, after his grandfather's denial, he tries to maintain his cold, unforgiving attitude. "As for Nelson," O'Connor writes, "his *mind* had frozen around his grandfather's treachery as if he were trying to preserve it intact to present at the final judgement . . . but every now and then his mouth would twitch and this was when he felt, from some remote place inside himself, a black mysterious form reach up as if it would melt his frozen vision in one hot grasp" (p. 267; italics added). The association of white, cold, and the head or conscious self is projected into the landscape just before the encounter with the statue, for in an elegant suburb the "big white houses were like partially submerged icebergs in the distance" (p. 267). But it is blackness, warmth and mystery that triumph as the little Negro statue dissolves Nelson's hatred, a melting revealed only by "a strange shivering about his mouth" (p. 269).

That Nelson cannot finally resist the "nigger" within himself rescues both the boy and his grandfather from the coldness of his proud contempt. Meanwhile, Mr. Head is making a related discovery about his own dark self. Feeling intensely his own shame and Nelson's punishing hatred, the old man "knew that now he was wandering into a *black* strange place where nothing was like it had ever been before" (p. 267; italics added). It is misery Mr. Head experiences, agony for the first time in his life, a suffering he recognizes incarnated in the little plaster statue. Erected by whites on the lawn of a big house, "he was meant to look happy," but part of the victory Mr. Head senses in him has been the triumph over stereotype, his becoming a genuine monument to the true condition of the blacks —which is miserable (pp. 268–69). Despite all the majesty of his clothes and bearing, the aging Negro they had seen on the train had had a sad face. Without realizing the connection, Mr. Head, "ancient child" that he is, has come to share in the condition of that other old man. In the little statue grandfather and grandson encounter the embodiment of the saving darkness in themselves, and the very fresh-

87

ness of the "black light" brought out by the moon that presides over their rural garden suggests that as they return home they have lost their original innocence for good.

Very closely associated with the blacks and with the city is O'Connor's use of the Dantean imagery of hell. It is forecast in the third paragraph of the story with the reference to Mr. Head looking as if he might be a great "guide of men," a "Vergil summoned in the middle of the night to go to Dante" (p. 250), but O'Connor does not really begin exploiting the allusion until the journey itself begins. And then its use seems at first a disappointingly flat one, pat and allegorical. The conductor "with the face of an ancient bloated bulldog," the sleeping passengers sprawled in painfully unnatural positions like tormented creatures, the ghostlike reflections in the train windows, Mr. Head's circling of the railway station dome always "to the left"—all of this seems a rather mechanical application of some of Dante's better-known motifs. The journey to the city as descent into hell reaches its climax with Mr. Head's absurd description of the urban sewer system, "how a man could slide into it and be sucked along down endless pitchblack tunnels." The lesson is not lost on Nelson: "He connected the sewer passages with the entrance to hell and understood for the first time how the world was put together in its lower parts." But it is at this moment too that O'Connor, having established the Dantean analogy, begins to shift its direction and significance. When Nelson rebelliously objects, "Yes, but you can stay away from the holes" (p. 259), he is of course right, and from this point on the apparent identification of Atlanta with the city of Dis ceases. Mr. Head stops circling the station dome (thereby getting them lost), and only then does the story make its real approach to the descent into hell. When the Dantean imagery reappears, it does so with another weight altogether.

For of course the city itself is not hell—except to Mr. Head, a man who as yet has no sense of what hell might truly be like. The allusions that seem to turn the trip to Atlanta into a journey to the underworld are a projection of the old man's assumptions into the exterior landscape of the story. Both he and Nelson anticipate that this day's excursion will provide, for better or worse, nothing more than the boy's exposure to the city he glamorizes, and his grandfather aims to see that it is for the worse. The challenges, as it turns out, cut deeper, and in the story's reversal it is the self-appointed guide who becomes the principal initiate. But while the urban scene is a necessarily alien and frightening testing ground that evokes from these two country mice responses of which their heads had remained unaware, the city itself has essentially only the values they bring to it. And those values quickly prove inadequate. Mr. Head, convinced that hell is "out there," identified with the landscape of the city (and when he calls it a "nigger heaven" he reveals just how hellish he believes it to be!), is totally unprepared for more intimate manifestations of the infernal.[16]

It is Nelson who receives the first hint that from the strangeness of this external world will come challenges which are actually internal. Gazing at the large Negro woman he suddenly feels "as if he were reeling down through a pitchblack tunnel" (p. 262), an abyss far more difficult to avoid than the sewer entrances. But the boy is frightened at his own reaction and in a gesture of humility grasps his grandfather's hand. Mr. Head, however, has proudly refused all knowledge of his own deeper impulses, and when his test comes he fails it—and Nelson—at once. Immediately he senses his entrance into a genuine inner hell: "Ahead of him he saw nothing but a hollow tunnel that had once been the street" (p. 265). His betrayal has converted the boy into his private demon, with eyes that pierce the old man "like pitchfork prongs," and when Nelson disdains to drink with his grandfather, Mr. Head moves fully into the inferno, that "black strange place" where he "los[es] all hope" and foresees his own death as "welcome because it would be the end" (pp. 266–67). This is indeed the very center of hell, Cocytus, the realm of the great betrayers, a sphere not of fire but of ice, where Nelson's frozen vision of hatred is objectified in the setting of houses like icebergs with drives that "wound around and around in endless ridiculous circles" (p. 267).

Precisely at this point O'Connor plays with the imagery of hell as exterior place and as interior state and makes clear where the burden of the story rests. When a man with two bulldogs approaches and gives directions which will lead them home again, "Mr. Head stared as if he were slowly returning from the dead" (p. 268). The bulldogs recall the metaphorical Cerberus who ushered them into this journey, the train conductor "with the face of an ancient bloated bulldog," and thus would seem to signal their emergence from the urban underworld. However, these are literal dogs, not mythologized monsters—we are still under that sun where "everything looked like exactly what it was"—and the return from an interior hell is not so easy as the escape from an infernal Atlanta. At the news that they are going to get home, Nelson remains "triumphantly cold," and Mr. Head touches bottom. "He felt he knew now what time would be like without seasons and what heat would be like without light and what man would be like without salvation" (p. 268). It is from this depth that he discovers the plaster statue which accomplishes what neither Mr. Head, Nelson, nor the man with the bulldogs could, restoring grandfather and grandson to each other with an altered awareness of themselves and of the world. And it creates for them a sense of their home as a paradise regained, earned, this time, through the struggle and suffering each has undergone.

Yet the Edenic scene they return to and the explicit invocation of a paradise beyond the local setting are made possible only through touching the depths of a personal hell. So too do the other major antithetical motifs of the story (sun and moon, youth and age, black and white, exterior landscape and interior world) repeatedly turn in on one another, each in the pairs of opposites transforming the other as they touch. The result is the uniqueness of "The Artificial Nigger" among O'Connor's works: a story that ends not in violent death or estrangement or in an apocalyptic vision, but in human reconciliation and the promise of a genuine future in this world for the protagonists. Yet the tale exhibits all of the features of her later fiction that were examined above: the use of polar images, the dualities of the literal and the symbolic, of matter and spirit, the grotesque merging of the comic and the frightening. What, then, makes "The Artificial Nigger" one of her mildest and most benign stories? Surely the answer is that here alone has O'Connor imagined an action in which the central figures (and particularly Mr. Head) are forced to face their inadequacies during the course of the story, to acknowledge them, and—most important—to suffer intensely for them. With his denial of Nelson, the old man is stripped of all his pretensions: he can no longer evade recognition of himself as a bare forked animal whose agonized sense of damnation is entirely justified.

Thus "The Artificial Nigger" contains a double action which appears nowhere else—the reductive movement toward unmasking and the pain of awareness, the redemptive movement toward abnegation and atonement.[17] The result, as we have seen, is that the characteristic tensions of O'Connor's vision here produce an anguished but healing restoration rather than a violent sundering, and life, transformed, goes on.

The humanist reader may well wonder about that transformation. What after all have the Heads really learned by the end of "The Artificial Nigger"? How have their attitudes toward blacks been altered? What is one to make of Nelson's concluding assertion, "I'll never go back again" to the city?[18] Perhaps one answer to such questions is suggested in O'Connor's comment on the wolf of Gubbio that St. Francis is said to have converted: "The moral of this story, to me at least," she said, "is that the wolf, in spite of his improved character, always remained a wolf" (Mystery and Manners, p. 169). The Heads will not become liberals, they will still use the term nigger, they will remain backwoods yokels. O'Connor's devotion to the actual and the given is too firm, her sense of human limitations too strong to make a radical social metamorphosis credible to her. Whatever conversions may occur in her fiction, it is never the nature of the beast itself that is transformed.[19]

Yet for all that, the Heads have been altered, even, in a sense, on the social level. Hearing his own absurd comment before the plaster statue, Mr. Head suddenly recognizes the shallow falseness of all he has claimed as his worldly wisdom, and Nelson has been forced to face not only his grandfather's weaknesses but his own limitations. The real changes are of course psychological, moral, spiritual, changes which cut deeply enough to bring about a cautious restoration of the relationship that Mr. Head so desires. For there is a secret mainspring to the action of "The Artificial Nigger," a hidden pathos that Mr. Head, in his pride, will not articulate even to himself: his terror that the boy will fulfill his threats, will go off to the city he idealizes and abandon him in his old age. That his attempt to avert this outcome almost brings about what he most fears and that only his defeat and humiliation produce the desired alteration in Nelson are of course central ironies in the story. But he must first touch his own depths in order to have a glimpse of the heights and only then, grasping both poles, can he achieve the double vision that leads to reconciliation and enables life to continue.

III

At the moment of literalness in "The Artificial Nigger," that moment when "everything looked like exactly what it was," the principal character in the scene is revealed not as simply human, all too human, but as considerably less than that. "Hunched like an old monkey on the garbage can lid," the self-sufficient Mr. Head begins to move away from the human level, to be absorbed into Enoch Emery's world of animals, which here opens up into a view of the inferno. The vision of the literal in O'Connor is paradoxically also the vision of the grotesque, and in the case of Mr. Head that vision moves him downward, towards the realm of the inhuman and the demonic.

The grotesque, O'Connor contended, "always brings with it a slight hint of death to the ego, a kind of memento mori."[20] Certainly in the images applied to Mr. Head at this moment that death is perceptible, not only a destruction of the grandiose self-conception with which "The Artificial Nigger" opens, but a denial of those attributes which would identify him as distinctively human at all. Similarly, ancient "General" Sash of "A Late Encounter with the Enemy," in reducing his existence to egoistic appearances at ceremonial spectacles, becomes hardly distinguishable from the historical relics that surround him at these rituals. Wheeled out like some family heirloom usually consigned to the attic, "every year on Confederate Memorial Day, he was bundled up and lent to the Capitol City Museum where he was displayed from one to four in a musty room full of old photographs, old uniforms, old artillery, and historic documents. . . . There was nothing about him to indicate that he was alive except an occasional movement in his milky gray eyes" (p. 139).

But if the grotesque can produce these reductive images, absorbing the human to the level of animals and things, proclaiming the frightening emptiness of apparently engulfing matter, so can it also, with

equal terror, suggest the radical warping of the human by the numinous, the twisted deformity of the otherworldly. The hideous clubfoot that Rufus Johnson brandishes throughout "The Lame Shall
Enter First" is repeatedly clothed in Gothic images ("the end of an
empty sock protruded like a gray tongue from a severed head," "the
unsheathed mass of foot in the dirty sock," "an animal still half
alive" [pp. 450, 470]), but to Johnson the foot is at once a part of himself and independent, a confirmation of his tie with the vibrant
world of mystery, the center of his prophetic specialness. He treats it
"like a sacred object," and when a shoe for which it has been measured proves too small, he insists that the foot has grown, "as if,
in expanding, the foot had acted on some inspiration of its own"
(pp. 459, 466). Johnson's monstrous deformity is the inevitable sign
of human entrapment in matter, but as a sacramental object it twists
him to a dimension that is beyond this world altogether.

Caught within the dualistic pincers of the grotesque, O'Connor's
characters are all etched in images which deny them human completeness and which carry unmistakable reminders of death. For in
her vision death is both the ultimate absorption of the human into
matter—ashes to ashes, dust to dust—and the entrance into a dimension that is either utter negation or final wholeness. The world
of her fiction shimmers with these dualities, and her landscapes are
marked by views and objects that bear the overtones of her concern
with last things. But after *Wise Blood* that ultimate horizon shifts
and expands. At the heart of her first novel lay the museum with its
shrivelled mummy, emblems of the world of that book. At the heart
of the farm of the later story "The Displaced Person" lies the analogous symbol of Mrs. McIntyre's countryside domain, "the graveyard
where the Judge lay grinning under his desecrated monument"
(p. 224). Yet this story also contains—and there is no equivalent
image in the novel—the insistent peacock with its clear burden of a
universe transfigured. Similarly, "Revelation" is a story full of de-
meaning and reductive hogs, but the "transparent intensity" of the
final landscape is irrevocably apocalyptic, and even the despised
hogs have a crucial part to play in bringing about Mrs. Turpin's
revelation.

The tension between the hylic and the numinous, between the

less than human and the more than human, between the pull toward a reductive matter and the thrust of deforming spirit pervades O'Connor's vision after *Wise Blood*, expressing itself in the very images—the metaphors, the objects, the landscapes—that most intimately embody that vision. Yet that tension also reveals itself in the central conception of action in her stories, in the fierce confrontations between deeply opposed characters. From these confrontations a very traditional configuration emerges, but it is a configuration that is pushed, typically, to an untraditional and deeply discomforting extreme.

CHAPTER THREE

The Double

Conflict, often violent conflict, is at the very center of Flannery O'Connor's fiction. Characters mutter, snarl, and rage at one another until the rising pressure of the action forces a climactic clash, a bursting of tensions often both physical and deadly. Yet those same angry figures are viewed from a comic distance so severe that they hover on the edge of—and sometimes fall over into—caricature. O'Connor's people are among the least introspective in modern fiction, with minds at once so unaware and so absurdly assured that they have refused to acknowledge any deeper self. None of them are interested in what one character calls his "underhead," and the result is the very fury of their responses, for the unconscious exists in O'Connor's fiction not as a psychic area to be probed but as a violent force denied. The ironic upshot of their denial is that her characters thereby become obsessive figures, clinging in outrage to their narrowly rigid self-definitions in the face of all challenges. Incapable of doubt or self-questioning, her protagonists are incapable of the flexibility of development, and the climaxes of the stories confront them with the startling image of all they have denied. Their eyes are finally "shocked clean," but the shock is sometimes sufficient to kill them as well.

As the screw of the action turns and tensions rise, again and again there appears before those self-denying characters a creature both strange and yet in some way familiar, like a distorting mirror whose image they at once repudiate but cannot quite turn away from—in short, a double figure. An expression in character and action of

O'Connor's characteristic duality, the pattern recurs so often that it can only be called obsessive. Albert J. Guerard has justly remarked that "the word *double* is embarrassingly vague as used in literary criticism,"[1] but in her work the configuration always takes one of two classic forms. Either one character discovers that another is a replica of himself, an almost identical reflection—here the paradigm would be twins—or, much more often, one character is presented as the alter ego of another, the embodiment of qualities suppressed or ignored by the first, a mirror image or inverse reflection. Here the paradigm perhaps receives its best expression in the myth of the *Symposium* that for each of us there exists a complementary self to which we were once physically attached; Freud's observation that two dramatized figures may together constitute a complete personality is its psycholiterary counterpart.[2] Yet whichever form the double takes, he signals a widening split within the protagonist and is felt as an opposing self. The sense of uncanniness that always marks his appearance is sometimes muted in O'Connor, for since most of her works focus on relationships within a family the double figure may retain a surface plausibility. But the dismaying discovery of unwanted kinship can extend well beyond the family, and in fact beyond the human world altogether.

The heroes of both of the novels are deeply split within themselves. Almost inevitably, it seems, they also encounter everywhere *Doppelgängers* who reflect aspects of their self-division. In the more compressed form of the story the central figures may not be so obviously dramatized as internally divided, but they are nevertheless forced again and again to gaze into an appalling mirror.[3] Language and imagery heralding the *Doppelgänger* abounds. "That was your black double" (p. 419) the son of "Everything That Rises Must Converge" archly confides to his dying mother, without considering the implications for himself; for if the large Negro woman of this story embodies a side of life his mother has refused to see, then to whom does her dependent little boy correspond? Old Mark Fortune of "A View of the Woods" complacently recognizes in his granddaughter a "small replica" of himself, a recognition that becomes intolerable when at the story's end "his own image" turns "triumphant and hostile" (pp. 336, 355). The only literal twins in O'Connor's fiction are the mysterious brothers of "Greenleaf," but it is no accident, as we shall see, that the protagonist of "The Comforts of Home" is called Thomas, a name which means "twin." From twins it is but a short step to brothers: near the beginning of "The Artificial Nigger," we recall, Mr. Head and Nelson "looked enough alike to be brothers and brothers not too far apart in age," and near the end of that story they stare at their saving alter ego, the little statue, in attitudes which are called "identical." In "Judgement Day" old Tanner gazes at the black exconvict Coleman and sees a "negative image of himself, as if clownishness and captivity had been their common lot" (p. 538–39). In "The Lame Shall Enter First" the social worker Sheppard discovers that Rufus Johnson's eyes have become "distorting mirrors in which he saw himself made hideous and grotesque" (p. 474).

Double, replica, twin, brother, negative image, mirror—this is the classic language of the *Doppelgänger* motif. Of the traditional terms, only *shadow* seems to be missing; yet one recollects her comment on the appearance of the Negro in southern literature as "a figure for our darker selves, our shadow side," and certainly the image of the shadow is notably employed in both novels and in "The Artificial Nigger." While Hazel Motes strides through Taulkinham spewing forth blasphemies, he trails behind him "a thin nervous shadow walking backwards" (*Wise Blood*, p. 37), and both Tarwater and the Heads discover "ghost-like" transparencies in train and store windows, shadowy selves that appear to have a being of their own. These last seem images of what Otto Rank called "the double as immortal self,"[4] a spiritual shadow that is deeply disturbing because it is part of a dimension not contained by the everyday world these characters prefer to think is all that exists.

But the double configuration need not appear only in these traditional ways. To take a minor (and undeveloped) example, O'Connor suggests it swiftly and subtly in the once-identical sunhats worn by Mrs. Cope and Mrs. Pritchard at the opening of "A Circle in the Fire." Mrs. Pritchard's is "faded and out of shape" while Mrs. Cope's is "still stiff and bright green" (p. 175), images which imply succinctly the opposed temperaments of the two women. Yet Mrs. Cope's frightened turning away from suffering and evil and Mrs. Pritchard's morbid delight in their graphic details are equally a denial of everything *sun* implies in this story, and different as the condition of the two hats is, they both serve to shield the women from its rays. Thus the hat image immediately adumbrates their roles as embodiments of a false polarity challenged by the appearance of the three boys. Similarly, in "The Partridge Festival" O'Connor surrounds both the protagonist, Calhoun, and his female counterpart, Mary Elizabeth, with echoing images of infantilism to suggest from the start what the characters themselves only reluctantly come to admit: that in childishly claiming they are "spiritual kin" to the criminal Singleton, "a kinship with each other was unavoidable" (pp. 436, 441). But in that immature assertion of kinship with the mad murderer, they discover—and it destroys their callow theorizing for good—there lurks an inescapable bond with the despised Partridge, the great world itself.

In such a story as "The Partridge Festival" the blending of the psychological and symbolic motif of the double with the social and cultural theme of kinship emerges clearly. Matters of kin are a natural enough subject for any southern writer, but, as has often been noted, O'Connor is especially preoccupied with the tensions and ambiguities of family relationships, particularly those between parent and child. The motif of kinship need not, however, be confined to blood ties. Perhaps the most poignant moment in *Wise Blood* is Hazel Motes's confession late in the novel, "My people are all dead" (p. 217), a remark that reverberates in the surrounding silence to reach beyond his lost family and touch on some more essential aloneness. And of course the best-known recognition scene in O'Connor's fiction is the grandmother's discovery in "A Good Man Is Hard to Find" that The Misfit is "one of [her] babies . . . one of [her] own children" (p. 132), a discovery that produces her instantaneous death, one senses, precisely because he feels it to be mysteriously true.

In the ominous and uncanny materialization of The Misfit out of the distant landscape, in the grandmother's "peculiar feeling" both that "she had known him all her life" and that "she could not recall who he was" (p. 126), and in that final recognition scene the shadow of the double motif seems to make itself felt. In any case, there is no difficulty in identifying it at work in "Revelation." Mrs. Turpin's comically furious cry, "How am I a hog and me both?" focuses her humbling discovery that her closest kin is not human at all, that her deepest nature, denied in her fantasies of election and in her good works, is reflected in that old sow in her up-to-date pig parlor—and that however sanitized, a hog is a hog. But here as elsewhere in O'Connor the unveiling of true kinship is as self-estranging as it is self-revealing, for the climactic vision opens up to Mrs. Turpin a dimension in which even her virtues, which she had smugly taken for her deepest self, "were being burned away" (p. 508). Between the old sense of self and the new and dismaying knowledge, there opens a chasm hardly to be bridged.

Inherent in the very use of the double motif is a dualistic conception of the self, of character so deeply divided that an essential part can be embodied in an independent figure. That the configuration recurs throughout her fiction, as even this brief survey suggests, indicates how central to Flannery O'Connor's imagination it was. Yet the variety of changes she was able to ring on this basic construct is remarkable, and two somewhat more extended examples may help to give some sense of her inventiveness within an obsession. Here the stories which will serve, one from each of the collections she published, are precisely those glanced at in the previous chapter as illustrations of differing symbolic treatments of landscape: "A View of the Woods" and "Good Country People."

Although written later, "A View of the Woods" is the simpler (and the lesser) of these two works; it is also perhaps, of all O'Connor's stories, the one that most overtly makes use of the double motif. In her own terse words, "Mary Fortune and the old man [are] images of each other but opposite in the end" (*The Habit of Being*, p. 190). For this metamorphosis of an apparent replica into a genuine alter ego, the pivot on which the action turns is the process of denial. Like a number of her other protagonists, seventy-nine-year-old Mark Fortune tries to reject the finality of his own death, in this case by "insur[ing] the future." Aware that the family over which he exercises an absolute despotism is "waiting impatiently for the day when they could put him in a hole eight feet deep and cover him up with dirt" (p. 337), he has attempted to perpetuate himself indefinitely in two ways. First, he has so dedicated himself to material progress that he expects the town being built mostly on his former property to be called Fortune, Georgia (his present project, in which a machine digs a hole out of the soft clay, is his symbolic resistance to that other and final hole). Second, he has trained his favorite granddaughter and heiress, Mary Fortune, to be in every way another edition of him. "A View of the Woods" presents what happens when these two schemes for self-perpetuation suddenly come into conflict.[5]

The opening pages of the story repeatedly stress Mr. Fortune's awareness of the remarkable resemblance his granddaughter bears to him. Not only is she physically "a small replica of the old man," but "she was like him on the inside too. She had, to a singular degree, his intelligence, his strong will, and his push and drive." Despite the difference in their ages, "the spiritual distance between them was slight" (p. 336). All of this is a source of great satisfaction to the old man, who politely ignores the fact that Mary Fortune bears the family name Pitts and habitually speaks of the Pittses as if they are some tribe foreign to the two of them. "He liked to think of her," O'Connor writes, "as being thoroughly of his clay" (p. 338), made, presumably, of the same stuff as the rest of his property. And insofar as clay suggests his earth-bound vision, he seems to be right. Bearing "his unmistakable likeness," the child at first appears a precise copy of her grandfather, a clone that has unaccountably skipped a generation.

But it emerges that Mr. Fortune detects in her "one failure of character," which to him means "one point in which she did not resemble him" (pp. 346, 343). When her father summons Mary Fortune outside for a whipping, Mr. Fortune sees on her face a look "foreign" to it—a look, that is, that he cannot recognize as one he would be capable of—"part terror and part respect and part something else, something very like cooperation" (p. 340). When he berates the child for her submission, he cannot understand her ritualistic denial, "nobody's ever beaten me in my life and if anybody did, I'd kill him," although he dimly sees that these episodes are "Pitts's revenge on him," Pitts's indirect retaliation for the cruel power the old man holds over him (pp. 340–41). Nonetheless, this one flaw in an otherwise perfect child—perfect, of course, in her resemblance to him— remains for Mr. Fortune "an ugly mystery" (p. 346).

That flaw becomes the fissure that widens between them when Mary Fortune unexpectedly opposes his scheme to sell off the field in front of their house, a growing division in which the use of names, and thus of identity, is the central weapon. When early in the story the old man recalls the naming of the child Mary Fortune and refers to "the Pittses" as a group apart from "you and me," grandfather and granddaughter seem two versions of the same person, identical twins separated less by space and sex than by the time lapse of seventy years. But as she stubbornly sets herself against the projected sale, he finds himself telling her, "You act more like a Pitts than a Fortune" (p. 347), his lowest insult and one he immediately regrets. Nevertheless, she perseveres in her resistance until he is driven to confront her:

> "Are you a Fortune," he said, "or are you a Pitts? Make up your mind."
> Her voice was loud and positive and belligerent.
> "I'm Mary—Fortune—Pitts," she said.
> "Well I," he shouted, "am PURE Fortune!" [p. 351]

The trumping of her claim to mixed identity is a challenge that she answers with physical violence, and when she momentarily bests him in their fight, as "pale identical eye looked into pale identical eye," she informs him, "You been whipped . . . by me . . . and I'm PURE Pitts." Enraged that "the face that was his own . . . had dared to call itself Pitts," with a surge of fury the old man crushes her head against a rock, saying, "There's not an ounce of Pitts in me" (p. 355).

It is an idle and self-defeating boast. Beneath the varieties of pride and family loyalty conveyed in the manipulations of these names, the very words themselves suggest irreconcilable values. *Fortune* proclaims the Faustian self—an identity dramatized in the old man's pact with the snakelike Tillman (p. 352)—the assertion of the egoistic seeker of power, self-inflating and self-aggrandizing, devotee of the ancient bitch-goddess of this world, projecting himself infinitely through time, "gorging" himself on earthly "clay" (p. 335). *Pitts*, however, expresses a knowledge that is biblical rather than Faustian: the Psalmist's pit of powerlessness and suffering, of pain, loss, and worldly defeat, from which opens an appalling glimpse of the bottomless pit and the inescapable awareness of that earthly pit to which we all go. Thus when Mary Fortune confronts her grandfather with his own image and labels it Pitts, the old man finds this alter ego intolerable precisely because, like The Misfit at the end of "A Good Man Is Hard to Find," he senses that it is true. It is Mr. Fortune, after all, who has had the momentary vision of the woods full of blood, wounds, and "hellish red trunks"; it is Mr. Fortune who has been so challenged by the child's opposition that he has repeatedly had to marshal his "principles" to carry on with the sale; it is Mr. Fortune whose unacknowledged terror of his own obliteration lies behind both his many property deals and his attempts to view the child as merely another edition of himself. And Mary Fortune has just given him a taste of the Pitts condition, attacking him "like a pack of small demons" until he "began to roll like a man on fire" (pp. 354–55). No wonder "he seemed to see his own face coming to bite him," for the child here enacts not the replica of the worldly successful Fortune, but the revolt of the buried self, the despised Pitts.

Paradoxically, at the moment she defeats him and identifies herself as "PURE Pitts," she has never been more Fortune-like in her position of power, while he has been forced into the subjugated posture of the humbled Pittses. But so unyielding is the old man's refusal to accept the Pitts within that he *must* reverse their roles, even at the expense of her life. "There's not an ounce of Pitts in me" is only the last of his many denials, the final rejection of a dimension of himself and of existence that his ravenous ego will not acknowledge. The battle has a wryly ironic upshot, for in his frenzy to erase the Pitts from his own identity, Mr. Fortune has not insured the future but destroyed it, thereby presumably delivering into the hands of the despised Pittses all his worldly clay. In devoting himself to the material kingdoms of the world—"the Whore of Babylon," Mary Fortune has humorously but pertinently called him—he has lost them all except the one impossible to escape, the pit where there squats his genuine replica, the mechanical "monster . . . as stationary as he was, gorging itself on clay" (p. 356).

"Good Country People" also presents a generational relationship within a family, in this case mother and daughter, but essential as that pairing is, it is not at the dramatic center of the story. The pivotal action is of course Joy-Hulga's encounter with the Bible salesman, a confrontation that focuses and ironically reflects the other relationships in the story, that between the two older women, Mrs. Hopewell and Mrs. Freeman, and those of the girl with each of them.

For Mrs. Hopewell, life is apparently summed up in her stock of clichés, and the dialogues with Mrs. Freeman that begin the story are exercises in hackneyed oneupmanship:

> "Everybody is different," Mrs. Hopewell said.
> "Yes, most people is," Mrs. Freeman said.
> "It takes all kinds to make the world."
> "I always said it did myself." [p. 273]

Mrs. Hopewell's supply of platitudes runs to the genteel and the uplifting. On her outraged daughter she urges the virtues of a "pleasant expression," a "pleasant" manner, and such cheery advice as "a smile never hurt anyone," but to her bewildered dismay, the girl responds to none of this. "It seemed to Mrs. Hopewell that every year she grew less like other people and more like herself—bloated, rude and squint-eyed" (p. 276).

This evolution is of course precisely what her daughter intends. As in "A View of the Woods," naming again defines the shift: Joy's changing her name to Hulga is a deliberate defiance of her mother, a self-definition that sets her against everything Mrs. Hopewell stands for. "She saw it," O'Connor writes, "as the name of her highest creative act. One of her major triumphs was that her mother had not been able to turn her dust into Joy, but the greater one was that she had been able to turn it herself into Hulga" (p. 275). In this self-created rebirth, the girl believes, the ugly name acts as a mask for a private inner sense of identity: "She had a vision of the name working like the ugly sweating Vulcan who stayed in the furnace and to whom, presumably, the goddess [Venus] had to come when called." Cut off from the possibility of physical beauty by her "hulking" body and her wooden leg, Hulga emphasizes her outer ugliness in dress, manner, and action, but she secretly cherishes the vision of an inner self that is beautifully unique.

Forced by her physical disabilities to live at home, the girl's existence has become one continuous gesture of outraged rejection of the life around her. If her mother refuses to deal with anything but the genteel surfaces of life, Hulga scorns those surfaces and plunges into the "depths," acquiring a Ph.D. in philosophy and disdaining "any close attention to her surroundings" (p. 287). If Mrs. Hopewell approaches life with a naïve optimism, her daughter embraces atheistic nihilism, "see[ing] *through*" the surfaces of things "to nothing" (p. 287). Point by point, the girl has, she thinks, defined a self that is the antithesis of her mother's.

The mysterious appearance of the Bible salesman at the Hopewell home provides the first real test of that self called Hulga. As he presents himself, he seems a living embodiment of Mrs. Hopewell's most cherished clichés. "Honest," "sincere," "genuine," "simple," "earnest," "the salt of the earth," with his Bible-quoting and his missionary aspirations, he convinces the girl that at last she is "face to face with real innocence" (p. 289). Towards that innocence her feelings are deeply ambivalent. What she tells herself is that he is clay to be molded by her own "deeper understanding of life," an "inferior mind" to be instructed by "true genius," and she vaguely projects the aftermath of a seduction in which she transforms his inevitable remorse into "something useful" (p. 284). But what these fantasies of superiority reckon without is her unadmitted desire that someone pay homage to the goddess within.

The Bible salesman says that their meeting must have been fated "on account of what all [we] got in common" (p. 284), but all that they seem to have in common is a potentially fatal heart condition. Their apparent roles are a typical set of O'Connor antitheses—the academic and the country bumpkin, the sophisticate and the innocent, the cynical atheist and the naïve Christian—antitheses that reach their comic high point in the barn where, as the boy whines for a declaration of love, the girl gives him a crash course in nihilist epistemology. But in the sudden role reversal that takes place in that barn, we discover what a genuine *Doppelgänger* this Bible salesman is.

The boy says of the wooden leg (which she treats "as someone else would his soul, in private and almost with her own eyes turned away"), "It's what makes you different. You ain't like anybody else." It is then that her outer cynicism drops and the girl reveals her underlying belief in real innocence: "This boy, with an instinct that came from beyond wisdom, had touched the truth about her." The shrine of the goddess has been approached at last and with an attitude apparently "entirely reverent" (pp. 288–89). Her surrender to him is thus of more than her body, it is of her entire sense of self; and when she allows him to remove the leg, she becomes dependent on him for more than physical wholeness. Now he reveals to her who the true innocent is.

For the girl has not, as she thinks, escaped her mother and her mother's values: the entire identity of Hulga is built on them. Her academic nihilism is riddled with such clichés as "We are all damned . . . but some of us have taken off our blindfolds and see that there's nothing to see. It's a kind of salvation" (p. 288). If the language is more sophisticated than any at Mrs. Hopewell's command, it is no less trite, and the smug self-deception underlying it ("I don't have illusions") is, if anything, greater. Willfully blind to the world around her and complacent in her notion of self-created uniqueness, she has gained her sense of disdainful superiority precisely from her contemptuous acceptance of her mother's view of things. In kissing the boy, as we have seen, she falls into a parody of the maternal role, and when his childlike innocence becomes no longer credible, she asks, "Aren't you . . . aren't you just good country people?" (p. 290). The question is the ironic equivalent of Mrs. Hopewell's conviction that he is exactly that—a conviction her daughter has clearly shared.

As the mask of Hulga drops and reveals beneath it none other than Mrs. Hopewell's little girl Joy, it does so in response to the disappearance of the mask of the Bible salesman, of Manley Pointer, as he has called himself. And the face that looks forth from beneath *that* mask is the face of the nihilist the girl has claimed to be. She has pretended to be reborn into nothingness, but *he* has "been believing in nothing ever since I was born" (p. 291). Although we get only a glimpse of what lives beneath that mask—apparently, like The Misfit, the Bible salesman thrives on "meanness," in this case with a flair for the fetishistic—we see enough to grasp how uncannily mask and reality correspond to the Joy and Hulga identities of the girl. As the roles reverse themselves and his assumed innocence disappears into cynicism, so her superficial worldliness gives way to sentimental naïveté. If Manley Pointer turns out to be as hollow as the Bible he reveals in the barn, so Hulga is as empty as the wooden leg it was based on. "Like one presenting offerings at the shrine of a goddess" (p. 289), he takes from that Bible and places before her the contraceptives, whiskey, and pornographic cards that are a cruelly fitting devotion to the deified self. That self had been a sham; it is the girl, not the Bible salesman, who has the innocence of the child. Although he piously cites the text "He who losest his life shall find it," she is the one who truly believes in such a possibility, secularized though it is. For when she surrenders to him the privacy of the leg, "it was like losing her own life and finding it again, miraculously, in his" (p. 289). The text, of course, works here ironically: it is the precise formula for their exchange of apparent identities.

The climax of his role as mocking double comes in a vicious parody of the intellectual clichés the girl has earlier mouthed at him. Accused of hypocrisy, he replies indignantly, "I hope you don't think . . . that I believe in that crap! I may sell Bibles, but I know which end is up and I wasn't born yesterday and I know where I'm going!" (p. 290). But if the values here are the nihilistic ones the girl has professed, the idiom is the folk cliché so dear to Mrs. Hopewell, and the wedding of the two exposes with resonant finality how closely identified mother and daughter in truth are. Indeed, on this level "Good Country People" inverts the action of "A View of the Woods," for when Hulga is revealed as Joy, this apparent antithesis of her mother emerges as virtually a replica. The intricate set of reflections does not, however, end here, for the Bible salesman is not the only representative of those "good country people" in the story.

Mrs. Hopewell is of the opinion that Mrs. Freeman is also one of these "real genuine folks," and all the evidence ironically supports her. As Mrs. Freeman herself remarks, "Some people are more alike than others" (p. 282). Like the Bible salesman, she thrives on the exploitation of others' suffering—"Mrs. Freeman had a special fondness for the details of secret infections, hidden deformities, assaults upon children. Of diseases, she preferred the lingering or incurable" (p. 275)—and her persistent fascination with the girl's artificial leg is reflected and fulfilled in his successful theft of it. Even her "beady steel-pointed eyes" reappear at a higher pitch of intensity in his, "like two steel spikes" (pp. 275, 289) as they leer at the filched trophy. If Joy at last turns out to be truly her mother's daughter, so Mrs. Freeman emerges as a symbolic mother to the Bible salesman. And as he is given the last triumphant word in his duel with the girl, so Mrs. Freeman, characteristically pulling an "evil-smelling onion shoot" from the ground, has the final ironic word in the story:

" 'Some can't be that simple [as the Bible salesman appeared to be]
she said. 'I know I never could' " (p. 291).

The relationship between the two women which frames the central action thus turns out to be a less sinister version of the encounter between their real and symbolic children. Like her daughter,
Mrs. Hopewell persuades herself that she is in control of the situation, and like her she is self-deceived, for it is Mrs. Freeman with her
mechanical, "driving" gaze, her imperviousness, and her ability always to get the last word who dominates their relationship. If "Good
Country People" does not quite present parallel plots—the central
encounter becomes a dramatic reversal, the framing action remains
static and ongoing—it does set before us four characters in interlocking reflective relationship, like facing mirrors slightly askew.
The Bible salesman has the role of the classic double figure, but he is
only the center of the set of images and identities that cast back
mocking versions of one another. "Everybody is different," all agree,
whether as folk banality or as the secret nourishing of the hidden
self; but what the story dramatizes is how appallingly small and superficial those differences are. Some people are indeed more alike
than others.[6]

"A View of the Woods" and "Good Country People," then, employ
the double motif in almost directly contrary ways. The former opens
with the assertion that Mary Fortune Pitts is a replica of her grandfather and then gradually turns her into his alter ego, pure Pitts
in deadly combat with pure Fortune. The latter story begins with
Hulga as an antiself to her mother and then reveals the Joy hidden
beneath, but it does so through an exchange of apparent identities
between the girl and the *Doppelgänger* of the Bible salesman, and
further reflects *that* relationship in the comic mirror of Mrs. Hopewell and Mrs. Freeman's framing interchanges. Each story flashes at
the protagonist a revelation of the unacknowledged self and thus
hurls a decisive challenge at a cherished self-definition, but where
one insists on differentiation, the other denies it. The effect on the
protagonists cannot be other than shattering, but the difference between the disastrous ending of "A View of the Woods" and the comic
climax of "Good Country People" is that between a refusal to recognize the double figure and the inability *not* to recognize him.

The differences here are genuine and important, yet underlying them is a pattern which is disturbingly characteristic of O'Connor's use of the double motif. The *Doppelgänger* by definition creates a configuration of antitheses, of the acknowledged and the unacknowledged, of conscious and denied selves. But in O'Connor's tales this antithesis undergoes an intense pressure which drives it toward destruction; the result is a radical sundering which proclaims the failure of self-reconciliation. In both "A View of the Woods" and "Good Country People" what does not happen is underlined by its very inclusion, late in each story, as a momentary possibility. When, for instance, the child calls herself "Mary—Fortune—Pitts" she defines an integration of the warring selves designated by those names, but the story sweeps on to the mutual destruction of pure polarities. Analogously, Joy Hopewell's fantasy of "losing her life and finding it again, miraculously, in his" takes the practical form of "she would run away with him and . . . every night he would take the leg off and every morning put it back on again" (p. 289), an image of a kind of marriage in interdependence, a merging of the knowledge of Hulga with the innocence of Manley Pointer; but the action moves quickly to the girl's devastating defeat. In both works, of course, O'Connor has presented irreconcilable antagonists: between the attributes of Fortune and Pitts there is no point of meeting, and the only possible relationship between sentimental optimism and nihilistic hedonism is one of exploitation. Nevertheless, the child and the Bible salesman do embody denied sides of the self, the unrecognized Pitts and Joy within, and the failure—indeed, impossibility—of reconciliation in each story points once again to the extremity of O'Connor's imagination. The very typical quality of these two stories can perhaps be shown by an extended look at one more, a work in which her use of the double motif is at its most central: "The Comforts of Home."

II

The plot of "The Comforts of Home" is surely one of the least convincing O'Connor ever devised. Thomas, the protagonist, is a thirty-five-year-old historian who lives and works in the childhood home his widowed mother continues to make comfortable for him. But the old lady has another interest as well: she is addicted to helping the "unfortunate," and when a girl who calls herself Star Drake is arrested for passing a bad check, she bends all her efforts to rehabilitating this outcast. To Thomas's fury and dismay, "Star"—whose real name, he discovers, is Sarah Ham—eventually becomes installed in the spare bedroom, from which her empty-headed laughter and leering sexual innuendo seem to emerge to threaten his every comfort. Ineffectual in dealing with the situation himself, he finds the image of the dead father he had despised appearing to him to offer ruthless advice on how to get rid of the girl. Thomas at first rejects these distasteful suggestions, but when he discovers a gun missing from his desk, he follows the old man's directive to call in the sheriff. Just as that worthy has promised to investigate, however, Thomas finds that the gun has been returned, and in his attempt to plant it in the girl's purse, she discovers him. There is a scene, then a struggle, and just as the sheriff arrives Thomas fires the gun, only to discover that he has shot not Sarah Ham, but his mother.

Bald summary makes the story sound more preposterous than it is, but even in a direct encounter with O'Connor's commanding prose, it remains rather implausible. The awkward business of the disappearance and reappearance of the gun, for instance, crucial to the action as a means of involving the sheriff and setting up the violent denouement, is never explained. Far worse, the two pivotal figures are both overdrawn. Thomas, the aging historian with an inordinate attachment to his electric blanket, is hardly the most convincing portrait in O'Connor's gallery of intellectuals, and his opposite number, Sarah Ham, is an only sporadically believable presentation of a moral moron. Yet the very excesses in the rendering of these central characters underscore what is essential in their conception: they have been designed as polar extremes. Thomas's tightly buttoned life, with its antiseptic devotion to history, moderation, and order, is played off against the girl's disheveled mindlessness and blatant sexuality. In this antithesis lies her power to disrupt, for she embodies those aspects of the psyche that Thomas has repressed in himself. His mother's clichéd comment on Star reflects with unwitting irony on Thomas himself: "We don't know how the other half lives" (p. 387).

It must be apparent even from the summary above that "The Comforts of Home" seems to demand a "psychological" reading—so much so, in fact, that one suspects Flannery O'Connor of parodying the very material she is exploiting.[7] "Oh boy," says Sarah Ham of Thomas, "is he a case" (p. 403), and so he is, one so insistently classic (or stereotyped) and yet treated with such mocking irony that "The Comforts of Home" seems both to pay tribute to the findings of psychoanalysis and to deride its claims of encompassing the whole of any human situation. Yet whatever one makes of O'Connor's tone, the story does initially emerge as a psychic drama with Sarah Ham as its catalyst and center. In her congenital amorality, her repeated schemes and stratagems for seducing the mildly genteel Thomas, even in her hair, which is cut "like a dog or an elf's," she seems an almost comically literal embodiment of Jung's "anima," that female component of the male psyche that a man ignores at his peril. The anima, says Jung, is an "elfin being" which is "full of snares and traps, in order that man should fall, should reach the earth, and stay caught, so that life should be lived. . . . She is the serpent in the paradise of the harmless man with good resolutions and still better intentions. . . . The anima lives beyond all categories and can therefore dispense with blame as well as with praise."[8] This ambiguous, dangerous figure, beyond consciousness or control yet "the very stuff of life," points to an irremediable chaos, yet, says Jung, within this chaos there may lie a mysterious wisdom and purpose: "It is just the most unexpected, the most terrifyingly chaotic things which reveal a deeper meaning."[9] But although Thomas realizes that "the girl had caused a disturbance in the depths of his being, somewhere out of the reach of his power of analysis" (p. 393), his revulsion is so immediate and so complete that he refuses her all recognition. His mother sees more deeply: "I keep thinking it might be you," she says mystically, but this leads to no insight in her son. Thomas feels only "a deep unbearable loathing for himself as if he were turning slowly into the girl" (p. 385).

In Jung's language, then, Sarah Ham is the "anima-projection" of which Thomas is the "persona"; psychoanalytically viewed, the two characters are complementary figures, obverse doubles, alter egos. The arrival of the girl thus inevitably exacerbates all those psychic tensions which have lain dormant beneath Thomas's bland exterior. His attachment to his mother and hatred of his father is of course thunderingly Oedipal, but with his mother's adoption of Sarah Ham, an ominous shifting begins to occur. Jung states that the mother is the first bearer of the son's anima-image; she "protects him against the dangers that threaten from the darkness of his psyche,"[10] and the mother complex is typified by the failure to detach this image and thereby achieve some measure of genuine selfhood. Thomas has clearly continued to expect his mother to protect him from his deeper impulses, to provide him with internal as well as external comforts. And this the old lady has done, both by assuring him that he has "no bad inclinations, nothing bad you were born with" (p. 393) and by unwittingly furnishing the easy resting place for his anima-projection. But Sarah Ham's arrival and her repeated sexual challenges shatter Thomas's infantile world, and the instrument of this upheaval is the very mother on whom he has depended for his freedom from the disorder of psychical and sexual maturation. She has betrayed him.

With the failure of his mother to sustain the cherished order of his life, the image of the father he had hated ironically surfaces to advise Thomas of the means to its restoration. As he falls increasingly under the influence of this parental voice, it becomes evident that Thomas has refused the challenge of self-realization which Sarah Ham presents; he has merely substituted domination by the father for attachment to the mother.[11] The crucial act is his mother's return to the house with Sarah Ham. He has flung the gauntlet—"You can choose—her or me" (p. 383)—but even his mother's apparent choice cannot move him. At this moment, "He was like a man handed a knife and told to operate on himself if he wished to live" (p. 399). But the surgery proves too painful to face, and Thomas succumbs entirely to the will of his father, becoming a bumbling imitation of the old man.

It is just at this point, late in the story, that a second *Doppelgänger* appears bearing the blatant name Farebrother. Sheriff of the town and sinister exponent of a violent orderliness, he seems to materialize only when the chinks in Thomas's battered ego widen sufficiently to allow him recognition (in Jung's system, he would correspond to the "shadow" side of the self). In his desperate flight from all that Sarah Ham represents, Thomas thus capitulates to those darker impulses in himself that Farebrother embodies. The resemblance between the two can hardly be missed: both men have "pale blue eyes," and Sarah Ham early in the story has pointed out Thomas's likeness to a "cop." The sheriff's sneer at Thomas's anxious officiousness, "Want to swap jobs?" (p. 401), thus becomes an invitation the historian disastrously accepts, for with the fatal gunshot he takes to himself final authority for dispensing law and order, and Farebrother ironically turns chronicler for the event. If the sheriff is "another edition of Thomas's father," so too is Thomas by the end of the story. In refusing to acknowledge himself in Sarah Ham, Thomas unconsciously chooses the despised and more dangerous double of Farebrother.

The conflation of himself with Farebrother is thus for Thomas the outward sign of his submitting to the father's voice within, a submission that does nothing to free him from the sexual anxiety created by Sarah Ham's presence. The example of the father is a direct challenge to his masculinity ("You ain't like me. Not enough to be a man" [p. 393], the voice mocks); under his goading, Thomas's life of comfortable impotence is ended forever. The key symbol here is the gun—yet another of O'Connor's classic psychoanalytic devices—"an inheritance from the old man" that Thomas himself has never used. Sarah Ham's apparent theft of it is a symbolic prelude to her nude invasion of his bedroom, but her return of it seems an implicit invitation which, guided by his father, Thomas unconsciously accepts. His placing it in her "red pocket-book" which has a "skin-like feel to his touch" and gives off "an unmistakable odor of the girl" (p. 402) is a blatant acting out of the sexual fantasy his consciousness so violently denies. And when he is discovered, first by Sarah Ham and then, more crucially, by his mother, the guilt of the child caught in forbidden sex play contributes to the disaster that follows.

Psychologically, of course, the fatal shooting that is the climax of "The Comforts of Home" is not at all accidental. Thomas may believe he is aiming at Sarah Ham, but, as we have been told, "his fury was directed not at the little slut but at his mother" (p. 397). Her death satisfies more fundamental psychic needs than merely revenge for her betrayal: it is an attempt to remove the guilt of the symbolic sex act by eliminating the parental censor; it is the violent consummation of repressed Oedipal desires; and, simultaneously, it removes the figure who, as the source of the Oedipal attachment, blocks the normal sexual outlet the unconscious desires. Thomas's total repression of his own sexuality thus leads to the acting out of a destructive parody of eroticism: the attempt to deny the unconscious life has brought only its grotesquely perverse triumph. Farebrother's final vision that "the killer and the slut were about to collapse into each other's arms" (p. 404), absurd as literal truth, is symbolically just both as the ironic representation of their sexual "union" and, more important, as the expression of a completeness of personality of which the two characters form the splintered parts. For with the fatal act, the recognition of Sarah Ham as Thomas's instinctual double can no longer be refused.

If "The Comforts of Home" rests on this psychological base, that level hardly exhausts the implications of the story. Indeed, according to O'Connor, in her own work "the meaning of a story does not begin except at a depth where adequate motivation and adequate psychology and the various determinations have been exhausted" (*Mystery and Manners*, pp. 41–42). In a post-Freudian, post-Jungian time she may well have felt that for the writer such psychology was exhausted in another sense, susceptible, if drawn on at all, only of a broadly comic treatment. At any rate, "The Comforts of Home" is surely a tale of spiritual as well as psychological crisis; but although language and imagery point clearly to suprapsychological issues, the levels are so intertwined that they cannot finally be divorced.

Thomas's devotion to the ideal of total consciousness, the "principle of order," may be a psychic aberration, but it is also a moral and ultimately metaphysical stance, and the story both dramatizes and evaluates the terms of his commitment. As a historian concerned with "the long slow processes of time," Thomas begins as one of O'Connor's many moderates. Blandly certain that "a moderation of good produces likewise a moderation in evil" (p. 386), he rejects the excessive and "irrational" as at best foolish and useless, at worst dangerous. But the intrusion of Sarah Ham into his life opens up for this historian apocalyptic perspectives, perspectives in which he does not, of course, truly believe ("The devil for Thomas was only a manner of speaking"). At first, recognizing that the chaos of the girl's personality is "the most unendurable form of innocence," "he asked himself what the attitude of God was to this, meaning if possible to adopt it" (p. 390). But as her amorality seems to become more and more directed at him, he senses "about him forces, invisible currents entirely out of his control" (p. 385) which he immediately labels "demonic." Like Mr. Head, Thomas is sure that evil is external, and that it is synonymous with uncontrollable. As a result he ironically becomes the prey of the devil within. For the image of his father that Thomas conjures up is not only the manifestation of a regressive parent-complex, but a demonic figure, the biblical old man, the fallen Adam, who like Satan himself "had lived his lie" (p. 393).[12] His mother's charity to Sarah Ham thus becomes literally and ironically what Thomas calls it: daredevil.

As in all of O'Connor's work, the moderate center will not hold, and the story pits the extreme of the mother's "pure idiot mystery" against the extreme of the father's "reasonable ruthlessness" in a battle for the son's allegiance. The counters in this struggle are precisely those double figures each advances for Thomas's recognition. His mother insists that Sarah Ham "might be you"; his "father" repeatedly cries, "See the sheriff!" In a sentence dropped from the final version of the story, Thomas was made to sense that when his mother speaks of the girl, "all her compassion appeared to be directed at him, as if he were somehow involved, as if since he might have been such a freak himself, it was he she mourned for, he she was trying to save."[13] In the violence of his rigidity, the very irrationality of his insistence on reason, he *is* freakish, but it is the obverse of the grotesqueness of Sarah Ham. She is so repugnant to Thomas's conception of himself that even at their first encounter he greets her "in a tone of such loathing that he was shocked at the sound of it" (p. 389), and the vehemence of his rejection of the girl finally drives him before the mirror of the sinister Farebrother.

In a key sentence, Thomas complacently speculates that "if Anthony of Egypt had stayed at home and attended to his sister, no devils would have plagued him" (p. 386). Multilayered in its irony, the allusion suggests both the shallowness of Thomas's notions of virtue and order, which avoid the challenge of the genuinely lived life, and the foolishness of looking anywhere but within oneself for the source of the most dangerous devils. But the deepest irony is that if Thomas had had a more profound grasp of his perception, he might have turned it into a personal truth. Familiar with the outer form of Christian history, he remains unaware of its inner import, for although he does indeed stay at home, it is precisely his refusal to recognize Sarah Ham as his sister that brings the devils upon him. Thomas's life thus becomes a travesty of the saint's: as his pilgrimage to Farebrother mocks that of Anthony to his "brother" the hermit Paul, so his repressions burlesque the saint's monasticism, for Anthony well knew that the fount of his temptations, including the famous hog (Ham?), was within himself.

Thomas sees that Sarah Ham's "corruption" is irresponsible and therefore "blameless," but he thinks of her always as "the little slut," a choice of language that repudiates any kinship between them and so allows himself no such plea of guiltlessness. With the sure instinct that "the peace of perfect order" is created by removing the ultimate source of chaos, he shoots his mother. As in Wallace Stevens's adage, "A violent order is disorder"; no connoisseur of chaos, Thomas has been unable to contemplate the possibility of Stevens's corollary, "A great disorder is an order." For in abandoning "the long slow processes of time," Thomas has leaped beyond the human level altogether. Rather than merely adopting "the attitude of God," he has usurped to himself His millenial prerogatives. As the undisturbed "peace of perfect order" parodies the establishment of the Heavenly Kingdom, so the gunshot that will usher in such peace, a blast "meant to bring an end to evil in the world" (p. 403), is Thomas's mock Apocalypse. The imitation of Omnipotence inevitably produces, as Hawthorne knew, its demonic opposite; thus Farebrother is the appropriate figure to preside in gloating malice over the catastrophic climax of the story. His closing vision of the embrace of "the killer and the slut" therefore becomes more than psychologically apt, for the tabloid language reduces Thomas to the moral level of Sarah Ham and insists on the secret bond between them that Thomas has so violently denied.

Both psychologically and morally, not to recognize Sarah Ham is for Thomas the equivalent of not recognizing himself in all his freakishness. The image of the embrace with which "The Comforts of Home" ends exists of course only in the mind of the sheriff, and it points ironically to the disastrous failure of reconciliation not only between two characters, but between opposing sides of the self. In this respect it is like those momentary suggestions of integrated selves that arise late in "A View of the Woods" and "Good Country People" before those stories sweep on to the sundering of the protagonist and his double, an ironic glimpse of wholeness that for O'Connor never becomes a reality. Traditionally, the appearance of the *Doppelgänger* almost always causes a profound disruption—it can hardly be otherwise—but the final failure of self-reconciliation, one finds time after time in O'Connor, is by no means a necessary feature of the literature of the double. Some of the wider implications of her insistent and peculiar use of this motif need to be explored.

III

O'Connor's imagination seems usually to have begun its workings on a rather isolated, abrasive social context composed of the members of a family or the dwellers on a small farm, and then to have moved in one of two directions to bring about the dissolution or re-ordering of the original relationships. These two deeper movements, easily discernible beneath the variety of the surface actions of her stories, are versions of archetypal literary patterns hardly peculiar to O'Connor, but striking in the almost obsessive frequency with which they recur in her work. One is the movement outward, the journey; the other, its obverse, might be termed a movement inward, whereby an alien figure invades the initial context. Opposed as structures of action, both of these movements create for O'Connor's protagonists unprecedented situations, sudden crises which at their end often unveil the same image: the mocking face of the unsuspected double.

The strange and unknown intruders who turn up on the doorsteps of O'Connor's more respectable characters—beyond Bible salesmen and moronic nymphomaniacs, they may range from juvenile delinquents to stray bulls, from clubfooted fundamentalists to European refugees—are matched by the dark figures encountered at the climaxes of journeys, whether escaped convicts, angry black mothers, insane murderers, or statues of little Negroes. They make up a diverse group, certainly, extending from the apparently saintly to the clearly demonic, from the uncomprehending to the shrewdly knowing, from the masked confidence man to the blatantly leering mocker, from animal through human artifact. Yet different as their functions may be in individual stories, they possess in common an energy, a force: they become the galvanic centers of the works they inhabit, and in contrast to the more conventional protagonists they confront, they radiate an almost anarchic power. All are in some sense foreign, for they seem to embody a kind of knowledge the protagonists have lost touch with, and the most compelling are etched with the numinous, as if they are in contact with a mysterious country the more rational and "civilized" have never visited. They seem to demand recognition from the bemused intellectuals and genteel matrons they face: "Know me," they appear to threaten, "or be destroyed"; or, even more terrifying, "Know me *and* be destroyed."

Now of course that country is a familiar one in O'Connor's fiction, and since these alien figures often come bearing a clear burden of religiosity, we might conclude quickly that her distinctive contribution to the modern tradition of the double is to give the motif a weight that is theological rather than psychological or simply moral. Yet her art is not, I think, so univalent. As "The Comforts of Home" alone shows, introducing the theological does not demand expelling the psychological. Quite the reverse: the revelations in O'Connor's works, so often precipitated by those double figures, come only when the consciousness of the protagonist, with all its presuppositions and defenses, is finally overthrown and a deeper awareness forces its way through. O'Connor clearly saw the human unconscious not only as, say, the repository of repressed sexual and aggressive urges, but as a realm of inherent theological dimension from which could come intimations of the demonic and the divine.[14] Those potent doubles thus embody the link between the unknown within the self and the unknown beyond it, between the "other" hidden inside and that Other dimension which transcends the self, between the deepest roots of one's being and the furthest reaches of Being. As *Doppelgängers* they thereby themselves acquire a double reference, pointing at once to the denials of the opposite numbers they face and to an unsuspected world beyond.

For this reason, O'Connor's more extreme characters tend to a curious family likeness whatever their precise theological weight. Criminals all, the ungovernable Sarah Ham, the murderous Misfit, and the old prophet Mason Tarwater, different as their functions may be, resemble one another far more closely than they do those apostles of moderation—Thomas, the grandmother, and the schoolteacher Rayber—that each of them confronts. And many readers have had trouble deciding whether Rufus Johnson of "The Lame Shall Enter First" is a demonic avenger or a prophetic savior. What this uncertainty suggests is that such distinctions are not in fact primary, that as imaginative figures O'Connor's doubles all spring from the same region of her creative mind and emerge with a Dionysian force that is anterior to whatever theological role they are asked to play. Invested with a mysterious power, their immediate and unvarying function is to intrude the perilous unknown into the bland surfaces of ordinary life.

It is as outsiders, radically antisocial and dangerous, often literally outlaws, that these dark figures proclaim their links with the tradition of the *Doppelgänger* and make it hardly surprising that O'Connor acknowledged (however slightingly) Poe and (more warmly) Conrad and James among her literary forebears. The tradition has been persistent enough in the fiction of the past two centuries to establish some familiar contours, and seen in that larger context one telling characteristic of O'Connor's use of the motif leaps into sharp focus. What typically occurs in the relationship between the protagonist and his double is some form of intimate interaction, an increasing closeness, however hazardous or undesired, an expanding involvement that constitutes at least a tacit recognition of the claims of the second self.[15] The captain of Conrad's "The Secret Sharer" can hardly bear to surrender his double, Leggatt, even though both his command of the ship and his sanity are threatened by the presence of the other; Spencer Brydon of James's "The Jolly Corner" feels a strong and growing interaction with his ghostly alter ego long before he encounters him face to face; the terrible Hyde waxes apace in the Dr. Jekyll of Stevenson's famous parable; and even the narrator of Poe's "William Wilson," for all his furious attempts to deny his meddling double, can never fully expunge either his feelings of affinity with the other Wilson or the memory of recognizing his own features on that foreign face. But one never finds this process in Flannery O'Connor. Possessing, as we have seen, much self-assurance but little real self-awareness, her protagonists meet the challenge of the double only with repudiation, outraged resistance, an increased hardening of attitude that presses the tensions of her stories to the bursting point. There is no gradual awakening, no glimmer or growth of recognition, only the sudden, shocking revelation as the veil is ripped aside.

Indeed, the characteristic action in O'Connor's fiction is the reverse of a process of confrontation between protagonist and "other": it is a progressive stiffening into "the extreme situation" (*Mystery and Manners*, p. 113), the movement toward polar positions. The upshot of this is that her protagonists never truly reach either of the classic conclusions of the double tale: a final disintegration of personality (madness, suicide), or the reintegration and strengthening of the self. Images suggesting the reconciliation of self and other that do appear are highly ironic, as in that final paragraph of "The Comforts of Home" or in the analogous ending of "Greenleaf" where Mrs. May and the bull lie in a deadly embrace. Again, it is "The Artificial Nigger" that seems to provide the exception, a genuine reconciliation, but on closer examination the story turns out to confirm the rule. Mr. Head is indeed driven to an acceptance of the guilty self he has refused to know, the projection of "nigger" that the little statue both embodies and transforms, but rather than being integrated into his conscious identity, into all that is implied by *Head*, the new sense of self simply replaces the old. The "action of mercy" released by the statue both reveals to the old man his true identity as "a great sinner" and "cover[s] his pride like a flame and consume[s] it" (pp. 269–70). In glimpsing both the divine love that comes from beyond the self and his own "true depravity," Mr. Head emerges from the story grasping the poles of a saving vision that has revealed to him his own incompleteness.

Yet O'Connor's stories rarely go this far. Much more typical are the two patterns noted earlier: a fatal refusal to recognize the double figure—pure Fortune destroys pure Pitts and dooms himself, Thomas denies Sarah Ham and shoots his mother—or conversely, a recognition that cannot finally be avoided, yet which leaves the protagonist adrift among the shattered bits of his inadequate self-definition—Joy Hopewell stripped of her symbolic leg, Sheppard of "The Lame Shall Enter First" bereft of both his son and his secular liberalism. One comes to feel finally that the two sides of the self are so deeply inimical that no prolonged confrontation is possible, that O'Connor could hardly imagine a full reconciliation, that the fierce clash renewed in story after story had no permanent resolution this side of the grave. Psychologically, at least, Flannery O'Connor seems to have been an inveterate "Manichean."

Now it might be objected that the endings of those latter stories, for example, do open just such a possibility of reconciliation, that Joy Hopewell or Sheppard, freed of illusion through their encounters with the dark double, are at last capable of achieving a deeper, more genuinely integrated self. The strong sense of closure in these stories would not seem to invite speculation beyond their endings— although once begun, of course, anyone can play: isn't despair as likely a sequel as the more optimistic one outlined above?[16] But whatever might be supposed to take place after a story's conclusion, it is obviously not *that* action that engaged O'Connor's imagination. Her stories and novels characteristically do not close on images of harmony and reconciliation, all passion spent, but in pain and violence and a profound sense of displacement, of permanent exile from the known and familiar, including the final displacement of death. And it is the surfacing of this memento mori at the end of all her works, whether literally on the page before us or metaphorically in those annihilations of identity, that provides a final clue to her singular use of the *Doppelgänger* motif.

The protagonists of O'Connor's stories all cling to a narrow sense of order, whether the balanced social order of her many matrons or the dessicated rationalism of the intellectuals, for it allows them to feel safe from the terrors that they sense hover menacingly both within and without. The greatest of these terrors (for it ultimately includes all the others) is death, the chaos that swallows all human order along with the self that espouses it, that insists on the physical and finite nature of earthly existence. Here is the supreme triumph of the hylic, the final encompassing of the self by the world of matter. Much more comforting to deny death by projecting oneself into a perpetual future like Mr. Fortune, or by creating a new and beautifully unique self like Hulga Hopewell, or by retreating behind one's mother to develop a mastery over history like Thomas. If these are all attempts to transcend the common human fate, to achieve immortality, they are thereby also acts of hubris in which the mortal self usurps the powers of God. Thus the double figure is always a profound threat to the protagonist, for by definition he embodies all that has been denied in order to create the inflated invulnerable self.

And thus, too, for Flannery O'Connor there can be no final reconciliation between them, for the impulse to rebel against death, to assert the self in the face of annihilation, to insist on the power of
one's uniqueness can never be harmonized with the demand to submit, to risk the chaos of the physical, the dissolution of the self, and
the certainty of death.

The "theological" sense of the *Doppelgänger* motif is therefore
much broader than the question of whether individual figures can be
labeled divine or demonic. The double in O'Connor's fiction represents an ineluctable human dualism, the divided self that is the
inheritance of fallen man, who is thereby doomed not only to incompleteness but to rending conflict. It is little comfort that those
doubles often carry about them the overtones of the numinous, for
their advent brings only the harrowing violence which ends not in a
coming together but in a splitting apart, the sundering of the protagonist from his sense of himself and his world and even from life
itself. O'Connor repeatedly stressed her concern as a writer with the
operations of supernatural grace, but its workings, she said, are not
those of "a healing property," not "warm and binding," but deeply
"disruptive," "dark and divisive." The Christological passage she
most often cited (Matthew 10:34) gives a precise description of the
effect of her double figures: "Think not that I am come to send peace
on earth: I came not to send peace, but a sword."[17]

In a world of incomplete selves, we are thus led back to the grotesque not as a didactic metaphor of evil or Godlessness or false belief but as "an accurate description of the human condition, even at
its best."[18] That conclusion is implicit everywhere in O'Connor's
work, but it surfaces clearly in her play with a traditional image of
human wholeness. From Plato through the Renaissance to modern
psychologists and poets, the image of the hermaphrodite has represented an ideal of human completeness, a reconciliation of the divi-
sions within the self and between self and world. As Ernest Becker
has put it, "It is a desire for a healing of the ruptures of existence, the
dualism of self and body, self and other, self and world."[19] The recurrent myth of the androgyne places that condition in an unfallen
Golden Age or, sometimes using Galatians 3:28 ("There is neither
male nor female: for ye are all one in Christ Jesus") in a mystical or
future state. But when this androgynous ideal is incarnated in our

actual fallen world, as it is in "A Temple of the Holy Ghost," it can only appear as, quite literally, a freak. O'Connor's use of the image in this story thus cuts in two directions at once: it is both a characteristically extreme metaphor for the suffering and limitation inherent in an inescapably physical existence (part of which paradoxically is our own *single* sexuality) and, simultaneously, an evocation of the state in which hermaphrodism is not grotesque but ideal, a contrast extended symbolically in the story through juxtaposed images of the suffering and the resurrected Christ. But in "A Temple of the Holy Ghost," as everywhere in O'Connor, we are condemned to live in this world, and to live as divided and incomplete selves. The freak serves as a kind of limited double for the twelve-year-old prepubescent protagonist who would like to believe that she exists as a disembodied mind, but if he introduces her to the religious dimension of even the most grotesque body (as suggested in the Pauline title), he cannot of course make her one with it. There is no final reconciliation between self and other in this world: one of the protagonist's last perceptions, typical of her detached and "mean" intelligence, is a dry notation of the piglike obesity of another character (p. 248).

If for O'Connor this inner duality cannot finally be healed, there remains another possible way of at-onement: a denial so complete that it becomes an extirpation of one side of the self. Mr. Fortune's murder of his granddaughter in "A View of the Woods" expresses one form of this, the violent (and self-defeating) repudiation of the dark Pitts of the self. But the double figure may also embody the assertive consciousness, and when it does so its destruction is hardly less terrifying. This latter action is revealed most clearly not in the stories but in *The Violent Bear It Away*, a novel populated almost entirely by divided characters and *Doppelgängers*. The rending struggle within young Tarwater which is the burden of the book is resolved not in an act of reintegration but in a ritual exorcism, a self-purification by fire that consumes the grinning "friend" who has shadowed him from the start. That friend is of course overtly presented as demonic, but he also embodies the rational, skeptical, rebellious, ironic side of Tarwater, and his destruction is a violent repudiation of an essential part of the boy. Tarwater achieves at the end a singleness of self and purpose, but the cost of that achievement is appalling.

It is a cost that Flannery O'Connor as a writer could not have afforded to pay. In her copy of Emmanuel Mounier's *The Character of Man*, she marked approvingly this passage: "When we say that thought is dialogue, we mean this quite strictly. We never think alone. The unspoken thought is a dialogue with someone who questions, contradicts, or spurs one on. This inner debate," Mounier continues, "may last a lifetime."[20] Surely the radical tensions in O'Connor's fiction—its polar images, its extremities of conflict, its apocalyptic tendencies, its deeply self-divided heroes, and, not least, its numerous double figures—emerge from just such a creative inner dialogue, a dialogue that indeed seems to have lasted a lifetime. And if her fiction almost never presents images of self-integration, it is surely because, unlike young Tarwater, she could not still that ironic voice that questions and contradicts, that mocks and rebels and says no. "Does one's integrity ever lie in what he is not able to do?" she once asked rhetorically, and she responded, "I think that usually it does, for free will does not mean one will, but many wills conflicting in one man" (*Mystery and Manners*, p. 115). O'Connor's own integrity as a writer lay in her projecting those conflicts into her fiction, dramatizing and exploring the clash without pretending to a spurious reconciliation she could not feel. One result is the obsessive recurrence of the double motif, but that creative inner tension finds even broader expression in some of the larger strategies of her fiction.

CHAPTER FOUR

The Aesthetics of Incongruity

If the jangle of conflicting wills is at the core of Flannery O'Connor's stories of the double, that essentially internal battle is acted out on the surface of her many domestic dramas. In the recurrent context of a small family whose members are abrasively tied together, the chief antagonists become a parental figure and a child, whether the "parent" be a literal father or (almost always) mother or a surrogate such as a grandfather, and whether the "child" be the ten-year-old Nelson of "The Artificial Nigger" or the sixty-two-year-old Sally Poker Sash of "A Late Encounter with the Enemy." Whatever the variations played on the pattern, these family relationships always involve a struggle for power, a power the parent may assert simply by his continuing presence and which the child, bent on his own autonomy, is determined to wrest to himself. The mother and daughter of "A Circle in the Fire" speak in their own individual tones, but they capture the friction that underlies all of O'Connor's domestic stories: " 'Why do you have to look like an idiot?' [Mrs. Cope] asked. 'Suppose company were to come? When are you going to grow up? What's going to become of you?' . . . 'Leave me be,' the child said in a high irritated voice. 'Leave me be. Just leave me be. I ain't you' " (p. 190).[1]

In her presentation of these generational struggles O'Connor carefully maintains an emotional tension within the story. When the parent is as aggressively domineering as the grandmother of "A Good Man Is Hard to Find" or Mrs. May of "Greenleaf," for instance, the children are as unattractive as Bailey and his family in the former or as Mrs. May's sons, who are "different . . . as night and day" (p. 314) but equally unappealing, in the latter. If Asbury Fox's liberal clichés and aesthetic pretensions are subjected to a mocking tone in "The Enduring Chill," his mother's provincial practicality and officious optimism are treated with a comparable comic irony. And when we turn our gaze from individual works to this group of stories as a whole, an analogous detachment becomes visible: the protagonist in these tales, the central consciousness and focus of concern, may be equally either the parent or the child. No less obsessive a pattern than the *Doppelgänger* motif (with which, as we have seen, it sometimes overlaps), the family conflict is remarkable for the apparent ease with which O'Connor can shift her attention from one role to the other. Returning again and again to the situation, she reveals the depth of her involvement with, and her ability to detach herself from, both sides of the generational battle.

For the children (of whatever age) the struggle begins in the desire to be let alone, to be given room, to differentiate themselves in an arena dominated by a "parent" who complacently insists on his or her "own way of doing." As Asbury Fox reflects about his mother, "her way had simply been the air he breathed," and he had left home, as he melodramatically puts it, "to escape the slave's atmosphere," "to find freedom." His pompous accusation of her voices the rage of all these children: "Woman, why did you pinion me?" ("The Enduring Chill," pp. 365, 364). But since the parents show no inclination (or even ability) to surrender their positions of power, they are increasingly challenged by the children, and the stories resound with the discord of clashing wills. That discord is often resolved in a violent climax, but the upshot is virtually always the same: the protagonist, whether parent or rebellious child, is defeated and even broken in his willful assertion of self. On this level, it changes nothing that their opponents are sometimes literally destroyed, as are, for instance, Thomas's mother or Mary Fortune. That Thomas and Mr. Fortune have had to resort to murderous violence is in fact the final index of their frustration and failure. The will to power always fails in O'Connor, for it thrusts at last against a reality greater than itself.

As we saw in looking at the double motif, this drive for control is finally a desperate attempt to project the ego into the external world, to make life conform to the mind's conception of it. "This is my place" ("A Circle in the Fire," p. 186), O'Connor's farm matrons cry, implying more than the mere possession of property. Mrs. May of "Greenleaf" puts it explicitly: "When she looked out any window in her house, she saw the reflection of her own character" (p. 321). But the most articulate believers in the mind's control are not of course these parental figures, but the children, almost all of whom conceive of themselves as intellectuals, and their universal failure is perhaps best illuminated by setting them against the protagonist of one of the few stories in which the generational struggle plays no part, O. E. Parker of "Parker's Back."[2]

Among other things, Parker is one indication of the shift in O'Connor's work after *Wise Blood*, for he is essentially a sympathetic reworking of the "unconscious" figure exemplified in the novel by Enoch Emery. That Parker's life develops independently of and sometimes quite against his conscious desires make him of course comic, but he is not the buffoon Enoch was, nor is his end the mocking emptiness of the man in the gorilla suit. Far from being an intellectual, Parker is "a boy whose mouth habitually hung open"; he is "as ordinary as a loaf of bread" (p. 513). When at the age of fourteen he sees the tattooed man whose body seems "a single intricate design of brilliant color," the "motion of wonder" he feels sets him off immediately from the cerebral protagonists of so many other O'Connor stories: "Until he saw the man at the fair, it did not enter his head that there was anything out of the ordinary about the fact that he existed. *Even then it did not enter his head*, but a peculiar unease settled in him" (p. 513; italics added). The relation of the O'Connor intellectual to the world is the attempt, as old Tarwater says of Rayber, to "get everything inside his head" (*The Violent Bear It Away*, p. 76). Parker's initial desire is to appropriate the images of "everything" to his *body*, but in such a way as to retain their independent life: on the man at the fair "the arabesque of men and beasts and flowers on his skin appeared to have a subtle motion of its own" ("Parker's Back," p. 513).

What Parker wants, in short, is not to control the world but quite literally to em-body it, to incarnate the image of that design of things that exists beyond him. His impulse is thus aesthetic, not intellectual: his desire is to turn himself into a living work of art. But the tattoos of the created world with which he covers his front bring only chaos, a result "haphazard and botched." Not until he has the face of Christ etched on the *obverse* of that body and acknowledges for the first time the true identity of the creature who inhabits this microcosm as Obidiah Elihue (names meaning "servant of Yahweh" and "God is he") does he achieve the effect he has groped after for so long. As Parker whispers the suppressed name, "all at once he felt the light pouring through him, turning his spider web soul into a perfect arabesque of colors, a garden of trees and birds and beasts" (p. 528). Driven blindly by an instinct he does not comprehend, Parker discovers that if the dream of perfect beauty is unrealizable in this world one may nevertheless recover—at great cost—the vision of Eden within.

Parker himself may not know how to name this instinct, but in an early draft for "The Fiction Writer and His Country" O'Connor suggested its nature. "The writer's true country," she said, "is the world of innocence, which is to say, the world of the uncorrupted imagination. . . . Of course, we have all been expelled from the Garden of Eden . . . and this is why the world of the imagination is so hard for us to enter. . . . It demands a pull against gravity."[3] The imagination, for O'Connor, is not simply a vaguely creative faculty: in a fallen world, it is the power within us that apprehends, however dimly, the numinous dimension of the creation, that in Parker brings about the vision of paradise regained. He feels the "pull against gravity," the abnegation and pain and loss that this demands, but he knows intuitively that it must be followed: "Throughout his life, grumbling and sometimes cursing, often afraid, once in rapture, Parker had obeyed whatever instinct of this kind had come to him" (p. 527). His imagination works to create in him his most deeply authentic self, even if that self is not one that Parker, had he been asked, would have chosen. But the cost of that achievement is enormous, and the story's final sentence proclaims both a mourning for what has been lost and the birth of genuine identity: "There he was—who called himself Obadiah Elihue—leaning against the tree, crying like a baby" (p. 530).

The will to vision that Parker acts out is deeply opposed to the will to power that governs most of O'Connor's protagonists, an antagonism most clearly revealed in precisely those who pretend to live by "imagination," the would-be artists. Asbury Fox, Calhoun of "The Partridge Festival," and (more incidentally) Julian of "Everything That Rises Must Converge" all aspire to being writers, although only Asbury has produced anything at all to support his pretensions, and even he admits that his work is "lifeless." Asbury's lament, "I have no imagination. I have no talent. I can't create. I have nothing but the desire for these things" ("The Enduring Chill," p. 364) might serve for Julian and Calhoun as well, and they blame stifling parents or a hostile society for their failures. The real problem, of course, is that in rebelling against those parents they have adopted a role which, they think, opposes the older generation's philistinism without exploring their fitness to play that role—a domestic version of *épater les bourgeois*. Indeed, their most genuine selves may not be the "rebel-artist-mystic[s]" they would like to think they are, but the very epitome of those middle class traits they intellectually despise: this, at least, is the central meaning of Calhoun's revelation at the end of "The Partridge Festival." It is not, as Asbury moans, that they have "no imagination," but that they have suppressed the genuine imagination, and the genuine self, they do possess by imposing an arbitrary control on their lives. As Asbury steps from the train at the opening of "The Enduring Chill," he looks at his ordinary home town and momentarily feels "that he was about to witness a majestic transformation, that the flat of roofs might at any moment turn into the mounting turrets of some exotic temple for a god he didn't know." But provincial Timberboro is the embodiment of everything Asbury scorns, and he is "irked that he *had allowed himself*, even for an instant, to see an imaginary temple in this collapsing country junction" (pp. 357, 358; italics added). By the end of the story Asbury will no longer be able to suppress his imagination, but he will also discover that it is not simply a cosy artistic faculty when it opens him to the enduring vision of purifying terror.

The failure of these pseudoartists, then, is less their lack of imagination than their willful denial of it, their refusal to trust it, their attempts to coerce it, to lead rather than be led by it—their assumption, in short, that like all the forces in life it is subject to human control. It is the lumpish Parker, with no pretensions to "creativity," who comes closer to being a genuine artist than any of O'Connor's fashionably self-conscious young men. But in their will to power, Asbury, Calhoun, and Julian are essentially no different from O'Connor's other intellectuals nor, ironically, from those intensely practical parental figures against whom so many of them are in revolt. Their invariable failure to impose the ego upon the world thus can also be described as a refusal to submit to the imagination, to surrender to that faculty that might enable them to discover both the genuine self and the true dimensions of the universe they inhabit. Again and again O'Connor's fiction implies that the will to power and the will to vision are incompatible drives, that control and surrender are necessarily contradictory, that the reasonable and the unreasonable are ever at war.

But when we shift our attention from this pattern of action to the larger strategies of her fiction, or when we listen to the voice of the occasional prose, we encounter an apparent contradiction. "When I write," O'Connor remarked, "I feel I am engaged in the reasonable use of the unreasonable," adding, "In art the reason goes wherever the imagination goes."[4] "We write with the whole personality" (*Mystery and Manners*, p. 193), she noted, and once elaborated explicitly, "the conscious as well as the unconscious mind" (*Mystery and Manners*, p. 101). The deeply dualistic tendency of her thinking is evident in the language here—*reasonable* and *unreasonable*, *reason* and *imagination*, *conscious* and *unconscious* (at other times she would add *judgment* and *vision*, *mystery* and *manners*, or the theological terms *grace* and *nature* to the list)—but she always insisted that for her the act of writing was a reconciliation of these potentially discordant qualities. Yet it is surely more accurate to speak of tension rather than harmonious reconciliation in her fiction, for if the thematic implications bear down hard on one side of those dualities—on the unreasonable, on imagination and the unconscious—other features of her work witness her commitment as a writer to the reasonable and the conscious.

Whatever is suggested by the fates of her characters, O'Connor's fiction everywhere manifests her powerful control of her material. She had nothing but scorn for what she saw as the outpourings of "unrestrained feelings" by the "very vocal writers from San Francisco," and endorsed instead Aquinas's "cold" definition of art as "reason in making" (*Mystery and Manners*, p. 82). Elsewhere she said, "I belong to that literary generation whose education was in the hands of the New Critics or those influenced by them, and with these people the emphasis was on seeing that your thoughts and feelings—whatever they were—were aptly contained within your elected image."[5] Even without such an explicit acknowledgment, the evidence of her deliberate shaping power is everywhere. The chiseled sentences, the sense of pace and form, the probing for meaning within outrageous or ludicrous action, the manipulation of tone, all point to her absorption of that atmosphere in which craftsmanship was valued above spontaneity, where technique became a form of discovery. Indeed, even without the lectures and essays and letters, the sometimes voluminous drafts of the fiction, the impressive contents of the library, it is clear from the finished stories and novels themselves that Flannery O'Connor was a highly conscious, intelligent—even "intellectual"—writer. Thus if her stories imply the necessity of surrendering the intellect, the impulse to control the world, in order to confront the larger powers of the unreasonable and the imagination, the shape of her work as a whole makes it clear that for her as a writer any such surrender would have been entirely debilitating. For O'Connor to operate at all, both sides of the duality were essential. Her description of how "Good Country People" came into being—a process both unconscious ("seemingly mindless") and yet "under control throughout" (*Mystery and Manners*, p. 100)—presents the act of writing as a seamless web, a happy reconciliation of the reasonable and the unreasonable. Indeed, O'Connor herself suggested that it was only in the act of writing that she felt this sense of wholeness: "I never completely forget myself except when I am writing and I am never more completely myself than when I am writing" (*The Habit of Being*, p. 458).

Yet whatever was involved in the act of composition, the fiction encountered by the reader exhibits everywhere not a harmonious oneness but the tautness of *concordia discors*. If, like the motif of the double, the recurrent clash between parent and child almost never leads to a scene of reconciliation, this pattern of action has striking analogues on other levels. The litotes of the plain style and the hyperbole of gesture and action, the containment implied by the craft and control and the unleashing dramatized in the rampant feelings and violent plots, the manners of the local, the everyday, the ordinary and the mystery of the devastating intrusions of psychic and cosmic forces, the laughter induced by the comic and the terror evoked by violence—out of all these dualities comes that vibrant tension that gives her work its disturbing power. None is more unnerving than the apparent gap between manner and matter, the distance between, on the one hand, the spare coolness and control of style and voice and, on the other, the violence and melodrama that make up the substance of what that style and voice convey. Like one of her more memorable characters, O'Connor as narrator is "clear and detached and ironic . . . regarding [her materials] from a great distance" (p. 285). But those materials create a world of such abrasive energy that the landscape of her fiction is littered with thefts, strokes, car accidents, self-mutilations, shootings, drownings, beatings, crushings, hangings, and gorings. The climaxes of her stories and novels are often the stuff of the tabloids, unabashedly sensational, the renderings of nightmares and fantasies of violence and sudden death. But through the carefully regulated style which mediates these horrors, O'Connor herself appears to look on with ironic equanimity as she propels her characters toward their appalling ends. Like God Himself, she seems to preside in her fiction as both creator and derisive judge.

Stephen Dedalus articulated the main direction of modernist fiction when he theorized that the dramatic artist was godlike in his disappearance from his handiwork, aloof, invisible, "indifferent"; and O'Connor echoed Joyce in placing the modern author "behind the scenes, apparently disinterested" and in insisting that "a piece of fiction must be very much a self-contained dramatic unit" (*Mystery and Manners*, pp. 74, 75). Yet if she is clearly in the modernist mainstream in the formal absence of herself-as-author from her narratives, the lack of overt commentary is hardly synonymous with Dedalian indifference. O'Connor's narrative voice is never merely neutral, and at least some of the rhetorical power given up through the adoption of formal impersonality is recaptured through her manipulation of tone. She is quite capable, particularly in her later stories, of a rapid shifting of tone (demanding a comparable nimbleness in the reader), but her most characteristic voice is that of the ironist who speaks at a great emotional distance from her subject yet, paradoxically, with great intensity, as if, although her characters must be viewed as fools or worse, what happens to them *matters* enormously. With characteristic understatement, she drily assured one interviewer that few readers "claim to see themselves"[6] in her figures; in fact, her entire narrative stance is designed to short-circuit the empathic response. In forcing the reader away from the characters, the sharp irony leaves open no vantage point but that of the narrator herself. From this distance we often—and, in the later stories, increasingly—look through the eyes of the protagonist, but we look at and around him as well to discover not only his own absurdity but the frightening dimensions of the world he inhabits.

The act of looking demands distance, sharp vision requires removal from the object viewed. If O'Connor's detachment implies anything but indifference, the severity of her act of perception *is* inextricable from the disconcerting laughter that sounds through her fiction. For her view of man is incorrigibly comic, comic with the piercing insight that can suddenly flip up the dark underside of human folly to reveal the matching grin of the memento mori. The grandmother of "A Good Man Is Hard to Find," for example, dresses elaborately for the family trip so that "in case of an accident, anyone seeing her dead on the highway would know at once that she was a lady" (p. 118). The wild disproportion of the terms, the vapid composure that summons up the ultimate violence only to treat it as a rare social opportunity, and the cool irony with which O'Connor presents the sentence makes it both fearful and ludicrous. The ridiculous in her work is often etched in a withering dryness: "He intended to stretch the boy's mind by introducing him to his ancestor, the fish, and to all the great wastes of unexplored time" (*The Violent Bear It Away*, p. 140); "She was a good Christian woman with a large respect for religion, though she did not, of course, believe any of it was true" ("Greenleaf," p. 316). In passages such as these, the irony is so sharp, the exposure of folly so pitiless, that the revelation of emptiness and self-deception is as appalling as it is comic.

All comedy is perhaps in some measure cruel in its laughter, but O'Connor's fiction contains a comic perception that is frightening in its very relentlessness. The scorn, the astringency, the refusal to soften the harshness of the mocking outline, to compromise comic justice with mercy, is compelling in its fierce integrity, but it also contains the fearsomeness of that "guffawing peal of thunder" ("The Life You Save May Be Your Own," p. 156) cited earlier. O'Connor's comic range is of course not limited to any single effect; she moves easily from paradoxical wit to the confusions of farce, from sharp satire to dialect humor, from subtle ironies to broad laughter. The stories are not monochromatic: they possess shadings of tone, degrees of distance and sympathy, and the later works in particular require complex responses throughout. Yet even the most sympathetic figures are viewed by an austere eye that blinks at no human absurdity, that notes ironically the gestures that reveal the rampant ego. It is as if the characters demand being stripped bare, as if their pretensions and evasions and self-deceiving lies must be swept ruthlessly aside until they are shown for the Old Adam they are, naked before all-seeing eyes in a kind of fictional Last Judgment. But the mocking laughter this process evokes is chilling; it is little wonder that John Hawkes thought he detected the Satanic note in it.[7]

In the rhetorical sense, comedy is by its very nature cathartic. As Wylie Sypher says, "Like tragedy, comedy is homeopathic. It cures folly by folly."[8] But in O'Connor's fiction the purgative action seems to work not only on the reader, but by a strange metamorphosis on the characters as well. The aggressive component in purposive (as distinguished from harmless) jokes was long ago pointed out by Freud, and Eric Bentley has recently observed the element of violence, of "destructive force," in both kinds of purposive jokes, those designed to "smash" and those to "strip." These he argues, are at the root of the main tradition of scornful comedy, the tradition in which O'Connor obviously belongs.[9] In her work the gradual comic stripping away parallels the thrust of the action that in story after story drives the characters to an extremity of abasement or guilt which rips aside their illusions. The relentless laughter of the narrator and the frightening drama of the action seem to converge toward a single point, the unmasking of their evil and folly. They are finally driven to see themselves as she has seen them throughout. But at the violent climaxes of O'Connor's stories all laughter, but not all irony, drops away, for these glimpses of reality lay bare the pain and terror that has lurked beneath the comedy all along.

The implicit violence in comedy is the hidden link between manner and matter in O'Connor, between the freeing of laughter and the freezing of fear. As they touch at the ultimate horizon of her fiction, the terrifying and the comic create a tension analogous to the recurrent motif of unrecognized double figures, or the repeated clashes between parents and children. Yet this fundamental doubleness also makes itself felt in her pervasive use of that highly ironic narrative voice. The duality implicit in all irony is heightened and sustained in O'Connor's work. In insisting on the split between what the protagonist takes himself to be and what he actually is (which in turn is inseparable from what he takes his world to be as opposed to what *it* is), her narrator points not just to a misjudgment or incomplete awareness, but to a veritable chasm of self-deception. "You aren't who you think you are" ("Everything That Rises Must Converge," p. 419), one of those protagonists smugly tells his mother (neither, of course, is he), and the remark might serve as a motto for all her central figures. That gap between the fabricated and deeply false persona and the true self (whether or not embodied in a *Doppelgänger*) is already implied in the double consciousness of the ironic narrator, whose false speaking masks true knowing and who thereby creates a double consciousness in the reader as well.

Along with the poised distance of that ironic narrative voice and the sustained comic perception, the rigorous attention to craft and the sparely honed style help achieve in O'Connor's fiction that reasonableness of which she spoke, the powerful sense of discipline and control that seems at the opposite pole from—and so perhaps made possible—the unleashing of the dark unreasonable forces of the violent and terrifying. For at the heart of her imagination is an irremediable wildness, a deliberate pursuit of the "extreme situation" that for her seems to have demanded the craftsmanship and coolness and ironic comedy to bring her obsessive materials under control. She was clearly determined to make the violence she conjured up engage a larger meaning and thus point to a greater order, but much of the power of her work flows from the unimpeded intensity of deeply felt sources which she learned how to shape without suppressing. One of Flannery O'Connor's firmest convictions is that the vital centers of life, both within and beyond the self, are radically unreasonable, and in her fiction the nonrational expresses itself in violence.

As a result, the shocking climaxes of her stories are frequently appropriate to the action that precedes them without seeming entirely inevitable. O'Connor herself once described those moments as characterized by "an action or a gesture which was both totally right and totally unexpected" (*Mystery and Manners*, p. 111). Almost inescapably her plots have a melodramatic cast, sometimes sensationally so. The number of accidents in her fiction alone is an index of the bent of her imagination, from the overturned car of "A Good Man Is Hard to Find" to the runaway tractor that kills the displaced person, from the bull's goring of Mrs. May in "Greenleaf" to Thomas's shooting of his mother in "The Comforts of Home." But despite the gratuitousness inherent in melodramatic action, O'Connor's climaxes grow out of an incipient violence of language, imagery, and emotion which creates explosive pressures. In "A Circle in the Fire," for example, the increasing fierceness of the landscape, from the opening "black wall" of trees behind which "the sun was a livid glaring white" to that sun "swollen and flame-colored and hung in a net of ragged cloud as if it might burn through any second and fall into the woods" (pp. 175, 184), parallels the developing antagonism between the farm dwellers and the invading city boys. Yet this hostility is itself rooted in the obsessive fears and negations of the farm owner, Mrs. Cope—she tears at weeds "as if they were an evil sent directly by the devil to destroy the place" (p. 175)—which in turn increasingly evokes the boys' latent destructiveness; and the atmosphere of impending violence is further heightened by dialogue given over to discussions of fires, hurricanes, European boxcars, iron lungs, guns, fighting, stealing, and poisoning. When the story bursts into the climactic fire, that outcome immediately seems right if not inescapable.

O'Connor's use of melodramatic action is central to her strategy to make available in fiction that realm of mystery beyond manners.

"If art imitates life," Bentley has noted, "it should be added that while naturalistic art imitates the surfaces, 'melodramatic' art imitates what is beneath the surface."[10] Elsewhere he has elaborated on the capacity of melodrama to evoke fear, not the common-sense fear of the everyday world, but the fear that "perhaps none too rationally is called irrational. Savage superstitions, neurotic fantasies, and childhood imaginings spring to mind, and equally outside the bounds of common sense is the fear of God."[11] Peter Brooks has recently gone further in terms directly relevant to O'Connor. Tracing the rise of stage melodrama in the late eighteenth and early nineteenth centuries to the "desacralization" of the universe, the final breakup of a widely shared belief in Christianity, Brooks sees melodrama as an attempt to recover not the realm of the sacred, which is "no longer viable," but "the ethical imperatives that traditionally depended on it." In this effort, melodrama becomes "an emblem of the cosmic ethical drama, which by reflection illuminates life here below." Necessarily, the world of melodrama is sharply dualistic: "What we most retain from any consideration of melodramatic structures is the sense of fundamental bipolar contrast and clash. The world according to melodrama is built on an irreducible Manichaeism, the conflict of good and evil not subject to compromise. . . . The middle ground and middle condition are excluded." The melodramatic mode, Brooks argues, is by no means an outdated, Victorian excess, but "a central fact of the modern sensibility."[12]

If we recall O'Connor's own comments on the problem of the Christian writer in a time of no certain belief, an age which "doubts both fact and value," and of the "violent" fictional methods such a gap entails, Brooks's description of the plight of earlier figures like Balzac and James will sound in many ways quite familiar:

In the absence of a true Sacred . . . they continue to believe that what is most important in a man's life is his ethical drama and the ethical implications of his psychic drama. Yet here they are dealing in quantities and entities that have only an uncertain ontology and, especially an uncertain visibility: they are not necessarily seen in the same manner, if perceived at all, by an audience, since the social cohesion of an earlier society with a greater community of belief no longer obtains. In the manner of the melodramatist, such writers must locate, express, demonstrate, prove, the very terms in which they are dealing. They must wrest them forth from behind the facades of life, show their meaning and their opera-tion. Precisely to the extent that they feel themselves dealing in concepts and issues that have no certain status or justification, they have recourse to the demonstrative, heightened representations of melodrama.[13]

It is hardly necessary to add that the problem Brooks describes was anything but alleviated by the middle of the twentieth century, nor that, as *Mystery and Manners* shows, Flannery O'Connor had a re-markably clear grasp of it.

Yet of course her aims were not those of the earlier writers, and she took from melodrama only those elements she needed. For O'Connor's concern is not with the "ethical imperatives" of tradi-tional melodrama but with just that theological dimension from which the ethical traditionally derived. Her assault, in short, is pre-cisely on the sacred, which had seemed, in Brooks's words, "no longer viable" in literature. If, for instance, she borrows from melo-drama the clash of violently opposed and irreconcilable characters, those characters are not presented as the embodiments of good and evil or innocence and villainy—comically conceived, her villains apt to look like inverted heroes (witness The Misfit or Manley Pointer), and in O'Connor's fiction no one is truly innocent. Melo-drama opens in a world of bipolar contrast and clash and never leaves that world. O'Connor's stories, however, begin on the middle ground of manners. It is precisely the function of the action to open up the off-balance world of mystery, that dimension in which "the middle ground and middle condition are excluded," and to reveal it not as a "domain of moral imperatives," but as eschatological reality. Finally, her climaxes come closer to those of tragedy than of traditional melo-drama. Innocence never having truly existed, it can hardly be re-stored triumphantly: the wrenching encounters with the numinous in O'Connor, as we have seen, bring no sense of reconciliation, but only pain, loss, and displacement.

What O'Connor takes from melodrama, therefore, is not its style or presentation of character or its focus on the moral realm but its "radically hyperbolic," "bigger-than-life" conception of *action* in order to "reach in grandiose reference to a noumenal realm" of irrec-oncilable dualities.[14] She grasped early what Richard Chase called melodrama's "capacity to evoke ultimates and absolutes, in order to dramatize theological . . . ideology,"[15] and she praised Hawthorne, from whom she repeatedly claimed literary descent, for his "lean and dark" fiction, "characterized by a melodrama which somehow carried more weight than one would think such a frail vessel would support."[16] In her own hands, the violent shattering of ordinary verisimilitude, of everyday events and logical connections, allows us to glimpse through the surfaces of actuality the workings of irrational and suprarational powers and invests them again with the terror and awe which are their due.

If O'Connor unashamedly draws on the disjunctions of melodramatic action to propel her figures toward the "extreme situation," that movement characteristically manifests itself in violence. Most often, but by no means always, the violence in her stories springs from a human source. As her myopic protagonists find their single-minded approaches to existence increasingly challenged, they are driven to greater and greater intensity of defense. The grandmother of "A Good Man Is Hard to Find" falls into hysterical parodies of her claims to gentility, jolly Mrs. Turpin of "Revelation," the woman with a "good disposition," finds herself shaking a furious fist at God, and old Mark Fortune of "A View of the Woods" kills the very granddaughter he has doted on. At their ends the tales rupture into a moment of violence which either bursts from within as the protagonist's last implacable defense of his threatened ego or rushes from without, as if to fill or annihilate the internal vacuum which has invited it. The degree of climactic violence is carefully calibrated to the denials that evoke it—yet one more sign of the reasonableness of O'Connor's control. But even "The Artificial Nigger," which may contain her most beatific climax, closes in language that is by no means free of pain and violence. Mr. Head acknowledges his own "agony," he "burned with shame," "he stood appalled" while "the action of mercy covered his pride like a flame and consumed it" (pp. 269–70).

Mild as it is for O'Connor, that language is a reminder that not all the violence in her fiction springs from human origin. Nevertheless, she seems to have seen a central wildness, a radical "irrationalism," at the core of man which for both better and worse defines his inmost being. Violence carrying overtones of the demonic consistently grows out of the subrational, a point most ironically demonstrated by those intellectuals whose devotion to principles of reason involves them in fatal acts. When Thomas shoots his mother, for instance, or when Sheppard of "The Lame Shall Enter First" recognizes his own guilty part in his son's hanging, the supreme irony is not that reason has produced these terrible climaxes, but that both men in their rigid intellectualism have opened themselves to precisely the irrational sources their minds so contemptuously dismiss. Thomas insists on logic with his mother, but, as we have seen, what drives him toward the shooting is the disturbance deep within his psyche increasingly brought into play by the story's action; and Sheppard's determination to "save" the delinquent Rufus Johnson masks in rationalistic language a devouring egotism that helps send his own son to his death. In stories such as these the veneer of intellectualism is revealed as a flimsy covering for an essential and unrecognized selfishness which, when pressed, erupts violently through the thin rational surface. In their dangerous divorce of mind from deeper feelings and their denial of the explosive force of the unconscious, O'Connor's intellectuals come very close to enacting a modern version of the duality Hawthorne called head and heart. Typically, however, there are no reconciliations in her work: within the characters, at least, the dissociation of sensibility is complete.

Yet if for O'Connor the intellect is at best a useless defense against inherent human depravity, it is also a stumbling block to genuine vision, and while the outbreak of violence may reveal the demonic, it may also suggest the presence of the divine. The most obvious examples here are to be found in the novels, but we have already observed the irrationality of O. E. Parker, who moves on a level beneath the conscious as he is driven to the suffering of his tattoo of Christ and the violence it provokes. Under the pressures of the prophetic mission, the Tarwaters of *The Violent Bear It Away* lose their reason altogether, yet madness is here, as with the fanatical Mrs. Greenleaf in the story of that name, O'Connor's characteristically extreme and literal metaphor for the essential nonrationalism of belief. However, the violence which not only matches but surpasses man's is that of divine revelation itself, which descends in a whirlwind on the hapless characters below. If the deepest vitality of man has its roots in the irrational, O'Connor's God is a being suprarational, and the encounter of the human with the divine takes place beyond the categories of the intellect, in a timeless recognition where the mind's discursiveness gives way to paradoxical vision. The God of Wrath and the God of Love seem to be one: mercy and judgment, like the horns of the Greenleaf bull, come together in an awesomeness suggested in Asbury Fox's discovery that the Holy Ghost is a "purifying terror." O'Connor might well have agreed with Pascal that the apparent violence of God is a function of the evil in man: "We suffer only in proportion as the vice which is natural to us resists supernatural grace. . . . But it would be very unfair to impute this violence to God, who is drawing us on, instead of to the world, which is holding us back."[17] Yet "vice" *is* "natural to us," and no rationalization can dispel the dramatized experience of the stories, the immense disproportion of the human and the divine that causes them to meet with a terrifying shock. The fearful encounters with the ultimate Other produce in a stroke for the characters what the mocking laughter has all along suggested to the reader—the violent shattering of all the claims of the self. Out of these wrenching displacements emerge, again and again, the archetypal features of the Old Adam.

O'Connor thus learned early how to control the melodramatic tendencies of her imagination, how to turn her fascination with violence, mutilation, and sudden death into strategies that create meaning. The violence that erupts from man and that which descends from God are both terrifying and mysterious, finally beyond rationalization, and the stories that end in apparent salvation are hardly more comfortable than those that end in murder. As one moves toward the eschatological poles, the poles move toward each other. "Be saved in the Lord's fire or perish in your own!" (p. 135) cries the child evangelist in *The Violent Bear It Away*. The choice is real in O'Connor's work, but it's fire either way.

The form of tension we have been exploring—between comic perception and melodramatic plotting, ironic voice and violent action, the release of laughter and the constraint of fear—seems to return us inescapably to that center of the incongruous, the grotesque. It is little wonder that O'Connor happily accepted that term as descriptive of her fiction, for the grotesque is precisely that mode that achieves its effect not by reconciling conflicting forms and responses, but by holding them in insoluble suspension: its very nature is to be not simply comic *or* frightening, but both simultaneously, at once ludicrous and terrifying. In discovering early in her career that the grotesque was her true métier, O'Connor committed herself to an aesthetics of incongruity, to the exploration and exploitation of jarring disharmonies which by definition were not finally to be reconciled. Yet if this remains the mode of her fiction, she found a way, at the end of her career, to bring together on the level of character those very qualities that she had dramatized as at war throughout her fiction.

In her last published work, "Judgement Day," O'Connor presents a protagonist unique in her stories, one in whom control and surrender, will and imagination, are reconciled and made one. It begins this way: "Tanner was conserving all his strength for the trip home. He *meant* to walk as far as he could get and *trust* to the Almighty to get him the rest of the way" (p. 531; italics added). Tanner is an old man near death, and he knows it, and his single-minded desire to get home is informed by a perspective that has already moved beyond time and beyond the great dichotomy of existence, the underlying source of all human conflict. "Dead or alive," the old man thinks, "he would be home. Dead or alive. It was the being there that mattered; the dead or alive did not" (p. 532). The local and the eternal for him are one. In his imagination he arises from his coffin at his hometown railroad station to announce the end of time and the arrival of "Judgement Day." Being an O'Connor work, the story is not without its comedy and violence, its ironies and reversals, but if these necessarily qualify the old man's vision, they do not finally undercut it. In Tanner, O'Connor at the end of her own life reconciled those very impulses that form the basis of conflict throughout her earlier work. Not surprisingly, he is the most sympathetically handled adult protagonist in all her stories.

The calm assurance of this late work, the compassionate view of its central figure and the harmonizing in him what are elsewhere presented as battling conscious and unconscious forces may suggest that, had she lived, O'Connor's fiction would have moved into a mellower phase—a view that might be supported by pointing to "Parker's Back," to the surviving fragments of *Why Do the Heathen Rage?*, and to the complex emotional tonality in late versions of such recurrent figures as the mother ("The Comforts of Home," "Everything That Rises Must Converge") and the intellectual ("Revelation"). But as things stand, "Judgement Day" must be seen as a finale rather than a departure, and as such it is hardly representative of the fiction O'Connor did achieve. Much more typical are those stories in which the clash opens into a wider and wider breach, in which resolution but not reconciliation is achieved (and that only at terrible cost), in which antithetical figures glare at one another across an ever-increasing gap, as if those dichotomies were the fictional embodiments of Flannery O'Connor's own irreconcilable dualities—between parent and child, conscious and unconscious, the reasonable and the unreasonable—which, if she could not heal, she could in story after story at least make work for her under the pressure of her art. In this respect, far more instructive than "Judgement Day" is a story that lies at the other end of her mature canon, one published soon after *Wise Blood*: "A Good Man Is Hard to Find." Here, perhaps more starkly than ever again, O'Connor revealed and exploited, on all levels, the tensions that are most characteristic of her fiction.

II

"A Good Man Is Hard to Find" continues to be O'Connor's best-known work, the story most often chosen to represent her in anthologies now as during her lifetime. Yet, fine as it is, it is not self-evidently her best story: something more than quality must account for its repeated selection by textbook editors. One reason for its popularity may well be precisely that "A Good Man Is Hard to Find" writes large the representative O'Connor themes and methods—comedy, violence, theological concern—and thus makes them quickly and unmistakably available. But another, surely, is the primordial appeal of the story, for "A Good Man Is Hard to Find" captures a very old truth, that in the midst of life we are in death, in its most compelling modern form. The characteristic contemporary nightmare of the sudden onslaught of violent death, a death that chooses its victims without warning, impersonally, apparently at random, without either motivation or remorse, the victims helpless either to escape or to defend themselves—this scenario for some of our deepest, most instinctual fears is the very basis of the story and the source of its immediate hold on our imaginations.

Interestingly enough, O'Connor's own public remarks on the story dismiss this level almost entirely. Stressing its spiritual implications, she emphasizes the grandmother's final action while brushing aside everything that leads up to it, saying, "If I took out this gesture and what she says with it, I would have no story. What was left would not be worth your attention." Her advice to readers of "A Good Man Is Hard to Find" is, "You should be on the lookout for such things as the action of grace in the Grandmother's soul, and not for the dead bodies" (*Mystery and Manners*, pp. 112, 113).

This is all very high-minded, but it would seem a little difficult for the unprejudiced reader of "A Good Man Is Hard to Find" to ignore the dead bodies; and while one may agree with O'Connor that the story is "something more than an account of a family murdered on the way to Florida" (*Mystery and Manners*, p. 114), it surely is, most immediately, just that "account." Any full discussion of the story must deal with both the grandmother's soul and the dead bodies, and indeed with the tension between the two levels implied here, for that tension is at the very heart of the story.

It is The Misfit who, in stating his own dilemma, articulates the story's central metaphor in the most frequently quoted passage from O'Connor's fiction:

> "Jesus was the only One that ever raised the dead," The Misfit continued, "and He shouldn't have done it. He thown everything off balance. If He did what He said, then it's nothing for you to do but thow away everything and follow Him, and if He didn't, then it's nothing for you to do but enjoy the few minutes you got left the best way you can—by killing somebody or burning down his house or doing some other meanness to him. No pleasure but meanness," he said and his voice had become almost a snarl.[18]

In every sense, "A Good Man Is Hard to Find" dramatizes a world radically off balance. Precisely at the center of the story a pleasure trip to Florida suddenly becomes an extended encounter with death when the family's car flips over, thereby slicing the action of the story neatly in half. O'Connor makes no attempt to mask the melodrama of this turning point; indeed, she insists on it by having the children shriek not once but three times ("in a frenzy of delight"), "We've had an ACCIDENT!" (p. 125). It is left to the reader to try to reconcile the two halves of the story, to make them balance around this pivotal act.

And on the most obvious level, that of action, the two sections remain resolutely off balance.[19] The first half of "A Good Man Is Hard to Find" is apparently as random and purposeless as the lives of the family it focuses on: they are headed for Florida, but, as episode succeeds episode, it is far less clear where the story is headed. The characters talk on diverse topics, quibble, make observations on the scenery, the children play a game, the grandmother tells a story, they stop for lunch, June Star tap dances, and so on. As a mimetic technique, the impression of fragmentation in the opening half of the story is O'Connor's way of establishing the discordance and emptiness of their superficial lives. Beneath the surface, however, this section has a greater coherence than first appears. The silent juxtaposition of apparently unrelated episodes both further reveals their, and especially the grandmother's, values and binds this part of the story more firmly together on a level beyond action. Consider the following examples of one episode giving way to another so that the second forms an ironic comment on the first:

> "In my time," said the grandmother, folding her thin veined fingers, "children were more respectful of their native states and their parents and everything else. People did right then. *Oh look at the cute little pickaninny!" she said and pointed to a Negro child standing in the door of a shack.*

> He [Red Sammy] and the grandmother discussed better times. The old lady said that in her opinion Europe was entirely to blame for the way things were now. She said the way Europe acted you would think we were made of money and Red Sam said it was no use talking about it, she was exactly right. The children ran outside into the white sunlight and looked at the monkey in the lacy chinaberry tree. *He was busy catching fleas on himself and biting each one carefully between his teeth as if it were a delicacy.* [pp. 119, 122; italics added]

Nevertheless, the initial impression of the episodic and the directionless is functional in the story. When the grandmother notes the mileage on the car—she "wrote this down because she thought it would be interesting to say how many miles they had been when they got back" (p. 118)—she reveals the family's trip as mere empty movement through space. Only with the accident that ends the outer journey does the action take on coherence and direction. Now the true, inner journey begins, and its destination is not Florida but death. Exterior motion in the second half of the story is minimal; aside from the eloquently understated trips into the woods, all physical traveling is over. The characters are now so motionless that small gestures acquire a disproportionate expressiveness, and the focus shifts from actions to words, from the episodic movement toward Florida to the gradually unfolding dialogue between the grandmother and The Misfit.

That dialogue has a continuity and cumulative force that is precisely what the action of the first half of the story lacked. Through it O'Connor achieves the mutual unmasking of these central figures, a process necessarily different for each, but nonetheless parallel and wrought out of their mutual interaction. If the action of the first half of the story is that of random exterior movement, that of the second is a progressive motion toward the deepest interiors of these two characters. Both figures are subjected to the distinctive O'Connor pressure, that intensity of situation that strips away the accretions of the false self.

This gradual revelation is most evident in The Misfit; indeed, if we fail to recognize the progression in his unburdening, he will seem simply inconsistent. At first, for all the menace in his appearance, The Misfit is remarkably well-mannered toward his intended victims. He blushes at Bailey's "shocking" remark to the old woman, consoles her, apologizes for his half-dressed condition "before you ladies" and couches his murderous orders in a deferential gentility: "Would you mind stepping back in them woods . . ." But the grandmother's desperate flattery gradually moves him beyond mere politeness. At first her accolade, "I know you're a good man," produces only the formulaic, "I pre-chate that, lady," but a few moments later the same remark elicits a more carefully considered response: "Nome, I ain't a good man" (p. 128). With this, The Misfit shifts to another level, gradually uncovering the dimensions of his quest to "know why it is," a quest that has led him to the tomblike penitenti-

FLANNERY O'CONNOR

ary and a sense of the baffling injustice of life. But when the grandmother self-servingly introduces religion into the dialogue, she
forces another turn of the screw, although again the shift is not apparent at once:

> "If you would pray," the old lady said, "Jesus would help you."
> "That's right," The Misfit said.
> "Then why don't you pray?" she asked. . . .
> "I don't want no hep," he said. "I'm doing all right by myself." [p. 130]

The offhand acknowledgment here of the efficacy of Jesus and the
claim to self-sufficiency without Him gradually gives way to the famous passage already quoted where The Misfit confesses his doubt of
Jesus and poses his stark alternatives. There The Misfit shows himself as literally a rational animal, reasoning with a frighteningly icy
logic to arrive at a snarl like that of the family cat as he speaks his
doctrine of Jesus or meanness. But there is a still deeper self beyond
that. Pretensions to "doing all right by myself" drop away, and what
appears is the face of the anguished and angry child: "'It ain't right I
wasn't there [when Jesus claimed to have raised the dead]. . . . Listen
lady,' he said in a high voice, 'if I had of been there I would of known
and I wouldn't be like I am now'" (p. 132). The center has at last
been reached, and the painful uncertainty there is only confirmed by
his (and the story's) final line: "It's no real pleasure in life."

The revelation of The Misfit is a gradual one, the piercing through
of layer after layer until we arrive at the core of his torment.[20] The
unmasking of the grandmother follows a different curve, the rising
intensity of her habitual responses, which, reaching the point of hys-
teria, suddenly burst like a bubble; and out of the wreckage emerges
a more deeply authentic self. Her situation, at least, is symbolized by
the relative physical postures of the two antagonists. Whereas The
Misfit "squats" soon after his entrance into the story and does
not budge from that position until he leaps back to shoot the old
woman, the grandmother stands "looking down on him" through almost all of their dialogue. She begins with her genteel flattery—"I
know you're a good man . . . I know you must come from nice people!" (the line that had recently worked so well with Red Sammy)—
proceeds through advice for gaining middle-class security ("Think

how wonderful it would be to settle down and live a comfortable life"), and, all else failing, grasps frantically at her religiosity. Nothing silences the gunshots from the woods, and the grandmother's final attempt to stave off the inevitable is a hysterically garbled parody of all her arguments: "'Jesus!' the old lady cried. 'You've got good blood! I know you wouldn't shoot a lady! I know you come from nice people! Pray! Jesus, you ought not to shoot a lady. I'll give you all the money I've got!'" (pp. 132–33).

There is nowhere further to go in that direction, and amongst the shattered confusion of her customary values, she collapses from her position above The Misfit, literally sinking down to his level of anguish and uncertainty. She cannot answer his arguments, but, stripped of her middle-class pretensions and self-serving assurances, she can, and does, respond as a "grand-mother" (and she is given no other name)[21] to his suffering. Rather than attempting to manipulate those around her to her own ends, for the first time she "reach[es]" out to the need of this surrogate child. The Misfit, of course, shoots her at once. The mutual revelations thus come together: as he discloses his deepest torment, she responds with her deepest self. It is the convergence that the entire latter half of "A Good Man Is Hard to Find" has been moving relentlessly toward.

If the action of the two parts of the story is remarkably different both in kind and direction, O'Connor's control of narrative voice and tone works toward creating a sustained aesthetic whole. The dominant tone of the first half of "A Good Man Is Hard to Find" must certainly be called comic, but it is O'Connor at her most ironically astringent and sharply satirical, and the voice that, for example, presents the children's mother—her face "as broad and innocent as a cabbage and . . . tied around with a green head-kerchief that had two points on the top like a rabbit's ears" (p. 117)—is ruthlessly detached from her characters. The very chilliness of the comic distance here might itself be felt as a bit unnerving. Moreover, there is a darkly menacing undertone that runs throughout the first part of the story in the form of recurrent references to violence and death: the various allusions to the exploits of The Misfit which, more than foreshadowing his later appearance, suggest the inability of the characters genuinely to imagine what he represents; the grandmother's complacent fantasizing of her own violent death in a car accident or of her cat asphyxiating himself; the graveyard that is the occasion for an arch joke; the violence of those dreadful children toward each other and their father; the verbal aggressiveness of Red Sammy's wife; even the name of the town Toombsboro.[22]

This sinister undertone moves closer to the surface when the family turns off the main road—"The dirt road was hilly and there were sudden washes in it and sharp curves on dangerous embankments" (p. 124)—and deepens still further when the hidden cat springs "with a snarl" to precipitate the accident. With the threateningly slow appearance of The Misfit and his accomplices in the "hearse-like automobile," it spreads into the central action of the story, which it will dominate until the end.

As the menacing undercurrent of the first part of the story rises to dominate the second, the prevailing comedy of the first half sinks and darkens still further, but it does not disappear. The elaborate politeness of The Misfit has already been mentioned; in the midst of the ruthless death dealing, it repeatedly strikes a bizarrely incongruous note. Consider the exchange about The Misfit's improper attire which comes just after Bailey and his son have been escorted into the woods:

> "I'm sorry I don't have a shirt on before you ladies," he said, hunching his shoulders slightly. "We buried our clothes that we had on when we escaped and we're just making do until we can get better. We borrowed these from some folks we met," he explained.
> "That's perfectly all right," the grandmother said. "Maybe Bailey has an extra shirt in his suitcase."
> "I'll look and see terrectly," The Misfit said. [p. 129]

It is all very well bred, but since the story has begun with the grandmother admonishing her son to "read here what it says [The Misfit] did to these people," the context and the euphemistic *borrowed* makes the entire exchange horrifyingly ludicrous—black comedy indeed. And here as elsewhere the grandmother becomes not less but more absurd, for her sentimental gentilities were never so preposterously at odds with the actual situation.

The extension of comic perception throughout the sinister second part of the story is a reminder that the coolly observant narrator, the detached voice of the first part, is still present, noting the terrors of this family, and especially of the grandmother, from the same emotional distance that she reported their follies. When the grandmother first recognizes The Misfit, this passage occurs: " 'You wouldn't shoot a lady, would you?' the grandmother said and removed a clean handkerchief from her cuff and began to slap at her eyes with it" (p. 127). The old lady has just learned that she faces almost certain death and she is understandably frightened, but the precise notation of action and the single word *slap* preserve the narrative distance: no sympathy is added to her self-pity here. When the last of five pistol shots sounds from the woods, "the grandmother raised her head like a parched old turkey hen crying for water and called, 'Bailey Boy, Bailey Boy!' " (p. 132). Those pistol reports signify the end of her entire family, but the animal simile qualifies and contains the pathos inherent in the situation. The controlled detachment of the narrative voice perhaps makes the horror of the second half of the story bearable, but such unflappable poise is more than a little frightening in itself. In any case, the sustained consistency of that voice is a powerful means of binding the two sections of the story together.

O'Connor's use of tone and voice thus works toward reconciling the two halves of "A Good Man Is Hard to Find" despite the rather disparate action contained in each. Tonally the story maintains a mixture of the comic and the sinister throughout, with different emphases as demanded by the differing kinds of action, and the narrative voice preserves its ironic detachment with implacable consistency. More, however, remains to be said about precisely that incident which seems to snap the action of the story in two, the car accident, for of course that event is by no means as simple as I have suggested above.

If O'Connor at first glance appears to insist on the melodrama of the car's overturn by having the children underline it with their delighted screams, "A Good Man Is Hard to Find" does not allow the attentive reader to miss the sense in which that accident is not accidental at all, but the responsibility of the grandmother. We recall the story's opening in which, wanting to travel to Tennessee rather than Florida, she attempts to change the family's mind by a hypocritical use of the threat of The Misfit, and we particularly savor the irony of

"I wouldn't take my children in any direction with a criminal like that aloose in it. I couldn't answer to my conscience if I did" (p. 117). For this of course is exactly what she does. The detour that leads to that accident on a deserted dirt road is a response to her nostalgia for an antebellum mansion where, she fibs enticingly, legend holds that treasure is hidden—a house, she belatedly remembers (and again we note the irony), which is not in Georgia at all, but in Tennessee. The immediate cause of the accident is the cat she has smuggled along against her son's wishes "because he would miss her too much and she was afraid he might brush against one of the gas burners and accidentally asphyxiate himself" (p. 118). In all of this we recognize how the grandmother's rampant selfishness, her sentimentality, gentility, nostalgia, materialism, and uncertain hold on reality have contributed to the accident on this sinister back road. The ironies, up to this point in the story, are evident and a bit pat.

But through The Misfit the second half of "A Good Man Is Hard to Find" raises questions at another level altogether and invites a reevaluation of the import of the car accident. The first imbalance in the world that he had detected was not that introduced by Jesus. This prior one he articulates in explaining his act of self-naming:

> "I call myself The Misfit," he said, "because I can't make what all I done wrong fit with what all I gone through in punishment."
> There was a piercing scream from the woods, followed closely by a pistol report. "Does it seem right to you, lady, that one is punished a heap and another ain't punished at all?" [p. 131]

Again, we note the irony of the juxtaposition (although, given the premises The Misfit gradually reveals, the logic of his "mean" actions is frighteningly consistent), but the problem of justice he raises here bears directly on the upshot of the car accident. By any human standards, does it seem "right" that not only the grandmother herself but her entire family down to the baby should be murderously "punished" for "what all [she] done wrong"? Even if we grant that the old lady bears responsibility for the accident, is she also responsible for the fact that this dirt road, of all the dirt roads in Georgia, is the one that harbors The Misfit and his gang? In light of the consequences of the car wreck, that accident is, in a deeper sense, fully as melodramatic as it first appeared.

The form of "A Good Man Is Hard to Find" thus supports The Misfit's arguments, for to him life *is* melodrama: if he says his punishment exceeds his crimes, the two parts of the story show both this family's sins and the excessiveness of their punishment. Thus far, however, The Misfit has been considering the problem of suffering horizontally, as it were, finding it unresolvable by human reason, unamenable to the desire to make this world fit into coherent patterns. It is only now that he introduces the other possibility, the vertical dimension of another life through which such dilemmas might be resolved. Unlike the problem of justice horizontally considered, this question requires not the mental weighing of experiences, but the fullest commitment of the self—thus the off-balance demand which it forces. The choice is finally a stark either/or, which to The Misfit takes the form of Jesus or meanness.

O'Connor's own remarks on this story (and everywhere else) leave of course no doubt where she felt herself committed. Emphasizing the grandmother's recognition of The Misfit and calling it her "moment of grace," she insisted that the assumptions underlying her writing were those of "the central Christian mysteries" (*Mystery and Manners*, pp. 112, 109). And it would seem difficult, watching the grandmother reach out to The Misfit as "one of [her] own babies" or responding to the overtones of her final posture ("her legs crossed under her like a child's and her face smiling up at the cloudless sky"), seriously to dispute this element in the story. Nevertheless, however childlike or smiling, that final posture does belong to a corpse, the object not only of the acknowledged meanness of The Misfit, but of a more devious cruelty in the story.

O'Connor was once approached directly on the question of this tension in her work: "If the Redemption is a framework for your writing, how do you account for the brutality in your stories?" In reply, she cited "A Good Man Is Hard to Find": "There really isn't much brutality. . . . People keep referring to the brutality in the stories, but even 'A Good Man Is Hard to Find' is, in a way, a comic stylized thing. It is not naturalistic writing and so you can't really call it brutal."[23] Apparently taking *brutality* here to mean simply violent action, O'Connor's response, perhaps deliberately, evades the question, implying that one can speak of cruelty only in connection with identifiably naturalistic writing (recall her admonition to ignore "the dead bodies" in "A Good Man Is Hard to Find"!). Most interesting of all is her failure (or refusal) to recognize that the comic, far from automatically ruling out cruelty, may itself be simply a more subtle source of it.

As O'Connor herself seems here to acknowledge, "A Good Man Is Hard to Find" may well be her most violent story, but it is also one in which the comic tone is at its most astringent, the ironic voice at its most drily mocking. The first half of the story is given over to the narrator's relentless revelation of the selfishness, the vacuousness, the nastiness of this family, and especially of its key member, the grandmother. In the exposure of her smugness, pretentiousness, and hypocrisy, of her egoistic manipulation of others, of the role of all these qualities in the causing of the car accident, the presentation walks a fine tonal line between laughter and outrage. The manner of her portrayal in the opening part of the story creates the expectation that the sequel will provide her with some comeuppance, that she will be made to offer satisfaction for such behavior. If, as I have argued above, the punishment that does come seems by all reasonable standards excessive, nevertheless the sense of satisfaction is projected into the landscape of the story, for as the murderous gunshots begin to echo from the woods, the very sound of the wind in the trees becomes "like a long satisfied insuck of breath" (p. 129). It might indeed be argued that the violence of the second part of "A Good Man Is Hard to Find" is the transposition of the biting tone of the first onto the level of action. In any case, the climax of the story manages to have it both ways at once. The grandmother does indeed have what O'Connor calls her "special kind of triumph," her "moment of grace," but she is made to pay immediately not only for that moment but for all her conduct with her life. At this point the two poles of The Misfit's conundrum, Jesus and meanness, converge, and the ambivalence is captured in the final image of the grandmother as a beatific corpse in a puddle of blood.

The full resonance of The Misfit's shooting depends upon our recollection of the grandmother's position in her family, for "A Good

Man" is among the first of O'Connor's mature stories to revolve around the conflict between generations. The old lady's recognition of this criminal as "one of my own children" is made literally plausible by his donning of the same shirt her son Bailey had been wearing earlier, but in the imaginative economy of the story that shirt signifies the symbolic presence of the now-dead son through the rest of The Misfit's confrontation with the grandmother. Bailey's most salient trait, his edgy sullenness, is clearly the mask of suppressed anger toward his garrulous and manipulative mother, an anger that bursts through only once, in his "shocking" rebuke to her when she identifies The Misfit. That psychopath has of course his own reasons for shooting her, but when he does so he also symbolically acts out the rage that Bailey has smothered, the repayment of all her crafty domineering and self-serving hypocrisy, for the smuggled cat, the dirt road, the car accident, the blurting out of the name that ensures the family's doom. It is the first, but not the last, occasion in O'Connor's fiction when the confrontation between a mother and an angry child results in violent death.[24]

The encounter between the grandmother and The Misfit that occupies the second half of "A Good Man" is thus in one sense an extension and deepening of the more sporadic and superficial battle between the old lady and her family in the first half. Punctuated by the gunshots from the woods, their confrontation is also the most obvious source of the tensions within the story, and O'Connor uses the juxtaposition of this strangely mismatched pair to introduce those thematic misfits of crime and punishment, Jesus and meanness, and further echoes these dualities in a structure which divides the action midway with the car accident. Aesthetically, as we have seen, the story is sustained by the persistence of the coolly detached narrative voice throughout and by the careful control of comic and sinister tonal elements in both parts of the work. Nevertheless, O'Connor's use of melodramatic action is nowhere clearer than in "A Good Man Is Hard to Find," the tensions between violent material and comic treatment nowhere more blatantly exploited. At the climax of the story, we receive rapid successive glimpses of both the grandmother's soul and her dead body, an intimation of Jesus and an expression of meanness, the antithetical terms momentarily

brought together in the image of her smiling corpse. It is a paradoxical joining, but without these poles "A Good Man Is Hard to Find"
would not exist at all.

III

In her later essays and lectures, O'Connor repeatedly used the analogy of biblical prophecy to characterize the nature of fiction. For
herself as a Catholic, she left little doubt what the prophetic gift involved, as she saw it: "It is one of the functions of the Church to
transmit the prophetic vision that is good for all time, and when the
novelist has this as a part of his own vision, he has a powerful extension of sight" (*Mystery and Manners*, pp. 179–80). Later we must
consider more fully what this analogy seems to imply for her fiction
as a whole; at present we may confine ourselves to the observation
that her comments on the prophetic vision of the writer coincide
with her creation of some rather curious prophets as characters. Furthermore, certain aspects of the prophet that seem to have held great
significance for her suggest from a slightly different direction the
larger tensions of her work that this chapter has been exploring.

Early in 1960 she wrote to a correspondent, "I have been reading
what St. Thomas has to say in the *De veritate* on prophecy. He says
prophecy depends on the imaginative and not the moral faculty. It's a
matter of seeing."[25] Indeed, Aquinas says considerably more than
this: he insists that the prophetic gift "can be found indifferently in
good men and in evil men." "Man's goodness," Aquinas maintains,
"consists in charity," and "prophecy does not have any necessary
connection with charity." Since prophecy is a matter of the understanding and charity of the affections, "some [sinners] who lack
charity have minds more fit [than those of good men] to perceive
spiritual things, since they are free from carnal affections and
worldly cares and are gifted with a natural clarity of understanding."[26] Commenting on Aquinas's teachings on the nonrational
nature of the prophetic gift, Victor White underlines the rather startling implications of these views: "More shocking still perhaps to
sweet reasonableness is St. Thomas's emphasis that prophetic revelation is as such independent of good morals—let alone of personal

sanctity. For prophecy is required, he says tersely, not 'goodness of morals' (bonitas morum) but 'goodness of imagination' (bonitas imaginationis). . . . Aristotle, St. Thomas reminds us, had already remarked on the fact that it is not the best people who have the best dreams."[27]

Certainly the O'Connor characters from Hazel Motes onward who have the best dreams are hardly the best people, but Aquinas's distinction between the imaginative and the moral bears most illuminatingly on the prophetic figures who populate the later fiction. The sullen and murderous Tarwater of *The Violent Bear It Away*, the furious Mary Grace of "Revelation," that apparent epitome of blasphemous carnality, O. E. Parker—none of these clearly prophetic characters is presented as morally good, some are indeed viciously destructive, all are grotesque. Perhaps the most revealing of such figures in the short fiction is the leering, malevolent Rufus Johnson of "The Lame Shall Enter First."

In the presentation of Rufus Johnson, O'Connor has typically seized on the independence of the imaginative and the moral, pushed them to jarring extremes, and, with no apologies, left them unreconciled. Rufus enters the story bearing the Word in its least palatable form, in the rigid fundamentalist doctrines he has learned from his fanatical grandfather, and he never abandons them despite the short course in liberal humanism his benefactor Sheppard attempts to supply. Indeed, quite the contrary, for Sheppard's opposition not only confirms Johnson in his beliefs, but inspires him to use them in a malicious plan of revenge on the social worker. By the end of the story there is little doubt that Johnson has flowered into a full-fledged prophetic figure. At the dinner table, Sheppard challenges him one final time on his belief in the Bible:

> "I believe it!" Johnson said breathlessly. "I'll show you I believe it!" He opened the book in his lap and tore out a page of it and thrust it into his mouth. He fixed his eyes on Sheppard. His jaws worked furiously and the paper crackled as he chewed it. . . .
>
> Johnson swallowed what was in his mouth. His eyes widened as if a vision of splendor were opening up before him. "I've eaten it!" he breathed. "I've eaten it like Ezekiel and it was honey to my mouth!" . . .
>
> "I've eaten it!" the boy cried. Wonder transformed his face . . . .

The boy rose and picked up the Bible and started toward the hall with it. At the door he paused, a small black figure on the threshold of some dark apocalypse. "The devil has you in his power," he said in a jubilant voice and disappeared. [pp. 477–78]

The allusion here to Ezekiel (and the only slightly less overt evocation of Saint John, the boy's namesake), the emphasis on the imaginative nature of the experience (the "vision of splendor," the transforming "wonder"), and the final word of prophetic judgment confirm the nature of Johnson's role in the story.

At the same time, the paradoxical "dark apocalypse" captures the duality of the boy, for Johnson is presented throughout "The Lame Shall Enter First" as, in a moral sense, deeply evil. If in this scene he recognizes the grip of "the devil" on Sheppard, he has earlier passed the same judgment on himself. "Satan," Johnson confides at his first appearance in the story, "He has me in his power" (p. 450). It is a conviction from which he never deviates, and O'Connor's portrayal of him seems to bear out the boy's view. Gratuitously malicious, he is a plunderer of garbage cans and homes, his look is described as "predatory," he is likened to a rat and a crow. Most disturbingly, his vengeful desire to "show" Sheppard takes the form of luring the social worker's young son Norton to his death. Here the imaginative and the moral, the prophetic and the demonic, conspire to achieve Johnson's aim, for while there is no doubt of the maleficence in his motives, his means are those of the evangelical proselytizer. He entices Norton to self-destruction by assuring him of a heaven where, the child believes, he will again find his lost mother. Thus the death of Norton is deeply ambivalent, for in that hanging culminates both Johnson's personal, malevolent revenge on Sheppard and the process of conversion that is a prophetic punishment for the social worker's atheistic pride.

Rufus Johnson is one of the more ostentatiously grotesque characters in the O'Connor corpus, the bizarre mixture of hard-shell Protestantism and seemingly gratuitous malice in his behavior matched on the physical level by the "monstrous" clubfoot he sports. Although Sheppard, with his social scientist's assumptions, tries to make a simple equation between the boy's deformity and his delinquency—"His mischief was compensation for the foot"—he has a deeper and less comfortable insight as well: "He felt a momentary dull despair as if he were faced with some elementary warping of nature that had happened too long ago to be corrected now" (p. 450). In the biblical context evoked in the story, the "warping of nature" would seem to cut both ways. The hideous foot, which, as we have seen earlier, Johnson treats "like a sacred object," is the visible sign of the boy's prophetic role, warped to divine purposes, but it is also the palpable expression of his share in the Fall, the recognition of which lies at the bottom of Johnson's Satanism. Contrary to Sheppard's facile analysis, it is not compensation for but in a sense affirmation of the foot that produces the boy's apparently motiveless mischief. His intense awareness of his individual uniqueness, however deformed, is the perverse source of his pride, and the demonic impulse reveals itself as an egoistic cultivation of one's special traits:[28] "I lie and steal because I'm good at it," he sneers at the defeated social worker (p. 480).

Johnson's lying at least (we never observe him at his stealing) is a creative act, the ability to play out different roles—the hurt innocent, the grateful penitent—before the all too credulous audience that Sheppard provides, roles made believable largely through the boy's skillful manipulation of voice and tone. The ability is not, perhaps, very different from the fiction writer's power of creating character. "Why do you write?" O'Connor was once asked. She answered, "Because I'm good at it," and although she elaborated so as to seem to purge that response of all hint of personal pride—the ability to write is a "gift," "gratuitous and wholly undeserved," "a mystery in itself," and so on (Mystery and Manners, p. 81)—we can hardly fail to hear the direct echo of Rufus Johnson's affirmation of his special qualities: "I lie and steal because I'm good at it." O'Connor spoke of her writing in the religious language of vocation, but Johnson has no doubt that his own propensities are the work of the devil.

In speaking of freakish characters, O'Connor once confessed that the writer's "prophet-freak is an image of himself" (Mystery and Manners, p. 118). If it would be naïve to take such characters as literal self-portraits, it would perhaps be equally naïve to refuse to see that they are creative self-projections. In the separation between the imaginative and the moral that she so eagerly seized upon in Aquinas, and so explicitly dramatized in Rufus Johnson, O'Connor found articulated a justification for her own kind of fiction. If prophetic vision, the general substance of which was transmitted to her through the church, was essential to O'Connor, she was nonetheless sharply aware that to try to write out of religious conviction alone was inevitable disaster. The result, she said firmly, could only be "pious trash." When she insisted that "we write with the whole personality," she knew that some of the deepest springs in her own personality did not flow from Aquinas's order of charity. Preferring *Catholic* to *Christian* as a term for her own writing, she noted wryly, "The word Christian is no longer reliable. It has come to mean anyone with a golden heart. And a golden heart would be a positive interference in the writing of fiction" (*Mystery and Manners*, p. 192). In the ordinary sense of the word, she was lacking in compassion and knew it. Sometimes she ironically deprecated the universal insistence on this quality in writers; at others she responded by redefining the term. One such redefinition—compassion as "being in travail with and for creation"—is accompanied by this revealing comment: "This is a sense [of the word] which implies a horror of sin as it is found, first in oneself, and from oneself communicated to the world."[29]

If O'Connor could not follow Mauriac's dictum to "purify the source,"[30] she found in the Thomistic separation of prophetic vision and goodness that for the sake of her writing, at any rate, such personal sanctity was unnecessary. "St. Thomas Aquinas," she noted, "says that art does not require rectitude of the appetite, that it is wholly concerned with the good of that which is made" (*Mystery and Manners*, p. 171).[31] Finding within herself impulses she could hardly view as good, rather than suppressing them for the sake of her piety, she exploited them for the sake of her art. The "territory" of her fiction, she said once, "is held largely by the devil" (*Mystery and Manners*, p. 118), but what her work dramatizes again and again is the folly of looking for the devil anywhere but in the depths of the self. Evil is a potent force in her fiction—a felt presence, not merely an idea—precisely because she could find it within herself, and she turned that self-awareness to fictional advantage. As in Rufus Johnson, the tension between the moral and the imaginative, between

THE AESTHETICS OF INCONGRUITY

sensibility and belief, produces the jarring paradox of the lacerating faith, the destructive salvation that her work everywhere displays.

Earlier, borrowing from Joyce, I suggested the analogy of God for the enormous sense of detachment O'Connor creates in her narrative voice; now it seems more apt to adopt her own metaphor and call that voice "prophetic." To John Hawkes, on the other hand, it sounded like the voice of the devil, and for "The Lame Shall Enter First," at least, she was willing to admit that he was right (*The Habit of Being*, p. 464). Indeed, the figure of Rufus Johnson seems almost calculated to show these designations as not only compatible but sometimes almost indistinguishable: if analysis can begin to separate elements of the prophetic and the Satanic in his portrayal, he speaks with a single voice throughout "The Lame Shall Enter First." Similarly, when Hawkes points to O'Connor's "demolishing" syntax, to the satirical judgments implicit in her narrative voice as coming from her "devil," he might just as appropriately have attributed these qualities to her prophet, that traditionally radical figure speaking out of his knowledge of God's demands in judgment on the life around him, remarkably specific in his indictments of that life seen *sub specie aeternitatis*. Both devil and prophet stand outside ordinary human existence and look on the sins and follies of men in judgment, but whereas the devil presumably takes a mean pleasure in what he sees, the prophet finds only outrage.[32] As it would be hard to say whether a malicious meanness or a deep prophetic revulsion plays the larger part in Johnson's revenge on Sheppard, so it finally becomes impossible to separate the cruel comedy from the outrage in the voice of O'Connor's fiction. Devil and prophet conspire to contribute to the distinctive tension of her work: in her second novel they become not mere figures of speech but recognizable shapes with voices of their own.

CHAPTER FIVE
The Violent Bear It Away

see also
p. 63

The extraordinary tensions that we have observed O'Connor exploiting in her mature stories are fully developed and on clear view
in her second novel. At the same time, and despite her own coupling
of it with her first book,[1] *The Violent Bear It Away* is a measure of
the distance her later work travels from *Wise Blood*. To put the two
novels side by side is to discover dramatically what endures and
what is transformed in her vision after 1952.

What most patently remains is a conception of the novel essentially different from that of most of her contemporaries. Compared
with the heftier works of such writers as Bellow and Mailer, Updike
and Styron, the very leanness of *Wise Blood* and *The Violent Bear It
Away* suggests O'Connor's deliberate limitation of her form. Even
the briefest glance at the surviving work sheets and drafts for the
two books reveals a ruthless paring away of character and incident,
an intensifying of focus, a gradual discovery of structure and meaning through the elimination of distracting or peripheral material.
Whatever distinctions must be drawn between the two novels, they
are both short, intense, poetically conceived, highly condensed
works where the modern scene (or selected aspects of it) is refracted
into symbolic modes of expression rather than being observed, de-
lineated, analyzed in all its diverse and sometimes bewildering
abundance.

However this may seem to differ from contemporary practice,
there is a distinguished American tradition of just this kind of novel.
From Poe's *Narrative of Arthur Gordon Pym* and Hawthorne's *The*

160

Scarlet Letter on through Crane's *Red Badge of Courage*, Fitzgerald's *The Great Gatsby* and Nathanael West's *Miss Lonelyhearts*, these short, intense, symbolic works, different as they are, are among the least dispensable of American classics. The last of these writers, West, reached back to the first of them, Poe, in his defense of what he called the "lyric novel":

> Lyric novels can be written according to Poe's definition of a lyric poem. The short novel is a distinct form especially fitted for use in this country. France, Spain, Italy have a literature as well as the Scandinavian countries. For a hasty people we are too patient with the Bucks, Dreisers and Lewises. Thank God we are not all Scandinavians.
>
> Forget the epic, the masterwork. . . . Leave slow growth to the book reviewers, you only have time to explode. Remember William Carlos Williams' description of the pioneer women who shot their children against the wilderness like cannonballs. Do the same with your novels.[2]

The formative impact of West and Poe on O'Connor's early work, specifically *Wise Blood*, has been argued above, but she was also an admirer of Stephen Crane.[3] And it was Hawthorne whom she repeatedly claimed as her literary ancestor, praising his "lean" fiction as against the "cumbersome" British novel of manners.[4] As a novelist, the lyric work was clearly native to her grain.

But if West's term helps generally to separate O'Connor's two novels from the work of most of her contemporaries, it will not serve to distinguish them from one another. And indeed *The Violent Bear It Away* does resemble *Wise Blood* in one central and crucial respect: in both books the protagonist is a young fundamentalist in revolt against his religious heritage. As a result we must speak of O'Connor's most characteristic and extensively developed heroes as rebellious, obsessed, self-divided figures. Yet beyond this obvious likeness, the two novels are enormously different. Immediately striking is the far tighter narrative patterning of *The Violent Bear It Away*; the diversified, episodic action of *Wise Blood* has given way to a firmly limited plot whose close integration is epitomized by the interlocking of the three central figures in uncle-nephew relationships. Once again, the hero is shadowed by an antihero, but whereas the careers of Hazel Motes and Enoch Emery are for the most part separate and parallel, intersecting only for crucial confrontations, young Tarwater and Rayber move together through the long middle section of *The Violent Bear It Away*, and the schoolteacher looms large in the boy's mind both before and after their extended encounter.

This tighter narrative patterning seems also to limit the range and number of minor characters in the later book. The widely varied gallery of grotesques that created the sense of Taulkinham as an actively populated place is missing from *The Violent Bear It Away*, although almost half of this novel is also set in a large city. If the energy of that earlier book seems centrifugal, showering outward from the hero at its center in a profusion of minor figures and incidents, the drive of the later work appears centripetal, the action and secondary characters revolving firmly within the orbit of the boy who is at its core. Put simply, *The Violent Bear It Away* replaces the diversity of character and action of *Wise Blood* with an intense concentration.

O'Connor's second novel is thus a less wild, less totally dislocating and estranging work than its predecessor. The flat, external, and dehumanizing treatment of the characters, the starkly dramatized presentness of scene which marked the earlier book are gone; flashback, the stylized rendering of internal perception, and the use of shifting centers of consciousness place us in a more familiar fictional mode. The frighteningly detached simplicity of style has given way to a denser, more flexible medium with a greater range of tonal shifts. Perhaps most telling, the outlandish comic similes that are essential to the fabric of *Wise Blood* rarely appear here, and when they do occur they are firmly attached to a perceiving character, not to the narrative voice. Rayber's eyes looking "like something human trapped in a switch box" (*The Violent Bear It Away*, p. 154) is one of the few bizarre tropes that might have been lifted straight from the earlier novel, but the analogy is drawn by the proprietress of the Cherokee Lodge, not by the narrator. The difference in effect is crucial: it is the difference beween the estrangement of the character and the estrangement of the entire world of the novel. If *Wise Blood* in overall effect moves toward nightmare, *The Violent Bear It Away* moves toward myth, but myth clothed in the outer garments of plausibility and framed in more familiar conventions of narrative fiction.

In short, *The Violent Bear It Away* is a more traditional novel than *Wise Blood*. It confounds literary expectations less radically, less continuously, less absolutely, although it is startling enough. But if the later book must finally be judged a better novel than the earlier one—as it almost universally has been—it is surely not because it is a more successful fulfillment of aims that had somehow been botched in the previous work. The usual (and understandable) critical gambit of discussing the two books together and comparatively tends to obscure their important differences. *The Violent Bear It Away*, it is true, more completely realizes its aspirations than does *Wise Blood*, and it is informed by a richer, deeper, denser vision. But it is also a less piercingly original work, less exuberant, less totally comic and wildly inventive, more controlled but also more hermetic. Viewed as two different *kinds* of lyric novel, it is not obvious that all the advantages lie with the later book.

Analogies with other writings may help suggest the very different effects of these two novels. If *Wise Blood* takes the astringent comic perception, the episodic action, and the nonmimetic techniques of *Miss Lonelyhearts* and pushes them beyond West's boundaries, *The Violent Bear It Away*, with its dense concentration, exquisite sense of form and structure, and movement between the examination of inner struggle and dramatic scenes of confrontation, is reminiscent of the methods of Hawthorne's *The Scarlet Letter*. In fact, O'Connor may well have borrowed her central configuration of three complexly intertwined adults (if young Tarwater may for the moment be so considered) circling around a mysteriously supernatural child from her predecessor's masterpiece. In any case, that such diverse analogues spring to mind may suggest that in the eight years that separate *Wise Blood* from *The Violent Bear It Away* O'Connor has moved to a rather different conception of the form of the novel. There was good reason for her to do so, for she had something different to express.

The extent to which the later work subtly but decisively reverses the prevailing vision of the earlier can be seen by juxtaposing two strikingly parallel episodes. In both books the antihero (Enoch, Rayber) proposes to take the hero (Hazel Motes, Tarwater) to a museum, and in each case the visit requires a trip through a city park. We have seen how in the episode in *Wise Blood* O'Connor uses parody of religious ritual, animal imagery, and Enoch's instinctual "blood consciousness" to lead to an emblem of eternal death. At the heart of the park, which is the heart of the city, lies Enoch's secular mystery, the shriveled mummy which epitomizes the realm of nature in this novel. The round, mausoleumlike structure is the center of all circles here, and for all Enoch's reverence, it is a temple of death.

Although the museum is never reached in *The Violent Bear It Away*, it carries similar overtones there in its exhibition of "all the great wastes of unexplored time" (p. 140). But in the later novel the trip ends in the park, and the experience there is given us twice, first through Rayber's eyes and then through Tarwater's. They respond in quite distinct ways, but whereas in *Wise Blood* the park was the very essence of the city, a distillation of its meaning and values, in *The Violent Bear It Away* it stands in sharp opposition to its urban surroundings, an evocation for uncle and nephew of the countryside clearing of Powderhead that is so important to both of them. And for each the park becomes the scene of revelation—although of very different kinds. Rayber's "illumination" is characteristically intellectual: he suddenly "understands" that Tarwater has a "compulsion" to baptize Bishop, a "fixation" on the child. But Rayber's mind has become activated in response to a fit of "hated love" which has seized him in the park, the overwhelming desire to perceive "a world transfigured" that he can fight only with his intellect (pp. 141, 146, 114). Tarwater's frightened awareness is of precisely such a world. Immediately on entering the park he senses a preternatural "hush," feels "the approach of mystery," recognizes "the felt presence" when the sun emerges from a cloud to illumine Bishop's blondness: "His face might have been a mirror where the sun had stopped to watch its reflection" (pp. 163–64). The distance between uncle and nephew, between a determined mechanistic view and an unwilling animistic vision, is captured by the language in which the two perceive Bishop's dash toward the park fountain. To Rayber the child's arms are "flailing like a windmill"; for Tarwater they "flap" "like something released from a cage" (pp. 145, 164).

That fountain is the center of the park. Round ("a concrete circle") like the museum of *Wise Blood*, it nevertheless contains within it not the image of death but lifegiving water. Whereas Enoch's unconscious mockery of the Mass had denied that nature was capable of any genuine revelation, that sacramental vision in the world of *Wise Blood* was possible, both Rayber and Tarwater affirm its potency in *The Violent Bear It Away*. Tarwater feels the oppressive presence of the encroaching world of silence throughout the park scene, and he is all too afraid that the mirrored sun in Bishop's face is precisely the divine sign he has dreaded. Rayber's testimony to the sacramental possibilities of nature is the more powerful for his urgent struggle to suppress his awareness, the battle of his will and intellect to overcome vision and to "refuse to feel"; but his success here is also his defeat, prefiguring his inability to feel anything at all when Bishop dies. The two park scenes are thus paradigmatic: they epitomize the worlds of their novels. At "the heart of the park" are the shriveled mummy or the illumined fountain, the ceremony of ironic communion or the possibility of genuine baptism, the reductive landscape which leads only down to a final death or the resonant scene that vibrates with the presence of mystery. The "sacramental vision" of which O'Connor so often spoke is genuinely operative in *The Violent Bear It Away* in a way it is not in *Wise Blood*.

The deep antipathy toward matter that pervaded that first novel is gone in *The Violent Bear It Away*, or, more accurately, it is here (as in the stories) embodied in individual characters and viewed from an ironic distance. Rayber, for example, like all O'Connor intellectuals, is repelled by physical ugliness. When Bishop cries, "his face red and hideously distorted," the schoolteacher "turned his eyes away" (p. 147), and his distaste expresses his instability in dealing with the concrete world. It is the sight of Bishop's messy eating that elicits Tarwater's more violent revulsion. "He's like a hog," the boy sneers, invoking O'Connor's disgusting animal par excellence. "He eats like a hog and he don't think more than a hog and when he dies, he'll rot like a hog. . . . The only difference between me and you and a hog is me and you can calculate, but there ain't any difference between him and one" (pp. 116–17). But visceral aversion hardly exhausts their response to Bishop, for although both uncle and nephew would like to view the idiot child simply as a repellent "thing," the very strength of their antipathy is an index of the mysterious attraction the little boy holds for them.

As might be anticipated from our comparison of the park episodes, the treatment of landscape has undergone an even more startling metamorphosis since *Wise Blood*. With predictable consistency, of course, the urban scene is again presented as ugly and sinister. When Tarwater first approaches the city he sees "a hill covered with old used-car bodies. In the indistinct darkness, they seemed to be drowning into the ground, to be about half-submerged already. The city hung in front of them on the side of the mountain as if it were part of the same pile, not yet buried so deep" (p. 54). But even here the view of the city as deathly junk heap is transformed by the water metaphor into a mythic image of the return to primal chaos, and it thereby acquires a reverberation denied the flat and empty landscapes of *Wise Blood*. What's more, O'Connor pays very little attention to the city scene in *The Violent Bear It Away*; most of the landscapes rendered are natural rather than man-made and, like the park, they resonate with the sacramental view of nature. A group of trees in *Wise Blood* are noted as "painted white from the ground up four feet" so that they look "as if they had on ankle-socks" (p. 96). In *The Violent Bear It Away*, however, trees become "majestic and aloof, as if they belonged to an order that had never budged from its first allegiance in the days of creation" (p. 185). The divergent "as if" clauses are one measure of the distance between the two novels.

Whereas Hazel Motes had searched the world around him for a sign of his salvation but had avoided looking toward the sky, Tarwater reverses the process. If he is to receive the prophetic summons, "he wished it to be a voice from out of a clear and empty sky, the trumpet of the Lord God Almighty, untouched by any fleshly hand or breath" (*The Violent Bear It Away*, p. 22). On the other hand, he (like Rayber in his different way) desperately avoids the "threatened intimacy of creation." In *Wise Blood* the everyday countryside world contained neither promise nor menace: Haze had early decided that the way to avoid Jesus was to remain at home "with his two eyes open, and his hands always handling the familiar thing, his feet on the known track, and his tongue not too loose" (p. 22). But in *The Violent Bear It Away* it is precisely the "familiar thing" that

Tarwater most fears: "if he let his eye rest for an instant longer than was needed to place something—a spade, a hoe, the mule's hind quarters before his plow, the red furrow under him—[he was afraid] that the thing would suddenly stand before him, strange and terrifying, demanding that he name it and name it justly and be judged for the name he gave it" (p. 22). *(William Carlos Williams!)*

The deep differences in the protagonists' response to the physical world is of course also manifested in their attitudes toward their own bodies. Both of O'Connor's heroes are by nature profoundly ascetic, but Haze's revolt takes the form of an affirmation of the material world and especially of the body: it is his "blood," he claims, that has "set [him] free." Yet Tarwater fears—justifiably, it turns out—nothing more than his blood; his great-uncle's madness, he suspects, "might be passed down, might be hidden in the blood and might strike some day in him" (*The Violent Bear It Away*, p. 21). *(yes)* Haze ends, appropriately, with a fierce denial of the body that is also a final rejection of the unredeemable matter of *Wise Blood*. Tarwater, on the other hand, only learns by violence that he *has* a body, that his fate is to endure the physical world. The boy was "intolerant of unspiritual evils and with those of the flesh he had never truckled" (*The Violent Bear It Away*, p. 226), but he is literally brought to earth by rape, the most intimate violation of his proud, unworldly idea of himself. As a result, Tarwater can no longer deny his full participation in the created world, a world of flesh and blood as well as spirit, and *The Violent Bear It Away* ends with his commitment to it.

The reversal in vision between *Wise Blood* and *The Violent Bear It Away* between the O'Connor who viewed this world as a nightmarish excrescence of reductive and repellent matter and the O'Connor who saw it through her Christian sacramentalism, seems analogous to the "correction" Mason Tarwater recalls undergoing in the opening pages of *The Violent Bear It Away*:

> He had been called in his early youth and had set out for the city to proclaim the destruction awaiting a world that had abandoned its Saviour. [But time passes, and the announced apocalypse fails to arrive.] . . . Then one morning he saw to his joy a finger of fire coming out of [the sun] and before he could turn, before he could shout, the finger had touched *(beauty)*

ι and the destruction he had been waiting for had fallen in his own
n and his own body. His own blood had been burned dry and not the
ᴗʟᴏᴏd of the world.

[Since then he had] learned much by his own mistakes [until now] . . .
it was saving and not destruction he was seeking. He had learned enough
to hate the destruction that had to come and not all that was going to be
destroyed. [Pp. 5–6]

Flannery O'Connor, of course, proclaims nothing in this fashion,
but the passage does suggest her turn from a *contemptus mundi* to
an embrace, "for all its horror" (*Mystery and Manners*, p. 146), of the
exigencies of worldly existence.

The transformation in O'Connor's vision so dramatically revealed
by juxtaposing the two novels actually occurred more gradually, as
we saw in looking at the stories she published after *Wise Blood*. By
the time of *The Violent Bear It Away*, this shift in the use of image
and metaphor and all that it implies was as complete as it would become. Not surprisingly, there is a comparable change in her use of
the double motif which is common to both novels as well as to
many of the stories. If in *Wise Blood* a number of figures reflect back
at Hazel Motes's brief embodiments of his putative secular commitment—Asa Hawks, Hoover Shoats, Solace Layfield, even Sabbath
Lily and Mrs. Flood—only Enoch Emery is granted a development at
all comparable to Haze's in the novel. The use of the double theme
in *The Violent Bear It Away* more closely resembles that of the stories, where O'Connor's practice is intensive rather than extensive:
a close focus on mirrorlike figures who illuminate one another
through prolonged concentration on their likenesses and distinctions. All four major characters of *The Violent Bear It Away* are complexly related in this way, a multiplied doubling which is rendered
plausible by the close family ties among them.

The first double figure to appear (and the last to disappear) is not,
strictly speaking, a character at all, merely the harsh voice of a
stranger who emerges at the death of old Tarwater and gradually assumes the shadowy shape of young Tarwater's "friend." He is of course
the manifestation of the boy's dark rebellious self that springs forth
the moment the old man's influence is removed, but he is also trans-

168

parently the devil, and as such, one of the triumphs of the novel, a worthy modern heir to the comic tempters of folklore and medieval drama. As the ultimate confidence man, his bag of tricks is as full as ever. In traditional fashion, he can cite scripture for his purpose: "That old man was the stone before your door and the Lord has rolled it away. . . . Praise Him" (p. 47). Indeed, as *simia dei*, he is an adept at straight-faced parody. "You have to take hold and put temptation behind you," he exhorts Tarwater. "If it's an idiot this time, the next time it's liable to be a nigger. Save yourself while the hour of salvation is at hand" (p. 166). One of his earliest ploys is also one of his oldest: he insists on his own nonexistence. When Tarwater thinks his choice must be "Jesus or the devil," "No no no, the stranger said, there ain't no such thing as a devil. I can tell you that from my own self-experience. I know that for a fact. It ain't Jesus or the devil. It's Jesus or *you*" (p. 39). This brightly plausible bit of comedy identifies, if further identification be necessary, the demonic with the self-determining ego. As the ironic spokesman for skepticism, rationalism, and empiricism, his new friend thus counsels the boy in an easygoing worldliness: "I wouldn't pay too much attention to my Redemption if I was you. Some people take everything too hard" (p. 45).

Although this comic tempter is in one sense only an interior voice, in another sense he is legion, for (in a small reprise of the doubling technique of *Wise Blood*) his splintered incarnations appear briefly in such minor figures as the salesman Meeks, the tramp the boy encounters in the park, and the homosexual rapist, all of whom mouth versions of his creed of worldly independence. But this demonic adviser also bears more than a passing resemblance to the dominant side of Tarwater's uncle Rayber, whose rationalistic evangelism masks an internal division as deep as the boy's. Rayber reflects back at his nephew another version of the youngster's own ambivalence: his first sight of Tarwater shows him a face that "might have been a mirror thrust before him in a nightmare" (p. 99). Both attribute their inner split to the influence of old Mason Tarwater who has, they feel, injected a deep irrationalism into them, an idiocy that for both finds its focus and embodiment in little Bishop. *That* child thus appears as a purified reflection of old Tarwater; he is described as looking "like the old man grown backwards to the lowest form of innocence" (p. 111), a resemblance so unmistakable that the old prophet himself is shocked by it.

The symbolic relationships among the characters are intricate, but they are saved from confusion or mere ingenuity by stylization, by a language which constantly forces us beyond individual tone or expression to questions of final commitment. On this level, as inhabitants of O'Connor's sharply dualistic world, characters inevitably drift toward a polar position. One of these extremes is represented by Bishop, the paradox of whose being is captured by the image of the trashbasket containing a rock which he carries. If his idiocy is a manifestation of the reality of the Fall—he first appears in the novel "gnawing on a brown apple core" (p. 32)—it is at the same time the preserver of his incorruptibility. In a Christian context he is a terrible and moving gloss on the imperative to become again as a little child, for he is the refuse of this world and the foundation of the next, at once worthless and sacred. But if Bishop represents total annihilation of self, Tarwater's friend is the perfect realization of the other pole of total self-affirmation, of man's sufficiency to determine his own unlimited destiny, freely to create a world for himself on his own terms. Like inverse city-mouse, country-mouse reflections, Rayber and Tarwater act out their self-divisions, are torn by each of the extremes, until both find that they have made their commitments.

At its furthest reaches the elaborately conceived double motif extends into all aspects of *The Violent Bear It Away* to become one of its major unifying devices. As the characters mirror and parody one another, this doubling becomes incarnated in language and action to set up recurrent echoes which force the mind backward and forward over the entire range of the book. In short, a sense of *déjà vu* is one of the basic structural principles of the novel. Working against the thrust of the narrative, this echolalia invites the juxtaposition of two speeches, images, or actions which by their distinct likeness comment on one another to reveal hidden affinities or create ironic resonance. In a minor instance, both Meeks and Rayber suspect Tarwater of lying to them, and they interrogate the boy in almost identical language about what he expects to "find out" in the city. The parallel passages suggest the underlying kinship of the crudely cynical salesman and the sensitive intellectual humanist, for both men are, at bottom, skeptics and empiricists. In another vein, when old Tarwater's exhortation to the boy to stay in the clearing "with just as much light as the sun wants to let in" (p. 24) is followed a few pages later by the stranger's mocking observation that Tarwater has been left alone in an empty spot "with just as much light as that dwarf sun wants to let in" (p. 36), the addition of the single modifier measures at once both the closeness and the distance between acceptance and revolt, between the Christian response and its demonic parody.

The echoing is not, of course, confined to verbal repetition. The image of Rayber sitting in a boat, his hat pulled down "like a fanatical country preacher" (p. 174), immediately evokes the old prophet and recalls Tarwater's observation that the schoolteacher's voice revealed "a passion equal and opposite to the old man's" (p. 34). "I saved you to be free, your own self! . . . and not a piece of information inside his [Rayber's] head!" (p. 16), the old man thunders at the boy. Rayber counters coolly with, "I think you're chained to him [old Tarwater] right now. I think you're not going to be free of him without my help" (p. 169).

Even more extensive are the parallels O'Connor creates between the boy and his schoolteacher uncle. The close similarities in their baptism and instruction by old Tarwater and their rebellions against him at the identical age of fourteen underlie Rayber's conviction that the boy is merely another edition of himself. But the reflections that develop become mocking images rather than the perfect likenesses the uncle had hoped for. Tarwater's success in drowning Bishop echoes Rayber's failure in his similar attempt, as the boy's return to Powderhead recalls the schoolteacher's abortive attempt to revisit the clearing, but the close parallels serve only to magnify the ironic differences. And as we have seen, O'Connor even provides two versions of the episode in the park, one Rayber's and one Tarwater's; but the identity of action focuses the immense dissimilarity in what is seen and the language in which it is couched, as if to symbolize in a single event both the closeness of these two "nephews" and the enormous distance between them.

These are only some of the offspring in *The Violent Bear It Away* of O'Connor's use of the double motif. It might indeed be argued that the entire novel is structured by it. Tarwater's two departures from the burning clearing, his double baptism on head and buttocks as both source and prototype for the ambivalent baptism-drowning of Bishop, that action as a violent restatement of old Tarwater's kidnapping of his nephews, the repeated car rides with sinister strangers—these immediately come to mind as further possibilities for such a reading. To see the novel thus is to view it spatially, flattened on a plane, or on a series of intersecting planes, in which the temporal element of narrative becomes of secondary importance. This is one dimension of the experience of reading *The Violent Bear It Away*, and along with the recurrent imagery of fire, water, and hunger and the varieties of foreshadowing, which in this novel acquire the force of prophecy and fulfillment, it provides the book with a dense and complex inner unity.[5] But the action that Tarwater undergoes is also, in the strict sense, an ordeal; *The Violent Bear It Away* chronicles a heroic journey that gains its resonance from O'Connor's use of jarring myths whose clash provides the novel with one of its principal underlying sources of tension.

II

The Bible, particularly the Old Testament, is of course O'Connor's primary source of mythic reference in *The Violent Bear It Away*. Early on we are told that Tarwater's great-uncle has educated him in the prophetic view of history, "beginning with Adam expelled from the Garden and going on down through the presidents to Herbert Hoover and on in speculation toward the Second Coming and the Day of Judgment" (p. 4). Since the boy himself is being raised an apprentice prophet, both of the Tarwaters find Moses and Daniel at least as real as, say, Herman Talmadge, and their natural allusions to Joshua and Jonah, Elisha and Elijah, Abel and Habakkuk keep this level of analogy constantly before us. But O'Connor also draws on the Bible and Christianity less overtly throughout the novel: for instance, a controlling form in *The Violent Bear It Away* is the number three, the mystical number of the Trinity. The three major characters, bound in their interlocking uncle-nephew relationships, are reflected on the level of action in the three major phases of Tarwater's struggle, which is given its formal statement in O'Connor's division of the book into three sections. Each of these sections is dominated by one of the major figures: old Tarwater, Rayber, and young Tarwater respectively. The central movement of the novel is thus from the old man to the young man to the boy (circling, at the end, to the symbolic reconciliation of the boy and the old man). Clearly the Christian analogue is not far away, and since O'Connor in *The Violent Bear It Away*, unlike *Wise Blood*, is concerned to probe directly the inwardness of her central characters, Jung's "Psychological Approach to the Trinity" becomes useful in exploring the significance of Tarwater's experience.[6]

Yet if the biblical and Christian context dominates *The Violent Bear It Away*, the novel is, after all, focused precisely on the boy's rejection of that context, a rejection that becomes increasingly intense and even desperate as the action unfolds. Tarwater's only notion is to disburden himself of his unwanted mission, but O'Connor shapes his revolt into an archetypal form. Juxtaposed with the explicit Christian materials of the novel are the echoes of another set of myths, those of the legendary culture hero who in various guises undertakes the perilous journey or the road of trials to wrest for his world an otherwise unattainable boon. *The Violent Bear It Away* thus presents us with an initiatory experience, a *rite de passage* where, ironically, the boy's rebellion against his mission establishes his fitness to undertake it, where the refusal to seek the boon is precisely what secures it. O'Connor's use of the secular heroic myths paradoxically both extends the Christian context and furiously clashes against it.

The action of *The Violent Bear It Away* begins with the death of old Mason Tarwater, but the extensive flashbacks in part 1 create him as very much alive for the novel and particularly for his great-nephew. Indeed, he dominates the opening section of the book. The old prophet has been not merely the primary but virtually the only figure in the boy's short life, his guardian and teacher, the sole source of his knowledge. Although not Tarwater's actual father, he is the only figure of parental authority the boy knows, and as he repeatedly reminds his irritated listener, he stands as surrogate for the child's true Father. The period of the boy's life conveyed by flashback thus corresponds closely to the first stage of Jung's psychologized "Trinity," the stage of the "Father" when the child is "still dependent on a ready-made pattern of existence which is habitual and has the character of law."[7] Given the old man's domineering ways and the boy's rebellious nature, at old Tarwater's death the revolt breaks forth immediately. Significantly, Tarwater's first thought is of his freedom to relocate a barrier his great-uncle had defined: "He had always followed his uncle's customs up to this date but: if I want to move that fence before I bury him, it wouldn't be a soul to hinder me" (p. 13).

From the first Tarwater has been deeply ambivalent about the supposed prophetic vocation the old man has insisted will descend to him. When he thinks "of Moses who struck water from a rock, of Joshua who made the sun stand still, of Daniel who stared down lions in the pit" (p. 10), he is more than eager for the call, for they are his childhood heroes, apparently self-sufficient, godlike creatures who seem to contain some magical power within themselves. But when the old man has reminded him of "the sweat and stink of the cross," of the unglamorous fact that Jesus is the source, center and end of all prophecy, "the bread of life," Tarwater has felt only refusal: "In the darkest, most private part of his soul, hanging upside down like a sleeping bat, was the certain, undeniable knowledge that he was not hungry for the bread of life" (p. 21).

These underground rumblings burst into a quake of rebellion at the moment of old Tarwater's death as the boy's latent ambivalence erupts into an open split between Tarwater and the stranger, that voice which gradually assumes the form and shape of his friend. Since the old man's first injunction to the boy has been to provide him with Christian burial, the long temptation episode which ensues—the temptation to disobey the commandment of the "Father" figure—takes the form of a reenactment of the Fall. As Tarwater begins to dig the grave, the "wise" tempter watches "from the shade of the speckled tree shadows" (p. 38) and shrewdly argues the self-interest of disobedience. Throughout *The Violent Bear It Away* the clearing of Powderhead bears the overtones of a modern Eden, a backwoods haven in a world blasted by the original Fall and restored through the Incarnation. It may not be the Earthly Paradise itself—

174

that, after all, is gone forever—but the old man's commitment has made it consecrated land, "ground that the Lord . . . held" (p. 237). And if Tarwater may seem at first an unlikely Adam, we recall that he avoids the intimacy of the created world because he fears that, like the first man, he will be required to name justly every thing in it.

The mythic significance of this opening episode is focused in Tarwater's longest recollection, his first trip to the city. Set in the midst of the temptation scene, the flashback both illuminates that action and prefigures its outcome. Accompanying his great-uncle to a lawyer's office, the boy suddenly feels in the impersonal crowds the evil of the city and is outraged that the old man does not pause to prophesy against it. As he gazes out the skyscraper window of the lawyer's office, he is certain that he will be guilty of no such lapses: "When he was called, on that day when he returned, he would set the city astir, he would return with fire in his eyes. . . . When I come for good, he said to himself, I'll do something to make every eye stick on me, and leaning forward, he saw his new hat drop down gently, lost and casual, dallied slightly by the breeze on its way to be smashed in the tin river below. He clutched at his bare head and fell back inside the room" (p. 28). Like so many other O'Connor protagonists, Tarwater finds evil everywhere but in himself and so is tempted into a complacency that lures him to his own fall. The boy's hat (like Hazel Motes's) is the emblem of his deepest spiritual integrity, and its loss to "the pit of the street" both marks the result of his pride here and foreshadows the more devastating theft of its successor much later in the novel. With the onset of self-consciousness, his country-bred innocence is gone for good: the fall in the lawyer's office opens the way to the greater fall by the unfinished grave which is its symbolic equivalent.

In the Old Testament the failure in the Garden delivered mankind over to the rule of Law, and in the comic interplay that follows the loss of the hat O'Connor deftly recovers the biblical metaphor as the defining term for the fallen world. As his great-uncle and the lawyer argue the chances of altering the old man's will, Tarwater repeatedly intrudes to report, "My hat fell." The hat is gone for good; the law proves inflexible. "You might as well resign yourself to this will," the lawyer tells old Tarwater in unconscious parody of the Christian injunction. To the old man, who acknowledges only another will, the laws of this world are merely a form of bondage, symbolized by the "clay-colored books of law that fortressed [the lawyer's] office" (p. 29). After trudging to other lawyers, his irked nephew tells him, "It's only one law and it's nothing you can do about it" (p. 30). But it was the law that placed the old man in the asylum, that tried to force the boy into school, that now, through the will, would pass on Powderhead to the despised Rayber. In the "senselessness" of his vocation, old Tarwater has repeatedly found himself at odds with the laws of this world. In such a context, freedom finds its expression in criminal action: "He proceeded about the Lord's business like an experienced crook" (p. 62).

As the old man repeatedly tells his resentful charge, "You were born into bondage and baptized into freedom, into the death of the Lord, into the death of the Lord Jesus Christ" (p. 20), but civil law is only one of the forms in which bondage lingers on. Another, closer to home, is the relentlessly rationalistic mind of the schoolteacher, whose very face, according to old Tarwater, looks like "the outside of a penitentiary," and whose greatest desire, he claims, is to trap the likes of the boy "inside his head" (pp. 70, 16). But the old man himself has so seemed to restrict the boy's liberty that it is not hard for his new "friend" to persuade him by the end of the temptation scene that the real threat to his freedom is not Rayber, but precisely the old prophet. As Tarwater tastes the forbidden fruit of the still-liquor his great-uncle had brewed—and which he had always denied the boy—his tempter solemnly mocks him with the image of resurrection: "That old man was the stone before your door and the Lord has rolled it away. He ain't rolled it quite far enough, of course. You got to finish up yourself" (p. 47). That finishing up is the burning of the house that the boy believes still contains the corpse, an act which is the explicit refusal of old Tarwater's commandment to bury him and an implicit repudiation of the entire order the old man represents. But the fire that Tarwater intends as a purification of his great-uncle's influence appears nonetheless to confirm the old prophet's insistence that they are like Elijah and Elisha. As the boy flees Powderhead the flames seem to be "moving up through the black night like a whirling chariot" (p. 50). It is only the first of Tarwater's many double-edged actions.

The deep ambivalence in the boy, the conflict between the divine and the demonic, is, of course, what permits O'Connor to exploit the tensions within the two mythic strains of the Christian and the heroic.[8] The schism that has opened with his great-uncle's death, the gulf between the old man's Christian imperatives and Tarwater's sense of his inviolable selfhood (now embodied in and fostered by his friend), has threatened in every step of the child's existence. The boy is sure, for instance, that the uniqueness of his beginnings is the sign of a heroic future. " 'I'm out of the womb of a whore. I was born in a wreck.' He flung this forth as if he were declaring a royal birth" (p. 106). The aura here of the uncanny that traditionally surrounds the legendary heroic birth is unmistakable, but this royal mother is a far cry from the usual virgin: Tarwater, at least, never doubts that she was a whore. The inversion suggests a parody of heroic myth, yet even old Tarwater (while putting the emphasis elsewhere) sees the supernatural in this start, affirming that "the Lord had rescued him out of the womb of a whore." Nevertheless, "his uncle had never seemed to be aware of the importance of the way he had been born, only of how he had been born again" (p. 41). But Tarwater's rebirth is as duplicitous as his birth. While the old man had given him a traditional Christian baptism, Rayber had immediately followed with a blasphemous parody on his buttocks, a demonic consecration which, like a promissory note, will be collected many pages later by the homosexual rapist.

This strain of ambivalence, with its echoes from heroic myth, runs throughout Tarwater's childhood. In traditional fashion he has been spirited away to be raised by a foster parent in a spot distant from the scene of his ultimate mission. The tension between Christian and heroic myths here suggests that Powderhead is paradoxically both a modern Eden and a place of exile, and that the boy's flight from the clearing is thus both his expulsion into the fallen world and the beginning of the heroic return. His uncle has prepared him for a divine call, but what thrusts him out onto his road of trials is rather the heroic "call to adventure,"[9] signaled by the appearance of his guiding friend—a dark mockery of the call he is supposedly awaiting. The traditional heroic signs appear—the suggestion of new birth ("He began to feel that he was only just now meeting himself" [p. 35]), the ambiguous figure to announce the initiation of the

journey—but with a distinctly modern meaning, for here they signify the start of a quest to realize the uniqueness of the individual
self. In terms of the Christian myth, however, Tarwater's journey
parodies the true mission and is thus unmistakably demonic. Paradoxically, it is precisely this demonic parody that turns the boy into
a genuine hero, for only in the intensity of his struggle to reject the
divine burden does he achieve his stature.

In O'Connor's ambiguous mingling of myths, the Christian
tempter becomes one with the supernatural helper of heroic legend,
and since he is the devil, who can "take on any look that suited
him" (p. 55), he appears to Tarwater again and again as a friendly
guide and teacher—as Meeks, as a bum in the park, as the homosexual, as the rationalistic side of Rayber. The flight from Powderhead,
the beginning of the descent into the fallen world, is led by the first
of these, who, although he fails to impress the boy with his un-
solicited advice, proves nevertheless a fitting initiator. The night
journey into the unknown first throws up the image of a hellish fiery glow. "'That's the same fire we came from!' the boy said in a
high voice" (p. 51), a perception suggesting both that the name
of this city is Dis and that (as for Hazel Motes) mere movement
through space will provide no escape for Tarwater. The salesman's
literal reassurance that what he sees is only "the glow of the city
lights" stifles the boy's momentary vision, but his second view is at
least as sinister as the first. In a passage already quoted in full, Tarwater perceives the city as an extension of a pile of old car bodies,
"drowning into the ground . . . half-submerged already" (p. 54). The
language here suggests some primeval realm, a city of dreadful night
returning to aboriginal watery darkness, to a fearful disorder which
is the legendary habitat of monsters, dragons, and strange beasts. If
the city as Dis is drawn from Christian tradition, this evocation of
primordial chaos seems to owe more to other, chthonic myths. In
any event, the vision defines the boy's journey as a traditional descent, one marked by encounters with images of devouring beasts, a
series of trials to be met and faced, each of which carries with it an
unwanted revelation as if in reward—or perhaps in punishment—for
the struggle undertaken.

The first of these appears immediately on entering the city as
Meeks pulls up at the "gaping concrete mouth" of a filling station.

The country boy's wary entrance into this mouth presents him with a sinister device, a telephone from which emerge voices that seem to come "from beyond the grave." Out of that "black coiled machine" comes "a revelation he could not yet decipher," the sound of Bishop's breathing, "a kind of bubbling noise, the kind of noise someone would make who was struggling to breathe in water" (pp. 80–83). Shaken, he escapes one beast only to encounter another as his initial guide delivers him to his successor, the boy's school-teacher-uncle. Rayber's house is "a black shape crouched in a greater darkness," and as Tarwater approaches it he too becomes "absorbed into the darkness." Once again the revelation comes, this one clear, decisive, unambiguous: the recognition of that call he has so long anticipated. There is nothing spectacular or magical about it. When he first sees Bishop, he simply *knows*: "He did not look into the eyes of any fiery beast or see a burning bush. He only knew, with a certainty sunk in despair, that he was expected to baptize the child he saw and begin the life his great-uncle had prepared him for. He knew that he was called to be a prophet and that the ways of his prophecy would not be remarkable" (p. 91).

The Christian mission is now unmistakable, but so is the boy's refusal, his *non serviam*. The denial of the prophetic role that was implicit in the failure to bury the old man becomes fully conscious and deliberate in the stark "No!" the boy hurls "like a challenge . . . in the face of his silent adversary." With the full articulation of this defiance, old Tarwater disappears as the dominant presence in the novel. The time of the "Father" is over, that of the "Son" about to begin.

Part 2 of *The Violent Bear It Away* is Rayber's section, the direct counterweight to part 1, for the schoolteacher's commitments are the radical antitheses of old Tarwater's: he is as passionate an apostle of humanistic salvation as the old man was of the Christian variety.[10] The old prophet had proposed that the boy take his cue from his own career; Rayber goes even further and insists on *his* life as the precise model for his nephew. Late in the action of part 1, Tarwater had made the initial movement toward the second or "Son" stage of Jung's psychic "Trinity": "the change usually sets in when the son starts to put himself in his father's place. According to the archaic pattern, this takes the form of quasi-father murder—in other words, violent identification with the father followed by his liquidation."[11] But the ritualistic destruction of the old man in the burning cabin had only been a beginning. It is Rayber who fully embodies successful rebellion against old Tarwater and who thus has formed himself into an almost perfect image of Jung's "Son." In the full realization of this stage, Jung says, "quasi-father murder" is followed by "conscious differentiation from the father and from the habits represented by him. . . . Habit can only be replaced by a mode of life consciously chosen and acquired. . . . Only then the state of unreflecting awareness known as 'Father' changes into the reflective and rational state of consciousness known as 'Son.'" Rayber prides himself on having achieved this independence. Jung, however, continues in terms which, while still accurately describing the schoolteacher, do so in a tone less congratulatory than his own: "The 'Son' represents a transition stage, an intermediate state, part child, part adult. . . . This state is not only in opposition to the still-existing earlier state, but, by virtue of its conscious and rational nature, it also contains many latent possibilities of dissociation. . . . The stage of the 'Son' is therefore a conflict situation *par excellence*."[12]

Less comically conceived, Rayber's plight is a variation on the radical dissociation of sensibility O'Connor had dramatized in Enoch Emery. It is of the essence of his situation that he is highly aware of it, seeing himself "divided in two—a violent and a rational self" (p. 139). Committed to a rationalistic view of man and what he chooses to call "the real world" (pp. 70, 73), he is nevertheless conscious that deep within him rages the pain of an almost ungovernable love, an irrational impulse to worship a sacramental creation manifested even in his idiot child, but extending beyond him to "everything his reason hated" (p. 114). As we have seen, there is for O'Connor no healing of this violent split, no merging of the two sides of the self into a fulfilling whole. Through willed self-denial the schoolteacher has disciplined himself to a position of balance, a tightrope "between madness and emptiness" (p. 115), a life which he knows is limited but is, he feels, at least normal, possessing dignity. Recognizing an analogous division in Tarwater, he thinks he also sees in him "his own image" (p. 105), and that because of "kinship and similarity and experience" (p. 115) he is the one to guide the boy through his trials and, more than guide him, to save him.

Rayber's vision of Tarwater's future is thus a mirror image of his own life, an *imitatio Rayberi* that parodies the Christian pattern. If he conforms almost perfectly to the types of the psychological "Son" and the mythic guide, he also reveals himself as a spiritual type of the Antichrist.[13] His occupation of teacher recalls one of Christ's primary roles, and he zealously sets about instructing the boy in the terms of his psychological salvation. "If there's any way to be born again," he tells him, "it's a way that you accomplish yourself, an understanding about yourself that you reach after a long time" (p. 194). As rationalist guide and savior, he offers Tarwater the secular rebirth of release from bondage to the old man. "I think you're not going to be free of him without my help," Rayber solemnly warns (p. 169).

But, given his premises, Rayber can only define this freedom in a language that effectively denies it. For the schoolteacher, all life, human as well as nonhuman, is governed by intelligible laws—once more, the biblical metaphor for the bondage of the fallen world. "There are certain laws that determine every man's conduct," he earnestly tells the boy, and, "What we understand, we can control" (pp. 196, 194). Rayber's own control is symbolized in the box of his hearing aid, an emblem of imprisonment and death which both epitomizes his mechanistic faith and selects his version of reality: sounds that disturb him are simply switched off, and he retires into a mock heaven of peaceful silence.

If only to justify his own position, the schoolteacher is committed to saving others for the rationalistic faith, but in this travesty of Christianity the way is at least as narrow, the gate as strait to the realm of normalcy as they ever were to that other Kingdom. Even more ominously, if the keys to this kingdom are the laws of human knowledge, the believer is at the mercy of the dispenser of those laws, open to the analysis and control of the omniscient guide. "I can read you like a book!"[14] Rayber unguardedly blurts, and the words suggest the imperceptible passing of the would-be messiah towards his demonic opposite. The role of schoolteacher cuts duplicitously in *The Violent Bear It Away*, for if it mockingly recalls Christ, it also echoes Galatians 3 : 24–25: "Wherefore the law was our schoolmaster to bring us into Christ, that we might be justified by faith. But after faith is come, we are no longer under a schoolmaster." Rayber preaches freedom, but he is the very embodiment of law: the rationalist is merely the old Pharisee in modern dress.

With respect to Tarwater, Rayber stands in the novel as an articulate model of one possible solution to the boy's dilemma. As the perfect type of the stage of the "Son," he embodies the moderate way, the denial of the "Father" which is also what passes for normal. "You want to avoid extremes," he tells him. "They are for violent people"[15] (p. 145). But Tarwater seems inescapably a violent person, for Rayber's rationalism finally misses the essence of the boy's difficulty, that undesired need to accept the prophetic mission which lies deeper than questions of influence or compulsion. O'Connor's careful development of the mysterious and growing hunger in Tarwater, "a silence inside akin to the silence outside," suggests the presence of a force beyond the reach of clinical psychology. The boy himself tries to attribute his internal gnawing to the poor quality of city food, his friend suggests with mocking pertinence that it may be worms,[16] Rayber is sure that Tarwater is "eaten up with false guilt" (p. 174). But Tarwater's soul-hunger is not to be filled with a phrase, and the tensions it exacerbates force him further down his road of trials.

The devouring monsters that greeted him on his entrance to the dark city reappear in part 2 of the novel as inescapable ordeals. The test of the labyrinth thrusts the boy, with Rayber in pursuit, through twisting city alleyways to a grimy pentacostal tabernacle which glares out of the darkness like "some Biblical beast."[17] Again the revelation comes, this time in the austere lyricism of the child evangelist:

> "Jesus came on cold straw. . . . 'Who is this?' the world said, 'who is this blue-cold child and this woman, plain as the winter?' . . . The world said, 'Love cuts like the cold wind and the will of God is plain as the winter. Where is the summer will of God? Where are the green seasons of God's will?' . . . Jesus is coming again! Will you know the Lord Jesus then? . . . If you don't know him now, you won't know him then." [Pp. 131–33]

The severity of God's wintry love demands more than Tarwater is willing to surrender, and the sight of his uncle waiting outside this beast "seemed to afford him relief amounting to rescue" (p. 135). Rayber rescues him again the next day in the park when he snatches Bishop out of the fountain that Tarwater seems ready to use as a baptismal font. The beast here—the water pours from "the mouth of a stone lion's head"—is one that his great-uncle had warned him of: "Remember the Lord's lion set in the path of the false prophet!" (p. 24). And this incident too has brought its own sign, as his "friend" derisively reminds him, "the sun coming out from under a cloud and falling on the head of a dimwit" (p. 165).

As Tarwater's trials and temptations increase in intensity, they become ironically prefigured in the actions, or inactions, of Rayber. If the boy's rebellion drives him to the ordeals of the hero, Rayber inversely reflects his experience in the mirror of the antihero. The schoolteacher conceives of himself in grandiose terms—he boasts of his "human dignity," he has "conquered" (or anyway "for the most part conquered") the madness that threatens him, he is certain that "in silent ways he lived a heroic life" (pp. 112, 115)—but his deeds mock his pretensions. For Rayber believes in the power of the word: a confirmed intellectual, language (and highly abstract language) is his métier, and he confuses the unfleshed word with the act itself. When he informs Tarwater in front of the tabernacle that the Resurrection is merely a fiction, there is such "profound finality" in his voice that the building "might have been the carcass of a beast he has just brought down" (p. 110). Although his first name is George, the verbal slaying of this particular dragon proves premature. Following the boy in his labyrinthine journey that night, he discovers their destination, appropriately, through language, as he "read the mocking words, UNLESS YE BE BORN AGAIN . . ." (p. 123). Significantly, whereas Tarwater enters the jaws of this beast, Rayber remains outside, observing the meeting from a safe distance, through an open window.

Like Tarwater, the schoolteacher had been kidnapped by the old man to be instructed in the facts of his Redemption, and although he has long since rejected his uncle's vision as atavistic nonsense, the undertow in his blood remains ineradicable and drives him to trials which parallel the boy's. But in his commitment to the word, the deed is either botched or renounced for the sake of his uneasy equilibrium, his precarious sanity. He has, for instance, tried to drown

Bishop, that intimate reminder of the idiocy he perceives in the universe, and in himself, but when the child struggles with "primeval rage" ("he felt he was trying to hold a giant under"), Rayber loses his nerve (p. 142). As he rushes out of the water with the body, the heroic ordeal dissolves into the farce of a mock pietà-and-resurrection. A man in "Roman striped shorts" gives artificial respiration, "three wailing women and a photographer" appear, and a picture in the next day's paper showing Rayber "on his knees, watching with an agonized expression," bears the caption "OVERJOYED FATHER SEES SON REVIVED" (p. 143).

If this act is bungled, the schoolteacher is nevertheless offered the archetypal heroic trial, the descent into the underworld, with its risk of death and promise of renewed life. On a random drive with Bishop, Rayber finds himself without conscious intention taking the road to Powderhead, where "the embankments on either side had the look of forming the entrance to a region he would enter at his peril" (p. 183). At the edge of the wood "he picked the child a blackberry and handed it to him. The little boy studied it and then, with his fallen smile, returned it to him as if they were performing a ceremony. Rayber flung it away." With the rejection of the sibylline child's talisman, further journey becomes impossible; and although he irritably thinks, "Descending to speak with the shade of my uncle" (p. 184), he suddenly realizes that he dare not undertake this trial. The confrontation with his own past, with his deepest self, with everything his uncle implies, is too great a threat to his precarious stability—it would risk a psychic dislocation so profound as to be a kind of death. But with the challenge unmet, the possibility of rebirth averted, Rayber seems condemned to the sterility of his own ego.

If Rayber refuses the descent, Tarwater can hardly escape it. In one sense, his entire experience since fleeing Powderhead has been a night-sea journey: through his mythic vision all of the ordeals in the sinister city appear to have happened in a fearful underworld. Yet the real descent, the greatest trial is still to come: the confrontation with Bishop that should decisively initiate or cancel the prophetic mission. It occurs at a place for temporary stopovers, the Cherokee Lodge, which O'Connor turns into a primeval image of the world itself. Erected partly on land, partly on water, it is, like the seasonal movements of the creation ("a world that turned from green to white and green to white and green to white again") and like the child evangelist's winter and summer wills of God, painted white in its lower part and green in its upper. The facade of the building facing the highway is covered with worldly beer and cigarette signs (instruments of the devil, according to old Tarwater). But at the rear is a resonant lake, "glassy," yet, under the hot sun, "burning"—a setting of apocalyptic reverberation in which the novel's strains of fire and water images are fused.[18] This lake becomes a virtual sea of shifting suggestion through which O'Connor floats both the Christian and heroic myths of *The Violent Bear It Away.* As the destination for Rayber's planned fishing trip, it ironically provides the site for the evangelism implied by that biblical metaphor; in seeming to contain the sun and clouds which it reflects, it appears to image heaven itself; as Bishop is rowed across its surface "by the surly oarsman . . . to some mysterious destination" (p. 198), it becomes a Stygian underworld; and as Tarwater discovers, it is the habitat of legendary monsters of the deep.

The baptism-drowning of Bishop which climaxes the second section of the novel is primarily Tarwater's ordeal, but its significance for him is not explored until the next chapter. Instead, O'Connor rightly closes part 2 on the figure who has dominated it: the act is presented through Rayber's response to it. Waiting in the lodge for the boys to return, the schoolteacher's mind plays over past experiences and future plans, and his ruminations provide a summary statement of his rationalistic commitment, an ironic context which will focus the full meaning for him of his child's death. With the detached clarity the pause brings, he sees the past few days with Tarwater as a kind of madness, his own acts those of "an insane person." In his new-found understanding, he feels that indifference is the only worthy goal: "It seemed to him that this indifference was the most that human dignity could achieve. . . . To feel nothing was peace" (p. 200).

The restrained sarcasm of these passages barely escapes travesty, but if tone is not under full control here, imagery and action carry a convincing commentary on Rayber's position. The heaven-on-earth he imagines is a cold mockery that implies its opposite, and the "red moon" which appears in his window like "the sun rising on the upsidedown half of the world" suggests in its sinister inversion the real nature of the realm he has consciously chosen. In his life of "balance . . . between madness and emptiness" (p. 115), he had from the beginning decided "to lurch toward emptiness and fall on the side of his choice." More particularly, he has known that should anything happen to Bishop, "he would have to resist feeling anything at all" (p. 182) to preserve his sanity. Now, as the child's bellowing comes to him across the lake, Rayber successfully steels himself against "the intolerable hurt that was his due." Like Henry James's John Marcher, to whom his choice makes him spiritual kin, he collapses when he recognizes that the nothing he feels defines not only what he is, but what he has been. His hell is of his own devising, for although he has warned Tarwater to "avoid extremes," he has inevitably become one of the violent himself: through the very intensity of his nay-saying he has lost his balance. To O'Connor's dualistic imagination, moderation must finally prove an illusion. The only genuine image of balance in *The Violent Bear It Away* is that of old Tarwater's corpse at the breakfast table (p. 11), all conflicts resolved in death. Pushed to a characteristically revealing extremity, the freedom of rationalistic humanism thus proves the depths of bondage. Rayber's commitment to the laws of the intellect is now total and untainted, but it has trapped him in the nothing of his emancipated ego. This, then, is the unmasked essence of his dignity, freedom, peace—the emptiness of living death.

Yet, as O'Connor pointed out (*The Habit of Being*, p. 484), there is just the possibility that the collapse which ends Rayber's story brings not only self-recognition but, with it, the seeds of its own reversal. If so, he knows what the results will be: "the whole world would become his idiot child" (*The Violent Bear It Away*, p. 182). Whatever the likelihood of such a sequel for Rayber, the novel dramatizes the full flowering of an analogous frenzy in his nephew.

With the ending of part 2, Rayber's role is clearly played out, and although his influence, like the old man's, lingers on, in part 3 young Tarwater emerges as the unchallenged focus. Once more out on the highway, the boy this time is picked up by a "looming" truck, "huge and skeletal," where he blurts out to the uncomprehending driver his confession that he has both drowned and baptized the child. The baptism, he tells himself, was only a meaningless accident, empty verbalizing—"just some words that run out of my mouth and spilled in the water"—and Tarwater has ever scorned mere words. "I never wasted my life talking. I always done something," he boasts (pp. 209, 208). As Rayber has been committed to the power of the word, Tarwater's faith rests wholly in the efficacy of the deed. Now, however, his very voice seems to belie him, and as he tries to articulate his experience he speaks incoherently, his voice "entirely out of control . . . as if many more words would destroy it permanently" (pp. 208, 211). The act has been a thoroughly ambivalent one, word conspiring with deed to create a violent moment which is both destructive and creative, death-dealing and life-bringing. But in his insistence that only the deed matters, the boy risks losing his hold on the word for good.

O'Connor's presentation of the climactic scene with Bishop as a half-waking dream Tarwater relives in the cab of the truck underlines its mythic quality. "Standing like a guide in the boat," Tarwater's sinister friend has been in faithful attendance. He, at least, is well aware of the threat of the word to his intentions: "No finaler act than this," he tells the boy. "In dealing with the dead you have to act. There's no mere word sufficient to say NO." But the intensity in the violet eyes of this friend is matched by the fixity of the "fish-colored" eyes of the child, for Bishop seems to demand his baptism as insistently as the demonic guide demands his death. Both are accomplished, yet the act becomes a death and a birth for Tarwater too. In the "bottomless darkness" of his dream, the boy recalls how the bank "loomed" like "the brow of some leviathan," how the water seemed to slide out "like a broad black tongue," how the child had "caught him round the neck and climbed onto his back," forcing him into the water "as if the whole bank were pulling him down." As O'Connor shifts the scene back and forth from interior to exterior, from the visionary dream of the past to the anguished spasms of the present, the descent into the whale—to the "shores of the dead"—merges with the darkness of the "monstrous" truck until the struggling boy cries out the baptismal words, the sun rises "with a long red wingspread," and Tarwater is ejected from the "gigantic monster" to trudge the empty road home (pp. 214–17). In this death and rebirth, Tarwater is both actor and acted upon, both murderer and initiate, for in the mutual violence of the laying on of hands, Bishop fulfills his hierarchical name: the sacramental child confirms the manhood mission of the rebellious prophet.

But Tarwater will not accept the mythic truth of his dream. His ambivalence is not only unresolved, it is intensified by the duplicitous nature of the act which he had intended as a simple rejection, one which would leave him to the freedom of "his own inclinations." Now the entire world seems a threatening monster to the boy; he feels "as if he were walking on the back of a giant beast which might at any moment stretch a muscle and send him rolling into the ditch below" (p. 220). He tells himself that his ordeal has purified him of the old man's madness ("He returned tried in the fire of his refusal"), but his encounters on the road suggest that the trial is not yet over. A vision of silent eyes in a well drives him away in terror, his thirst unslaked;[19] the ironically appropriate "purple drink" that he requests from the woman at the local crossroads store is denied him. But what most deeply shakes his assurance is his failure to "answer for his freedom and make bold his acts" to this huge female figure of judgment. Suddenly the boy discovers that the word is no longer his to command: "to his horror what rushed from his lips, like the shriek of a bat, was an obscenity he had overheard once at a fair" (p. 225). And so the sleeping bat, that rejection of Jesus he had felt within him as a child, is at last fully loosed. It is a failure that matches the spilling of the baptismal words, a triumph for the demonic just as the earlier language had been its defeat, and deeply shocking to the fierce pride of this austere boy. But the bat is out now, and it wastes no time in claiming its own.

The encounter with the homosexual is the most melodramatic episode in *The Violent Bear It Away*. All the other key acts of the novel spring directly out of the struggle within young Tarwater: this incident is as naturalistically accidental as the overturned car of "A Good Man Is Hard to Find," but symbolically more inevitable.[20] Fully characteristic of the logic of O'Connor's imagination, it is the extreme action that makes violently clear the implications of the choice the boy believes he has made. What this "familiar"-looking "stranger" calls him to is acknowledgment of his devil worship, manifested in a black mass of mock sacraments, "special" cigarettes and whiskey.[21] Tarwater indulges with eager defiance. Significantly aided by a gift from Rayber, a corkscrew-bottleopener that the boy considers his talisman, he turns the key of this kingdom to bring upon himself the fullness of that uncle's legacy, a heritage that reaches back to the schoolteacher's baptismal consecration of the child's buttocks. Pronouncing the whiskey "better than the Bread of Life!" Tarwater immediately gains the total freedom he has desired: "he felt himself pleasantly deprived of responsibility or of the need for any effort to justify his actions" (p. 230). But the consent to the demonic pact exacts its price at once. As the mock sacraments do their work, the perverted Eucharist is carried to its fulfillment in homosexual rape. The merging of Christ with the communicant as bride, the spiritual nourishment of the freely given love feast, the restoration of the soul through grace—every aspect of the Mass is parodied in its all-too-physical inversion. In the demonic consummation, it is not of course the communicant who is fulfilled, nourished, restored: carrying the boy's hat and reclaiming the corkscrew-bottleopener, it is the stranger who emerges looking "as if he had refreshed himself on blood" (p. 231). In this most Gothic of his "devourings," Tarwater discovers that the cost of his notion of freedom is a vampirish violation of both body and spirit.[22]

But like all the other symbolic devourings in the novel, this one too brings its revelation. Stripped of his clothes, his hat gone, the boy has suffered his most devastating ordeal, the violent piercing of his proud unworldliness, the rape of the self-sufficient ego. He awakens to find himself tied and "propped up against a log that lay across a small open space between two very tall trees" (pp. 231–32). As the imagery suggests, this is the inescapable crucifixion in O'Connor's work, the discovery of the ineluctable body, the doom of the limitation and suffering of flesh and blood—a body, Tarwater discovers to his horror, that is open to violation by forces beyond individual control. This is the true "trial by fire," a furious purgation through which, his eyes at last "burned clean," they look "as if, touched with a coal like the lips of the prophet, they would never be used for ordinary sights again" (p. 233). As he had feared, this violent discovery that he fully participates in the physicalness of the created world forever displaces him from that world. The familiar countryside that he has known since infancy now turns "strange and alien," and Tarwater suddenly sees the apocalyptic nature of the creation—a road "like fire hardened," a shack "afloat" on a field, a bridge "like the skeleton of some prehistoric beast."

If the end is now in sight, the boy's ordeal is not yet complete. Approaching Powderhead, he ritualistically pauses at the forked tree that affords a view of the clearing below. Here, at the mythic "world tree" which implies in its formation a double-dimensioned universe springing from a single trunk, he encounters for the last time the grinning presence that has accompanied him throughout his journey. This time, however, Tarwater knows him, and the purification that follows is the active complement of the process he had earlier passively endured. Firing the area until "he saw that his adversary would soon be consumed in a roaring blaze," he flees to the descent that Rayber had refused, taking the downward path "through reddened tree trunks that gradually grew darker as the sun sank out of sight." The flaming pine bough that lights his journey may be more homely than the golden one, but it is as true a talisman, for as he reaches the field below, the vision of the ascent is already at hand: "planes of purpling red above the tree line stretched back like stairsteps to reach the dusk" (p. 238).

With the discovery of the cross that marks the old man's grave, the journey of initiation is complete, the circle closed. Confronting it, Tarwater finds his hands opening "stiffly as if he were dropping something he had been clutching all his life," and as he surrenders the last of his defiance, the defeated boy accepts finally the vocation he both hates and deeply desires. His reward is the vision of the dead promised the heroic voyager to the underworld, a vision which makes him "aware at last of the object of his hunger, aware that it was the same as the old man's and that nothing on earth would fill him." With the recognition of the correspondence between inner and outer worlds, between the hunger and its fulfillment, comes the knowledge that he has been doomed and chosen, one of those "who would wander in the world, strangers from that violent country where the silence is never broken except to shout the truth" (pp. 240–42). The deep ambiguity of language is at last revealed. As in Rayber, the word may be false or ineffectual, yet when rooted in the silence of Being itself, it is the vehicle of truth. The voiceless deed may be heroic, but, surrounded by human silence, it may also be demonic, the wordless drowning of an idiot child or the terrible stillness of a perverted rape. When Tarwater's command comes, "GO WARN THE CHILDREN OF GOD OF THE TERRIBLE SPEED OF MERCY," "the words were as silent as seeds opening one at a time in his blood" (p. 242). The prophetic Word takes on flesh to redeem language itself, for prophecy, as old Tarwater knew, is also a form of action. In the frenzy of evangelical vision, the word and the deed are one.[23]

Thus the call he has awaited in desire and dread comes at last to the boy, who can no longer resist it. Throwing himself on the ground "with his face against the dirt of the grave," he receives his mission, rises, and smears on his forehead a handful of the dirt from that grave before setting out for "the dark city" once more. The symbolic action is the conclusive death and rebirth in the novel, and the ritualistic marking at once penitential, initiatory, and emblematic of his acceptance of the prophetic role passed on to him through the old man. It is the signature of that moment, typical of all heroic ordeals, of "atonement with the father,"[24] a moment which also corresponds to the full flowering of Jung's third psychological stage of "the Holy Ghost": "[In] the third stage, the initial stage of the father is, as it were, recovered. . . . Adulthood is reached when the son reproduces his own childhood state by voluntarily submitting to a paternal authority. . . . Just as the transition from the first stage to the second demands the sacrifice of childish dependence, so, at the transition to the third stage, an exclusive independence has to be relinquished."[25]

But it is precisely at this point that *The Violent Bear It Away* diverges sharply from Jung's paradigm, and the way in which it does so helps throw into relief the disturbing implications of the novel. Since Jung's "Trinity" is concerned with developing a model of psychic integration, his third and final phase retains "everything won in the second stage—reason and reflection," yet now deeply modified by "recognition of the unconscious." Committed to the concept of "quaternity" as the sign of psychic harmony, Jung posits in this last phase a union of those opposites which appear split in the second stage as "Christ" and the "adversary."[26] O'Connor's version of Tarwater's threefold movement is at once religiously more orthodox and psychologically more radical. For when he unconditionally rejects his adversary and submits himself to the Father, he thereby surrenders reason and reflection altogether. The fiery purgation of the dark double figure is simultaneously a repudiation of the demonic and an act of psychic mutilation. The violence toward others is at last turned inward upon himself, and the furious NO that the boy had hurled against the very notion of a prophetic mission is at last internalized in a devastating ritual of self-denial. At the close of the novel Tarwater has been tempered into an instrument of divine purpose, but it is a process, in T. S. Eliot's words, "costing not less than everything."

We might linger a moment on the darker side of that conclusion since the overwhelming tendency has been to read it as a happy if not dogmatic ending and thus to see the novel generically as comedy.[27] And so, in part, it is, sealed even with the traditional climax of a communal feast, here dramatized in the boy's vision of the eating of the divine loaves and fishes. Yet to view *The Violent Bear It Away* simply as comedy is to ignore the extraordinary tension of that ending, to emphasize the next world rather than this one, to insist on Tarwater's vision and forget that the final paragraph of the novel sets him grimly on his return to the "dark city." Now doomed to a life in "the bleeding stinking mad shadow of Jesus," he has long known that "the ways of his prophecy would not be remarkable" (p. 91); as he moves again toward the city his eyes "seemed already to envision the fate that awaited him" (p. 243). Unlike Hazel Motes, who is dispatched at the end of his story, Tarwater is projected into a future of madness, vilification, and persecution. And from this perspective Northrop Frye's comment on the career of the tragic hero seems as appropriate as any comic analogue: "The discovery or *anagnorisis* which comes at the end of the tragic plot is not simply the knowledge by the hero of what has happened to him . . . but the recognition of the determined shape of the life he has created for himself, with an implicit comparison with the uncreated potential life he has forsaken."[28]

More disturbing than Tarwater's external fate at the hands of the "children of God" is the internal violence that has made it inescapable, the fiery extirpation of the rational self. To align oneself with the will of God requires a psychic ravaging so radical that the boy's recognition that he has been chosen leaves him, as O'Connor puts it earlier in the novel, "in despair" (p. 91), and his final acquiescence to that will renders him both "forever lost" to all "his own inclinations" but one (p. 221) and an outcast on the face of the earth. Merely to note that alienation from the world is traditionally Christian, as indeed it is, is to evade the mixed tone of the novel's ending and the dark coloration of O'Connor's fierce Christianity. A book that presents us with the comically sinister wiles of a recognizable devil and an unmistakable manifestation of God's purposes, *The Violent Bear It Away* reveals the divine to be at least as terrifying as the demonic.

Thus the doubleness of that ending—the excruciating loss that is the boy's triumph, the agonized victory that is his defeat—is deeply appropriate to the violent internal struggle that the novel has dramatized. It is inevitable, in fact, given the apocalyptic terms of that clash. If Tarwater's entire experience recalls the reluctance of the Hebrew prophets, the week of his passion also adumbrates the central biblical movement from a temptation and fall through a long and increasingly rebellious travail under the law to a crucifixion and, finally, a vision of revelation. But the boy's journey has been mythic in a non-Christian sense as well: imagery and action lend to his trials the overtones of the heroic initiation ordeal. There is a tension between these two strains of myth. They seem to work against one another as if O'Connor, somewhat like the Milton of *Paradise Lost*, were using them to distinguish between false and true heroism, for if Tarwater's battle against the prophetic calling is heroic, it is the rebellion of the Satanic hero. These distinctions are not irrelevant, but nothing more clearly marks *The Violent Bear It Away* as a modern work than the fact that a neat separation between true and false heroism cannot finally be made. It is only through the boy's fall into the demonic world that he comes to his vision of the divine and thus accepts his mission in that middle realm of earth; caught in the tensions from below and above, he assumes finally the burden of *this* world.[29] Tarwater's defiance no less than his submission, his furious revolt as much as his rending acceptance, confers on him at the end of the novel the stature of the authentic prophet-hero.

III

To call Tarwater a hero of any sort is to distinguish between him and the protagonists of O'Connor's stories. The grandmothers and hardworking farm ladies, the neglected or precocious children, the aging intellectuals and social workers, the pregnant women and cantankerous old men and itinerant carpenters—these various figures at the center of the stories make up what might be called "just folks," the ordinary people of her fictional world. As their tales open, they are seen living quite unexceptionable, everyday lives, preparing for a family vacation, trying to make ends meet on a farm, worrying about moving to a subdivision, enduring the pains of preadolescent loneliness, and so on. They have no grander sense of purpose than ridding their farms of nut grass or getting more work out of the hired help or going to Tennessee rather than Florida or coping with a sassy child; certainly they are not prepared for the strange and usually terrible things that happen to them. If O'Connor's narrative strategy discourages us from naïvely identifying with them, we at least recognize them at once.

The same cannot be said either of Tarwater or of Hazel Motes. The protagonists of the novels are not at all "just folks"—although they may think that is exactly what they want to be—and they are too outlandish to be immediately recognizable. Odd, angular, surly, and perverse, Haze and young Tarwater are obsessed by an overwhelming sense of purpose, of mission, that they would gladly shuck off if only they could. Their inability to do so is of course the burden of their stories and the confirmation of their extraordinariness. At the end of *The Violent Bear It Away* the burning clean of Tarwater's eyes assures that he will never behold ordinary sights again, and Hazel Motes's self-blinding burns his eyes so clean that they will never be used for earthly sights at all. But these stigmata only make manifest what those peculiar narratives have implied all along: that in her novels O'Connor is concerned not with ordinary folk, but with heroes.

That ancient and honorific term may sound rather strange applied to such eccentric figures; given O'Connor's treatment of Hazel Motes and Tarwater it would seem to demand qualification. But to say that they are both tragicomic characters, willful, surly, obsessive, ridiculous, is merely to begin to measure the affront they offer to conventional expectations. Despite the rather different methods of characterization, both Haze and Tarwater are designedly unnatural protagonists. It is probably a toss-up which is the less smoothly appealing, for O'Connor's strategy is to force us to grasp imaginatively, intellectually, and even viscerally rather than through an easy emotional identification the fullest significance of their experiences. To many readers they may not be lovable or even likable, but they are something more important for vital fiction: they are convincing, and convincing in a thoroughly modern way.

Part of their modernity is that in an irreligious time that views itself as hopelessly antiheroic, they are remarkably reluctant heroes who are trying to be just as irreligious as everyone else. They do not want their burdens, they undertake prolonged rebellious struggles to demonstrate their freedom from them, embark on journeys meant to deny any sense of mission—and so, absurdly and movingly, confirm their roles. But as grotesque heroes they also reveal the terrible cost of those roles. At the ends of the novels, Hazel Motes blinds himself and in ritualistic physical mortification seeks out death, while Tarwater turns his violence upon his inner nature and faces the supererogatory martyrdom of his futile prophesying. "There's no peace for the redeemed" (*Wise Blood*, p. 140), Hazel Motes had preached. He might have gone further and said that for O'Connor's defiant and defeated heroes, there is little that resembles a distinctively earthly life at all.

These devastating inverted affirmations are a radical and triumphant conception, although O'Connor's few public pronouncements on her novels have tended to narrow the scope of her ambition. Hazel Motes she referred to simply as a "Christian *malgré lui*," and she approvingly cited the comment of some nuns of her acquaintance that they could understand Tarwater because they too had struggled with their vocation. Pleased, she added, "That's all the understanding you could ask for."[30] Perhaps. But Haze is not merely a Christian in spite of himself, and the vocation Tarwater is called to is beyond the bounds of recognizable orthodoxy. Unlike *Wise Blood*, *The Violent Bear It Away* does have a representative of enduring Christian community, but it is Buford Munson, the Negro who finally gives the old man his proper burial, not the vehemently divided boy himself. Tarwater is, to borrow the language of his great-uncle, "more than a Christian, a prophet" (p. 15), and if the earlier novel contains no passage so explicit, Hazel Motes as much as the boy is finally something "more than a Christian." In a phrase that rings down the centuries, they are both Christian heroes. But that term has now a rather rusty sound, and inevitably any modern protagonist who could revive it would have to be significantly different from the heroes of Dante or Spenser, Bunyan or Milton, or even of Dostoyevski. Perhaps O'Connor's finest achievement in her novels is to have recovered for our times and in our terms a convincing image to fill that ancient phase.

Certainly Tarwater is, in the full sense of the term, a genuine culture hero. In the final paragraph of *The Violent Bear It Away*, he returns from his backwoods clearing to our world, to "the dark city," bearing the fruit of his agonized ordeal, the unwanted gift of the Word. In this he differs profoundly from Hazel Motes, who in his isolated integrity at the end of *Wise Blood* may be as truly heroic as Tarwater, but who inhabits a world so deeply corrupt that the most he can achieve is the desperate attempt at his own salvation, and that only through a total denial of the world. The proper symbol for his journey is the tunnel, for he is only passing through this life, and as he emerges from it self-blinded, his vision turns wholly, mystically inward. If Hazel Motes is the modern hero as saint, Tarwater is the hero as prophet, as maimingly ascetic in his way as Haze—and this is one meaning of the "violent" of the book's title—but doomed to action in this world. The proper symbol for *his* journey seems the circle—from country to city back round to country again—yet the spiral motion of the novel's final paragraph thrusts him again toward the city, toward those sleeping "children of God." We know, and he knows, the greeting he will receive there, but at least the emissary has come, and the ancient promise once more has been renewed.

O'Connor's two novels are, then, distinctively different from her stories, for whatever the experiences of her ordinary folk, the creation of these dreadful mutilated heroes, defining themselves through the archetypal motif of the journey-quest, clearly demanded the more spacious form the novel affords. We may not like the heroes we get, but perhaps we get the heroes we deserve. If Hazel Motes and young Tarwater seem too repellent, too grotesque—ignorant, violent, mad, murderers and outcasts—it may be worth reaching back over the centuries, back beyond familiar literary heroes, to an even older description of the servant of God: "He hath no form nor comeliness; and when we shall see him, there is no beauty that we should desire him. He is despised and rejected of men; a man of sorrows, and acquainted with grief: and we hid as it were our faces from him; he was despised and we esteemed him not. Surely he hath borne our griefs, and carried our sorrows; yet we did esteem him stricken, smitten of God, and afflicted" (Isaiah 53 : 2–4). This kind of hero is always an affront and an outrage. Perhaps the true wonder is not that he should be grotesque, but that he should come at all.

CHAPTER SIX
The Prophetic Imagination

Like most of Flannery O'Connor's critics, I have not been able to ignore the religious concerns of her fiction in the preceding chapters. Those concerns are, as she claimed, central rather than peripheral, so much so that they demand a more direct confrontation, an attempt to plot out the religious dimensions of her imagination. The issues her work raises *are* more questions of imagination than of belief in the usual sense, and the exploration which follows will be more occupied with aesthetic than with theological discriminations, with such matters as temperament, tone, feeling, form, and patterns of action rather than with precise doctrinal points. For a writer of fiction, these are the primary issues, and while O'Connor's work certainly allows for the drawing of technical theological inferences, these need to be determined within the larger imaginative structures of her fiction, not outside of them. She did not, after all, pretend to be a systematic theologian. In fact, quoting Pascal, she insisted that her immediate concern as a writer was with the existential, not the theological, with the "God of Abraham, Isaac, and Jacob and not of the philosophers and scholars" (*Mystery and Manners*, p. 161).

On the other hand, it is late in the day to profess that in Flannery O'Connor we are dealing with a writer wholly innocent of theology. Indeed, her often-quoted assertion, "I see from the standpoint of Christian orthodoxy" (*Mystery and Manners*, p. 32), has seemed to many of her critics not only decisive but self-explanatory: she was not just a Roman Catholic, but specifically a Thomist.[1] And certainly to browse through her occasional writings is to recognize again and again the assumptions and even the language of Scholasticism, derived either directly from Aquinas himself or by way of such neo-Thomists as Jacques Maritain. *Mystery and Manners* alone is full of it: fiction, we hear, begins where all human knowledge begins, with the senses; art is a "virtue of the practical intellect," it is "reason in making," it does not require "rectitude of the appetite," and so on (*Mystery and Manners*, pp. 67, 81, 82, 171). Both directly and indirectly, she repeatedly affirmed her allegiance to this central tradition of Catholicism, maintaining that the church vouchsafed to its writers "a powerful extension of sight." All of these passages seem to make persuasive her claim to a friend that "she was a Thomist through and through."[2]

In a number of her later essays, however, while always asserting her deep commitment to Catholicism, she tacitly admitted that although orthodoxy may be where such a writer begins, it is not necessarily where her fiction ends. Vision—that key metaphor in all her writing—was apparently not as simple a matter as she had earlier claimed. The writer who also considers himself a Christian, she said, sees in fact through two pair of eyes, his own and those of the church:

> It would be foolish to say there is no conflict between those two sets of eyes. There is a conflict, and it is a conflict which we escape at our peril, one which cannot be settled beforehand by theory or fiat or faith. We think that faith entitles us to avoid it, when in fact, faith prompts us to begin it, and to continue it until, like Jacob, we are marked. . . . The tensions of being a Catholic novelist are probably never balanced for the writer until the Church becomes so much a part of his personality that he can forget about her—in the same sense that when he writes, he forgets about himself. [*Mystery and Manners*, p. 180]

She added that such balance "is a condition we aim for, but one which is seldom achieved in this life, particularly by novelists." In another context, she put the conflict in spiritual terms: "It is only in the last stages of the mystical life that the body and soul—or with the novelist that the conviction and the sensibility—will function congenially together,"[3] and she clearly did not claim for herself any such exalted state. In one passing comment, she went further still: fiction, she remarked, being a human product, inevitably "escapes any orthodoxy we might set up for it" (*Mystery and Manners*, p. 192).

"We write with the whole personality" (*Mystery and Manners*, p. 193), O'Connor insisted, but these remarks suggest that her own personality was a battleground, the source and scene of intense struggle, of conflict renewed again and again. The central result for her fiction was violence and tension, the numerous double figures, the attraction to polarities, the unreconciled extremes—in short, the dualistic imagination that the previous chapters have tried to explore. When she wrote, with regard to Hazel Motes, "Free will does not mean one will, but many wills conflicting in one man" (*Mystery and Manners*, p. 115), she might have been speaking of herself, although what all of her work presents is not the chaos of many conflicting wills, but the drama of the divided will, straining toward opposed poles. However, she was also in that preface closely echoing Saint Augustine. While he too could speak of many "wills in conflict with one another," what he knew most intimately was the struggle of the ambivalent will, divided against itself: "Thus there are two wills in us, because neither of them is entire. . . . When I was deliberating about serving the Lord my God, as I had long meant to do, it was I who willed to do it, I who was unwilling. . . . Therefore I strove with myself and was distracted by myself."[4]

Focusing as it does on the dynamics of opposition, this passage from the *Confessions* is deeply characteristic of Augustine. Its reverberation in the preface to *Wise Blood*, so expressive of the workings of O'Connor's own mind, suggests that the essential cast of her imagination was far more Augustinian than Thomistic. Reconciliation and synthesis, the congruity of faith and human reason, the harmonious hierarchy of the faculties—the great accommodations of Thomistic thought seem curiously irrelevant to the central experience of O'Connor's fiction; whereas Augustine's disposition of the major contraries—grace and sin, spirit and flesh, God and self, the heavenly city and the earthly—immediately evokes the tensions and dualities of her work. Fascinated by violent oppositions and openly scornful of appeals to moderation, O'Connor shows little imaginative sympathy with the Aristotelian bias of the dominant tradition of Catholic humanism. On the other hand, since Augustine is claimed both by Catholicism and by the Reformation rebels against the church, it is little wonder that she responded so readily to certain expressions of Protestant belief. After all, as she herself was the first to point out, her imagination had received a lasting imprint from her growing up Catholic in the Protestant South.

But O'Connor's very particular brand of imaginative ecumenicism is not to be confused with any of the more liberal modern theological movements, whether Catholic or Protestant—nor, indeed, with the inclusive traditions of Christian humanism itself. Closely allied to the Augustinian cast of her mind is her profound and enduring affinity with the severer ascetic strain in the church, and particularly its most extreme forms, where it leads to the visionary and the apocalyptic. O'Connor's asceticism is, in fact, so pervasive that it reaches into every aspect of her fiction. Robert Fitzgerald has pointed out the aptness of the term for her style: "She would be sardonic over the word *ascesis*, but it seems to me a good one for the peculiar discipline of the O'Connor style. How much has been refrained from, and how much else has been cut out and thrown away, in order that the bald narrative sentences should present just what they present and in just this order!"[5] Yet that same deep commitment to austerity, discipline, purging away can be observed in her stylization of character, which moves swiftly to strip her figures to essences; in that severity of eye that rigorously refuses to "excuse all human weakness because human weakness is human" (*Mystery and Manners*, p. 43); in the ironic voice that relentlessly lays bare the expressions of pretension, pettiness, absurdity, and evil; and even, as we shall see, in the very shape of the action itself.

Central to the ascetic tradition is Christ's stark either/or: "If any man will come after me, let him deny himself, and take up his cross, and follow me. For whosoever will save his life shall lose it: and whosoever shall lose his life for my sake shall find it" (Matthew 16:24–25). Perhaps even more disturbing is the supplementary charge, "And if thine eye offend thee, pluck it out, and cast it from thee: it is better for thee to enter into life with one eye, rather than having two eyes to be cast into hell fire" (Matthew 18:9). The choice is both clear and all-encompassing: "To try and 'save one's life,' i.e. no doubt, to insist on leading a life of one's own and 'preserving the independence of one's person, ideas and tastes' (Lagrange), is to lose it. To save one's life, one must renounce everything—give up all attempt at making an impression on the world and forego the flowering of one's own personality—'for Christ's sake and the gospel's.'"[6]

This is the world of O'Connor's fiction, a world of pain dominated by the crucified, not the resurrected Christ, given over to sharp suffering and sudden death. It is indeed a world "made for the dead" (*The Violent Bear It Away*, p. 16), not for the accommodation of the living, and those who, like Mrs. May of "Greenleaf," evade the agonizing denial of self ("Jesus stab me in the heart!") are likely to find themselves brought to a violently literal death. The Christ who stalks this world is not the Comforter, the Reconciler, the Mediator, the Healer and Guardian, "gentle Jesus meek and mild"—not, as "Parker's Back" ticks off such reassuring images, "The Good Shepherd, Forbid Them Not, The Smiling Jesus, Jesus the Physician's Friend" (p. 522). He is rather (as that story again puts it) the "all-demanding" One, the Divider and Sunderer who, in O'Connor's favorite Christological passage, "came not to send peace, but a sword" (Matthew 11:34). And the most painful cleavages are not those within households, as in "Parker's Back," but those which cut through the center of an individual life and sunder a man from his entire familiar sense of himself. The Misfit, of course, had put it with Augustinian rigor—"If He did what He said, then it's nothing for you to do but throw away everything and follow Him, and if He didn't, then it's nothing for you to do but enjoy the few minutes you got left the best way you can" ("A Good Man Is Hard to Find," p. 132)—but it was not clear from that story just how precise the word *everything* was. "Jesus or the devil," mutters Tarwater of his ultimate choice. "Jesus or *you*," his friend corrects him (*The Violent Bear It Away*, p. 39). For O'Connor, the two formulations are finally one.

To note that this choice, simple and devastating, radical and all-consuming, underlies all of her fiction is perhaps to do little more than state the obvious. But it is just this insistence on the sharp divisiveness of the alternatives that separates her from the more inclusive strain of Christian humanism and places her firmly in the ascetic tradition. One commentator on the sense of pain inherent in that tradition might have been describing the central thrust of her work when he pointed out, "The aim of asceticism is not to produce decent, well-balanced citizens . . . its business is to keep the *scandalum Crucis* alive." Thus, as she herself seemed to realize, her deepest affinities were with the stark pre-Renaissance traditions of the church which had resisted the humanistic appeal. The "ideal of positive and immediate sanctification of the world" had, for instance, its attraction for the early church fathers, but they rejected it for the monastic standard of "systematic separation from the world." Renaissance humanism, however, struck a deep blow at ascetic ideals and practices, for the two strains were in essence incompatible "in so far as Christian asceticism entails the restriction of natural activity and almost the mutilation of nature." There were attempts at reconciliation, but the sense was lost of "the dynamic element in Christian asceticism, which makes it essentially a kind of folly, folly inspired by the cross."[7] Despite pockets of resistance to the humanistic tide that washed over all of Western culture, by the middle of the twentieth century the older forms of asceticism seemed effectively dead in mainstream Catholicism. Indeed, in a heavily psychoanalytic age, they often appeared rather an embarrassment.

O'Connor served notice both of her central commitment and of her recognition of its outrageousness to the humanist mind as early as *Wise Blood*. In an action typically literal and extreme, Hazel Motes finds that not one but both eyes offend him and proceeds, following the biblical injunction, to pluck them out. This act is incomprehensible to his worldly landlady, but when he goes on to wrap barbed wire around his chest and line his shoes with rocks and broken glass, she delivers herself of an obtuse but accurate protest: "It's something that people have quit doing—like boiling in oil or being a saint. . . . There's no reason for it. People have quit doing it." Haze himself may be only dimly aware that he is carrying on a tradition—"They ain't quit doing it as long as I'm doing it" (p. 224)—but Flannery O'Connor fully realized (and in this first novel flaunted) her allegiance to the most radical forms of Christian asceticism.

That she never employed traditional ascetic practices in such an overt—indeed, bizarre—way again is partly attributable to the basic shift in focus her work underwent after *Wise Blood*. However, she had also discovered in that first novel that she no longer needed them, that the very form of the work itself might embody the central ascetic impulse more profoundly than any specific images or actions. Within the varied situations that her stories and novels present on the surface, the characteristic O'Connor work is the imitation of an action of purgation. In her ironic tales, the purifying action works primarily for the reader; more often, it operates on the protagonist as well. In either case, the essential process of her fictions is to subject her protagonist to an extraordinary situation, an unprecedented action that brings increasing pressure to bear on his deepest sense of himself and that by the climax of the work has effected a cleansing of his most cherished illusions, or indeed of any living self at all. Although she would also endow a number of her later characters, as she had Hazel Motes, with a version of her own ascetic temperament (The Misfit, Tarwater, Rayber, and Sheppard, among others), she had more significantly learned how to project her deepest concerns into the very shape of the fiction so that all of her protagonists come to one variety or another of that agonizing crux, "Jesus or *you*."

Now some may, of course, decline to recognize that crux. In "The Life You Save May Be Your Own," for instance, Mr. Shiftlet's self-righteous prayer that the "slime" be cleansed from the earth produces the "guffawing peal of thunder," and in "A View of the Woods" Mr. Fortune's rejection of his painful vision leads directly to the killing of his granddaughter. But these very denials of the stark alternatives are themselves acts of choice. More frequently O'Connor's protagonists are driven out of their mockingly presented cocoons of illusion, purified by the very intensity of the action until they reach some recognition of the reality beyond the self. Now and again these wrenching eye-openings burst with the suddenness of an exploded balloon, as in "Good Country People" where the loss of the leg signals the unanticipated stripping away of the girl's entire Hulga identity. Usually, however—and "A Good Man Is Hard to Find" or "The Lame Shall Enter First" are clear examples—the protagonist is subjected to a prolonged pressure which gradually purges him of his familiar self. The essential process is perhaps most explicit in "The Enduring Chill." Under the combined forces of his mother's relentless determination, his doctor's assured persistence ("Slowly Lord but sure," he sings), an old priest's "battering" catechistical attack, and his own failure at "communion" with the black farmhands, Asbury Fox is finally left emptied of "old life," "shocked clean," prepared to undergo the "purifying terror" of an icy Holy Ghost.[8] Thus the disappearance of most of the outer trappings of asceticism after *Wise Blood* hardly signals the vanishing of the ascetic impulse from O'Connor's work. Transformed into the very shape of the action, it subjects her protagonists to a purging away of the extraneous and inessential and brings them to the cross of their final commitments.

This enduring ascetic strain in O'Connor's fiction would seem, on the surface, incompatible with the sacramentalism that develops in her work after *Wise Blood*. If the first derives from the Crucifixion and suggests self-denial and detachment from the world of things, the second stems from the Incarnation and affirms the presence of the divine within the created world. Hazel Motes's asceticism had indeed been an extreme version of the oldest contemplative ideals of the church. For the monks of the patristic period, "the business of asceticism was to free man from the trammels of life in this world, and life in this world was seen by the monks as something clogged and dulled by matter. . . .matter had . . . become a leaden carapace," stifling the aspirations of the spirit.[9] However, the mortifications that come down on O'Connor's later protagonists are cleansings of the doors of perception, purifications not of body, but of consciousness. They are returned *to* a world of matter through which spirit gleams: the ascetic action thus comes to reveal the sacramental vision. The situation of these characters is that described by Evelyn Underhill: "We see a sham world because we live a sham life. We do not know ourselves. . . . That world, which we have distorted by identifying it with our own self-regarding arrangements of its elements, has got to reassume for us the character of Reality, of God."[10] Out of the creative tension between the ascetic and the sacramental comes that mingled severity and radiance, the austere and the visionary, that marks the uniqueness of all O'Connor's later fiction.

Nevertheless, the ascetic process, however conceived, is by its very nature an anticipation of death. It is hardly too much to say that all of her mature work ends either in literal death or in that violent purging of the ego that is the death of the self. As she remarked, "Death has always been brother to my imagination. I can't imagine a story that doesn't properly end in it or in its foreshadowings."[11] Yet what preoccupies her characters is not merely the fact of death but the question of its finality: they are concerned not simply with the end of life but with the mysteries of eschatology. Hazel Motes is obsessed with the image of the coffin closing; for The Misfit the only question worth asking is whether or not Jesus raised the dead; "General" Sash of "A Late Encounter with the Enemy" makes "a desperate effort to see over" his death to find out what follows; and young Tarwater wants only to be convinced that the dead do not rise again. From *Wise Blood* on, death is the hinge of O'Connor's world, but gradually through the natural scene that is the ostensible focus of her work there begins to glimmer and then to glare the presence of the supernatural. The sacramental finally manifests itself in the great duality of the eschatological: we may be looking at this world, but the pressures of heaven and hell make themselves felt behind it. In the later work they burst into the phenomenal world to give undeniable evidence of their reality.

II

The dualities of an Augustinian cast of mind, the deeply ascetic temperament, the preoccupation with last things characterize all of Flannery O'Connor's mature fiction. Enduring traits, they help to define the parameters of an imagination that has committed itself to the religious sense of life. Yet her work is not static. As her career developed, certain issues and emphases in her fiction began to undergo a gradual change.

We have already seen from several perspectives the distinction of *Wise Blood* from the works that followed it. In that novel the inherent dualism of O'Connor's imagination is so radical that the deep revulsion against all forms of matter, the opposition of it to the spiritual, and the absolute separation of the worldly from the otherworldly results in a work that can only be called "Manichean." As a result of these cleavages, the central religious issue that faces Hazel Motes is the quite traditional one of faith versus doubt, although this is partly masked by O'Connor's presentation of him as an incarnate paradox whose violent rebellion seems to suggest a correspondingly strong sense of underlying conviction. However, although Haze both fears and secretly hopes that, as his grandfather had foretold, "Jesus would have him in the end" (p. 22), he is far from certain.

In fact, his entire blasphemous stance is designed to elicit a sign, some sacramental token that will convince him he inhabits a Christian universe; but the world of *Wise Blood* is capable of no such manifestation. Haze makes his leap of faith into a literal darkness at the end of the novel, but what he has really wanted all along is not faith but direct enlightenment—knowledge.

Haze's dilemma is essentially the one The Misfit also struggles with in the story that closely followed *Wise Blood* in publication. Here too, although the outcome is quite different, the issue is one of faith for a character who wants knowledge—"It ain't right I wasn't there [when Jesus claimed to have raised the dead] because if I had of been there I would of *known*" ("A Good Man Is Hard to Find," p. 132; italics added)—but The Misfit scans the blank sky of the story as fruitlessly as Haze had searched his world for a sign. "The River," published the same year as "A Good Man Is Hard to Find" (1953), presents the obverse of this situation. Baptized by a preacher whom he hears say that the "River of Pain" empties into the Kingdom of Christ, young Harry Ashfield decides to complete the process on his own. The child, who, O'Connor said, "hasn't reached the age of reason," never doubts that he will find "the Kingdom of Christ in the river" (p. 173) and thus drowns himself. "Children," Rayber will reflect bitterly, "are cursed with believing" (*The Violent Bear It Away*, p. 171). It would perhaps be more accurate to say that for the prerational there is no distinction between belief and knowledge.

It might at first seem inevitable that a writer such as O'Connor, for whom the central religious question is always "Jesus or *you*," should be concerned with problems of faith and doubt, belief and disbelief. In fact, however, she very soon began to move away from these questions towards something quite different: the rendering of visionary experience that would transform them altogether. Although the stories of *A Good Man Is Hard to Find* were all published rapidly between 1953 and 1955, one can trace there a gradual movement toward those climactic moments of revelation that would emerge fully in *Everything That Rises Must Converge* and *The Violent Bear It Away*. It is "A Late Encounter with the Enemy," another work published in 1953, that first strikes this note in her fiction. Near the end of the story she moves more intimately into the consciousness of old "General" Sash than she had with any of her earlier protagonists. As he sits angrily on the auditorium stage, stirred despite himself by the graduation speech he has had to endure, suddenly "the music swelled toward him," "the entire past opened up on him out of nowhere" (p. 143), and he is subjected to the rapid reliving of his long-forgotten early life. The old man's experience is hardly apocalyptic; nevertheless, it is O'Connor's first attempt at presenting her characteristically overpowering climactic moment as, quite literally, a vision.

In the stories of 1954 she began to experiment more ambitiously with the visionary mode. "A Temple of the Holy Ghost" employs once again the contents of the protagonist's memory, but now they are transformed into a dream-experience—the carnival freak, in an evangelistic setting, speaking of the sacredness of the body—around which the entire story turns. In "A Circle in the Fire" the final sentence suggests briefly and tentatively, in an "as if" clause, the apocalyptic possibilities of the revelatory moment: "She . . . could just catch in the distance a few wild high shrieks of joy as if the prophets were dancing in the fiery furnace, in the circle the angel had cleared for them" (p. 193). In the final story of that year, "The Displaced Person," O'Connor presented for the first time a fully rendered prophetic vision. However, Mrs. Shortley's Sunday-afternoon revelation comes out of a suspicious matrix of recollections of newsreels of concentration camps, dark distrust of all things foreign and Catholic, studies of the Bible that assure her of her importance to the divine plan, and heart spasms that "stopped her thought altogether" (p. 210). In other words, O'Connor leaves the status of this vision ambiguous: we are free to view it as an entirely subjective, self-gratifying experience of Mrs. Shortley's, even while recognizing the ironic fulfillment of her prophecy ("Who will remain whole?") in the circumstances of her own subsequent death. While all of the visions of the later works will also have their roots deep in the protagonist's personality, there will never again be any doubt that they are also genuine revelations.

With the gradual shift toward the visionary mode, the central human religious questions also undergo transformation. Once again, a juxtaposition of the novels provides perhaps the easiest and most dramatic way of pointing up important differences between early and later O'Connor. The climactic moments of the two heroes make evident enough the distinctions between the worlds they inhabit. Tarwater's great revelation at the end of *The Violent Bear It Away* has no counterpart in *Wise Blood*, where Hazel Motes confronts only "the blank gray sky" before leaping to his desperate penance. One consequence of this important dissimilarity is that the essential problems confronting the two are subtly but fundamentally different. Early in their respective books, both boys strike a similar stance: they place themselves on the alert for a sign that, as they have been instructed by their elders, God is deeply involved in their destinies. Neither discovers any such sign, and Haze will move through all of *Wise Blood* without finding one. Tarwater, however, before his first day is over, *knows* what his fate is to be: "The revelation came, silent, implacable, direct as a bullet. He did not look into the eyes of any fiery beast or see a burning bush. He only *knew*, with a *certainty* sunk in despair, that he was expected to baptize the child he saw and begin the life his great uncle had prepared him for. He *knew* that he was called to be a prophet and that the ways of his prophecy would not be remarkable" (*The Violent Bear It Away*, p. 91; italics added). An earlier version of this passage had been even more explicit: "His gift was neither faith, nor hope, nor love, but only knowledge. The boy knew, once and for ever, that everything his great-uncle had taught him was true." [12] It is into the face of this certainty that Tarwater hurls his desperate and defiant NO! The central tension in O'Connor's second novel is thus not between belief and apostasy, as in *Wise Blood*, but between acceptance and revolt.

Throughout the stories of *Everything That Rises Must Converge*, too, it is not the possibility of belief that is at issue, but the inescapability of knowledge, an appalling knowledge that comes to hapless protagonists who hardly thought that *that* was what they wanted. What they discover are the eschatological dimensions of the universe they inhabit. Their awareness may take the form of Julian's initiation into "the world of guilt and sorrow" in "Everything That Rises Must Converge" or, more damningly, of Sheppard's crushing recognition of the Satan in himself in "The Lame Shall Enter First." But these dark revelations of the radically fallen world are more than matched by those visions that come, like the descent of the Holy Ghost to the terrified Asbury Fox, from above. Mrs. May of "Greenleaf" finds her sudden blast of vision literally unbearable, and if Mrs. Turpin survives her revelation, she does so in the grim certainty of what she *knows*: her eyes at the end of the story are "fixed un-blinkingly on what lay ahead" ("Revelation," pp. 508–9). So perva-sive is the visionary mode in O'Connor's second collection that the ironic tale "The Comforts of Home" concludes with a parody of these moments of epiphany. Whatever awareness Thomas may achieve, Sheriff Farebrother, entering the scene in the final para-graphs of the story, has a tabloid revelation suddenly "flashed" to him: "Over [Thomas's mother's] body, the killer and the slut were about to collapse into each other's arms" (p. 404).

Thomas is of course one of O'Connor's many intellectuals, a his-torian, and his failure in "The Comforts of Home" sheds an oblique light on the nature of the visions that dominate the later work. Committed to "the long slow processes of time," as she had put it in an earlier draft of the story, "between heaven and hell, he felt there was no choice; limbo was all he asked," and she there passed her most scathing judgment on him: "His vision of the future was not apocalyptic."[13] A lukewarm apostle of moderation, rejecting the as-cetic demands the action places on him and the stark eschatological choice, this historian is granted no revelation. For protagonists less sluggishly resistant than Thomas, however, their visions are literally apocalyptic: a veil is pulled aside (and "The Enduring Chill" makes explicit use of this image) so that they see at last. If what they see at those moments seems a glimpse of the full dimensions of Reality, the knowledge they gain is actually twofold, for the sudden es-chatological perspective reveals also their irreducible selves, beyond all deceptions of the ego. The apocalyptic strain that dominates the later fiction is thus not a concern with the end of time, but the reve-lation of the here and now *sub specie aeternitatis*. It is a matter not of belief but of *gnosis*.[14]

From the beginning, as we have seen, O'Connor was deeply oc-cupied with the problem of knowledge. Hazel Motes scans the land-scape for a sign that will evince the workings of Providence; The Misfit rejects Jesus because he cannot know whether He raised the dead. The mind, she saw, makes its own demands, insists on a ra-tionalistic satisfaction that will quiet the deep craving to know. Yet it is even more dangerous than this, for the great temptation of rea-son is the illusion it creates of self-sufficiency, of domination and control of the world beyond itself, of transcendence of the limitations of the body, of matter, indeed even of human mortality. It is for O'Connor the most seductive of the human faculties, for it both imitates and mocks the powers of God Himself. Thus as early as the young protagonist of "The Turkey" who is drawn to blasphemy because it is "something entirely of the mind," the stance of the intellect for her is always that of revolt, whether or not that revolt is conscious. The overweening mind enacts again and again the sin of the angel in her fiction, not only in the long parade of self-styled intellectuals, but even in such practical farm matrons as Mrs. May, who views her little word as "the reflection of her own character" ("Greenleaf," p. 321), or Mrs. Turpin, who busies her head with an ordering of the social scheme (and indeed of the universe) that secretly asserts her own power over it.

Now the conscious mind is not, of course, an autonomous faculty. O'Connor well knew that consciousness has its roots deep in unconscious life and that the will toward a proud self-reliance does not originate full blown in the intellect. Nevertheless, reason not only masks this deeper process but in a sense seems to endorse it, lends it plausibility and even an apparent nobleness. "Ye shall be as gods, knowing good and evil" (Genesis 3:5) is the oldest of temptations, but in a secularized universe it takes on the appearance of a necessary truth. Most of the protagonists of O'Connor's stories assume they inhabit such a universe, and they strike their godlike poses with comic complacency. For the heroes of the novels, however, no such unconscious ease is possible. Haze fears and Tarwater never really doubts that he lives in a theocentric world, and however humorous the homemade existentialism of the former or the rationalistic devil of the latter, both are forms of rebellion based on their claims to intellectual autonomy. "The devil," O'Connor once remarked, is "an evil intelligence determined on its own supremacy" (*Mystery and Manners*, p. 168), but since the only devil she was concerned with was the devil within, we might turn that statement around: the intelligence determined on its own supremacy becomes the habitat of the devil. In "The Comforts of Home," in fact, in the guise of the dead father who "take[s] up his station in Thomas's mind" (p. 395), it is quite literally that.

O'Connor's work thus dramatizes again and again the post-Descartian dissociation of sensibility, the conflict (to put it in the terms of religious man) between reason and faith, between the demands of the intellect and the hunger of the soul. The desire of such early characters as Ruller McFarney, Hazel Motes, and The Misfit for a sign is really for a kind of divine datum, a supernatural proof that would simultaneously appease the intellect and satisfy the spirit. They do not find such comforting signs, and indeed conceived as a tension between the demand to know and the will to believe, O'Connor finds the split unbridgeable: one side or the other—and the essential possibilities are dramatized in Haze and The Misfit— simply gives way. Yet almost from the start, the ascetic cast of her imagination had moved her toward another kind of resolution altogether.

As we have seen, all of O'Connor's central figures are dissociated creatures, versions of Enoch Emery whose "brain was divided into two parts" (*Wise Blood*, p. 87). One of these parts is the consciousness which, like Enoch's, is "stocked up with all kinds of words and phrases," the clichéd "trash" of the unexamined life; the other, of course, is the denied or forgotten, the ignored and suppressed side of the self—the unconscious, if you will. Psychologically considered, then, the ascetic action in the fiction works to purify, to burn away the contents of the conscious mind and so release the deepest response that has hidden behind it—to reveal, as she put it, "what we are essentially" (*Mystery and Manners*, p. 113). Precisely what is revealed can vary enormously, from the grandmother's gesture of love to Thomas's murderous fury, from Hulga Hopewell's childish trust to Tarwater's vision of the true object of his spiritual hunger. In some of these stories, the essence which emerges is that made familiar by modern psychology: the anger that lurks behind Thomas's placid exterior, for instance, or the childlike dependence masked by Hulga's and Julian's intellectual posturings, or the memories of his earlier life that old "General" Sash has forgotten. But in that last case, something more than the mechanics of repression seems suggested: the old man of "A Late Encounter with the Enemy" is made not merely to remember his past, but actively to reexperience it, to relive it in a brief but intensely emotional episode. The recovery of the past, in short, appears to involve more than bare recollection; sharply vivid, even physical, the images that assault him seem to signify a revival of his imagination. Certainly in the grandmother's final gesture, in her discovery in The Misfit of her own metaphorical child, we become aware of an imaginative release that enables her for the first time to see beyond the limits of her own ego. But these are early stories. The imagination, O'Connor discovered, might accomplish much more: it might become the channel of visionary awareness.

In her view of imagination and her distinction of it from reason O'Connor seems Thomistic indeed. Aquinas had argued not only the superiority of revelation to reason, but the imagination as the faculty by which man might directly receive that revelation. Human apprehension of the divine does not come through the clear and distinct processes of reason. "It proceeds by no measured steps, which can be checked by laws of logic and detached scientific observation; it is an *intuitus*, an intuition—a vision—more especially an inward vision or audition—an *instinctus*, an *inspiratio*." It is the imagination (*phantasia*), with its ability to withdraw itself from the immediate, to reform its sense impressions in its own way, and thus become a receptacle for the "'remote' in space or time" that is for Aquinas the vehicle of divine (or indeed, demonic) knowledge. The imagination can of course be directed by the will—as in the conscious creation of a work of art—but it seems most open to revelation when it is withdrawn, that is, when it is unconscious. In short, "it is through the subrational that the super-rational is brought to human consciousness."[15]

For O'Connor as for Aquinas, it is the imagination, with its roots deep in the human unconscious, that is the link between the depths of the self and the unseen reaches of the universe, that can reveal to finite man his apocalyptic destiny. As much a part of the "essential self" as the repressions revealed by modern psychology, the imagination for her is as dangerous a force as any named by Freud, for what it opens to, in those shattering climaxes when it achieves release, are the unwanted visions that ravage the lives of her protagonists. The early church fathers, in a metaphor deeply congenial to her, had spoken of "the eye of the soul," which, when awakened, opened to a direct awareness of the divine. Like them, she shows that the coming of visionary knowledge "leave[s] behind . . . the activities of the intellect."[16] But in her fiction the violence of the opposition between reason and imagination pushes the orthodox distinction between these faculties to its extreme limit. If the visions of her later work are a form of knowledge indeed, they are not only unavailable to but actively opposed by any motion of the discursive intellect. Reason leads not toward revelation but away from it: the rationalistic tendency is one of abstraction from the earth, from the body, from the concrete world altogether, an attempt to withdraw into a self-created and self-contained "mental bubble" ("Everything That Rises Must Converge," p. 411). The imagination, on the other hand, feeds on the world of the senses, and her climactic visions present their knowledge as experience, supernatural awareness that comes in the images of the natural world. This double affirmation of both the material and the spiritual, in opposition to the barren abstractions of reason, is perhaps O'Connor's ultimate fidelity to the sacramental commitment of her own imagination.

Thus, the desire for knowledge that had so dogged her early protagonists is fulfilled with a vengeance in the later work. Conforming to no reasonable expectation, answering no conscious desire, it is an altogether different knowledge from the signs sought by those early characters. O'Connor's visions are not a comforting proof of an ordered universe, but appalling, all-encompassing confrontations of the self with that dimension of Being which is also Other, the terrifying unveilings of genuine *gnosis*. None of O'Connor's characters seek *this* kind of knowledge. If, like Tarwater, they suspect its existence at all, they flee it with all their energy.

Throughout her mature work, the ascetic pressure of the action always thrusts her protagonists toward an eschatological extreme where the essential self declares its nature, where the habits of the conscious mind collapse under the violent onslaught of events and the imagination may be released. However, the limits of that extreme horizon shift as one moves from the earlier to the later fiction. The Misfit's epitaph for the grandmother, "She would of been a good woman . . . if it had been somebody there to shoot her every minute of her life," ("A Good Man Is Hard to Find," p. 133) suggests accurately that *Wise Blood* and the stories that immediately follow it move repeatedly to, but never beyond, death. Old "General" Sash is not the only one who makes "a desperate effort to see over it [death] and find out what comes after" ("A Late Encounter with the Enemy," p. 143), yet if any succeed, their discoveries are not part of their stories. But by the period of *Everything That Rises Must Converge* and *The Violent Bear It Away*, O'Connor has expanded her eschatological horizons, and if death continues to be present everywhere, so now are threatening intimations of the divine and the demonic and those final visions that move us toward the dimension beyond death. In her first mature work, Hazel Motes had been obsessed with the terrible finality of the closing coffin lid; in her last-published story, old Tanner imagines bursting free of his temporarily confining pine box. The title of that last story is "Judgement Day."

III

The powerful tensions of O'Connor's imagination seem to have drawn her inevitably toward the ascetic and eschatological poles, towards the complementary motions of denial and affirmation that mark all her work, and the development of her sacramental vision serves only to extend the apocalyptic dimensions of her fiction. However extreme these concerns, however outside the more moderate traditions of Christian humanism, they are not without precedent in the thought of the church. Augustine, Aquinas, and other early church fathers, to say nothing of the New Testament itself, could all supply justifying texts for these tendencies in her work. But O'Connor chose to identify herself with a role that, for the Catholic, would seem rather more questionable. As a writer of fiction she was, she said, a prophet.

Now the spirit may blow where it listeth, but as the institutional guardian of the prophetic Word, the church has hardly been hospitable to the individual voice crying, "Thus sayeth the Lord." O'Connor knew this very well: in affirming her link with a biblical type left undeveloped by historical Catholicism, she seems characteristically to have been asserting both her traditionalism and her independence. "The prophet," she declared, "is a man apart. He is not typical of a group." On the other hand, she had the curious conviction that if "you leave a man alone with his Bible and the Holy Ghost inspires him, he's going to be a Catholic one way or another" (*The Habit of Being*, p. 517). Furthermore, "for the Catholic novelist, the prophetic vision is not simply a matter of his personal imaginative gift; it is also a matter of the Church's gift" (*Mystery and Manners*, p. 179). To call herself a prophet, then, was apparently to affirm both her Catholicism and her individuality, the traditional and the innovative, the church's vision and her own.

It was vision O'Connor emphasized whenever she spoke of the figure of the prophet, and if Catholicism could provide her with nothing in the way of prophetic models, it did contain a well-developed tradition of that other type of visionary, the mystic (however suspiciously it often viewed this similarly extreme figure[17]). The mystic's final goal, ecstasy or union with the divine, seems foreign to O'Connor's temperament, but the earlier stages of the mystical way, purification and illumination, certainly were not. For prophetic experience she would have had to go directly to the Bible for precedents, but the mystics had left a considerable body of writing in which she read extensively,[18] and her fiction often blends the prophetical and mystical strains. In *The Violent Bear It Away*, to take the most obvious example, much of the prophetic material is directly on the surface. The boy protagonist's reluctance to assume his vocation is the novel's *donné*, and explicit references to Elisha and Elijah, Moses, Habbakuk, Jonah, Daniel, and so on establish the Tarwaters as heirs of the Old Testament prophets. But of course as post-Christian prophets, they make overt use of the New Testament as well. One of the most important of these latter references is to Jesus as the Bread of Life, which young Tarwater decides early on he is "not hungry for" (p. 21). The metaphor is pursued literally: when the boy arrives in the city, he becomes aware of a "strangeness in his stomach, a peculiar hunger" (p. 161) that first leaves him unsatisfied with ordinary food, then causes him to vomit, and finally prevents him from eating at all. Only in his final vision does he recognize the object of his hunger and sees that it unites him with "a line of men whose lives were chosen to sustain it," and that "nothing on earth would fill him" (pp. 242, 241).

Tarwater thus becomes linked with a wider tradition than the prophetic—with all those who *know* that their true country is elsewhere and will never be satisfied with anything less. But the metaphor through which O'Connor has dramatized his craving, that of insatiable hunger, was common to the mystics. Speaking of the illuminated soul, Ruysbroeck said: "Here there begins an eternal hunger, which shall never more be satisfied. . . . These men are poor indeed: for they are hungry and greedy, and their hunger is insatiable! Whatsoever they eat and drink they shall never be satisfied, for this hunger is eternal."[19] Even more pertinent, a number of mystics, among them Saint Catherine of Genoa and Saint Catherine of Siena, apparently underwent ordeals very much like Tarwater's. For periods they desired no ordinary food, and when they did attempt to eat, regurgitated. Of Saint Catherine of Siena we are told that "food became no longer necessary to her, and the attempt to swallow it was attended by extraordinary sufferings." That both of these saints could be assuaged only by the Eucharist is also relevant to Tarwater's hunger. For as a fundamentalist Protestant, with no such relief in the Sacrament, his unappeasable appetite starkly dramatizes Ruysbroeck's observation, "It is the inward craving and hankering of the affective power and created spirit after an Uncreated Good." Tarwater's vision is firmly within the prophetic tradition, but its specific contents are borrowed from the mystics.[20]

Yet in allying herself with that ancient tradition, O'Connor did so not simply by portraying prophetic characters but by declaring herself, as writer, to be a prophet—rather a different matter. She did not use the term in its popular sense of one who "predict[s] the future" (Mystery and Manners, p. 179), nor even in its common literary sense of one who uses fiction as the vehicle of an urgent moral message. In fact, neither observation of the prophetic figures in her fiction nor culling her remarks outside of it reveals her full conception of that role. The latter do little more than identify prophecy with imagination (rather than the moral sense) and generally speak of it in ways that make it sound interchangeable with sacramental vision. Yet when she insisted, "The fiction writer should be characterized by his vision. His kind of vision is prophetic vision" (Mystery and Manners, p. 179), she knew, with respect to her own work, whereof she spoke. However she may have come by it, Flannery O'Connor had an astonishing grasp not of modern versions of the prophetic, but of the biblical stance itself. The concept of prophecy both includes and extends those aspects of her work we have been observing to become, finally, the most encompassing metaphor for the religious dimensions of her fiction.

At its root prophecy is, as O'Connor repeatedly claimed, a matter of vision. Speaking of the biblical prophets, Abraham Heschel comments, "Prophecy may be described as *exegesis of existence from a divine perspective*." As a result, the prophet is possessed of a very particular kind of double vision: "His view is oblique. God is the focal point of his thought, and the world is seen as reflected in God. Indeed, the main task of prophetic thinking is to bring the world into divine focus. . . . He does not take a direct approach to things. It is not a straight line, spanning subject and object, but rather a triangle—through God to the object. . . . The prophet's eye is directed to the contemporary scene; the society and its conduct are the main theme of his speeches. Yet his ear is inclined to God. . . . his true greatness is his ability to hold God and man in a single thought."[21]

In O'Connor's fiction, this prophetic double focus, the "holding God and man in a single thought," results in the simultaneous satiric and apocalyptic perspectives of her work. The outrage and condemnation that the Old Testament prophets hurled at the apostasy of the Israelites becomes, in her hands, the acerbic irony and the mocking caricatures that reveal their modern equivalents, while the divine perspective, fierce, threatening, biding its time, is embodied in the landscape, seeming to lurk there awaiting the opportunity to reveal itself. From this point of view, the prophetic voice O'Connor adopts becomes the tonal equivalent of her native asceticism, that asceticism which on the level of action drives her characters toward their purgatorial eye-openings. "The prophet not only conveys; he reveals. He almost does unto others what God does unto him. In speaking, the prophet reveals God."[22] O'Connor's form of prophetic speaking is of course the entire expression of a story, and whatever may be unveiled to the protagonists, her stance reveals the divine perspective to the reader.

Once more we should note that the full dimensions of the prophetic vision do not appear in her work from the start. In *Wise Blood* the characteristic ironic voice and satiric perception, the sense of outrage, the use of caricature and parody emerge clearly, but the voice itself must carry the entire prophetic burden of the novel, for there the apocalyptic sense is so thoroughly otherworldly that it cannot be embodied in the texture of the work. It is, again, only with the development of the sacramental landscape and the visionary mode that O'Connor reaches the full development of her prophetic vision.

Yet if the full flowering comes only later, the essentials of that vision are apparent by 1952. The prophetic view is necessarily one of radical tensions; it inevitably presents a world off balance, in which only extremes have genuine existence. "The prophet hates the approximate, he shuns the middle of the road. Man must live on the summit to avoid the abyss. . . . Compromise is an attitude the prophet abhors." Making no concessions to human weakness, consumed by his revelation of divine imperatives, he is "an unbearable extremist."[23] From this perspective, sinful man has not merely fallen away from his proper role and duties; he is in active rebellion against God.[24] Augustine gave the classic Christian expression of this view in his identification of the inhabitants of his two cities: "So it is that two cities have been made by two loves; the earthly city by love of self to the exclusion of God, the heavenly by love of God to the exclusion of self."[25] In the laconic words of *The Violent Bear It Away*, "Jesus or *you*."

O'Connor's version of this essential prophetic view is her repeated portrayal of the divided self. The state of her protagonists as their stories begin is one of revolt against the divine order (whether they are aware of this or not), yet deep within, usually unacknowledged, they harbor an inherent desire for God. Here of course she follows orthodox Christian thinking; perhaps the expression of this human doubleness that comes closest to her own conception is that of Saint Bernard of Clairvaux: "The soul's essential nature, as Augustine taught, is to be an image of God. The fall of man was the obscuring of the divine image by a dissimilitude, an 'unlikeness' superimposed on it. But the image itself is indestructible: every man retains his 'capacity for the eternal.' . . . [Thus] the so-called 'annihilation' of self is the doing-away of the unlikeness; and since the image of God in becoming unlike God became unlike itself, the love which restores the divine similitude restores the soul to itself."[26] The ascetic purging away of the fallen self, then, reveals the indwelling "capacity for the eternal." But in the fallen state, the state of rebellion, that suppressed capacity can emerge in curious forms, the most outrageous of which is the figure of the pseudo-Christ.

From the "new jesus" of *Wise Blood* to the fantasy Jesus Mrs. Turpin conjures up in "Revelation" to confirm her self-satisfaction, O'Connor repeatedly dramatizes the revolt against God as the creation of human substitutes for Him. Mr. Shiftlet of "The Life You Save May Be Your Own" and Manley Pointer of "Good Country People" are versions of the pseudo-Christ as con man, easily betraying those who put their faith in them; Thomas of "The Comforts of

Home" attempts to adopt the attitude of God and ends with a gun in his hand; Rayber believes in salvation through human effort, but he saves himself only for emptiness; and Singleton of "The Partridge Festival" turns out to be not a Christ figure but a psychopath. In suggesting both the inherent human desire for God and the rebellion against Him that locates that desire in man himself, this series of "Christ-haunted" figures illustrates Jung's law of psychological compensation: "It is a psychological rule that when an archetype has lost its metaphysical hypostasis, it becomes identified with the conscious mind of the individual, which it influences and refashions in its own form. And since an archetype always possesses a certain numinosity, the integration of the numen generally produces an inflation of the subject."[27]

To the dualistic, prophetic consciousness, that inflation has an inevitable result: when the rebellion against God takes the form of projecting His image onto man, by ironic inversion the pseudo-Christ becomes an antichrist, the mock savior gives off the odor not of sanctity but of the pit. This perception is at the center of "The Lame Shall Enter First," that story of a "tin Jesus" who in attempting to play God proves to be inadequately human; incapable of admitting his own limitations, he becomes responsible for his child's death and thereby justifies Rufus Johnson's taunt, "Satan has you in his power" (p. 477). The central irony of the story lies in the contradiction between Sheppard's conscious and unconscious beliefs. As a modern intellectual atheist he rejects Johnson's fundamentalism as mere "rubbish," but so deeply "Christ-haunted" is he that he has unwittingly adopted the role himself. Thus Sheppard is not, as he thinks, free of Christianity; while consciously rejecting its tenets, he has unconsciously refashioned them in a secular context, with disastrous results. Like that other professing atheist Hulga Hopewell of "Good Country People," he has been unable to exist without a savior, but whereas "Hulga's" projection of that part onto the Bible salesman betrays only herself, Sheppard's abdication of his human role for a divine one leaves the body of his son as his accuser.

The inherent longing for the divine, unwanted, suppressed, often corresponding to no conscious desire, expresses itself in other forms than the "Christ-haunted" figure, from The Misfit's anguished awareness of the possibility of the Resurrection to O. E. Parker's need for the Byzantine tattoo, from Mr. Fortune's sudden vision of the transfigured woods to Asbury Fox's irritated perception of his home town transformed into a "temple for a god he didn't know" ("The Enduring Chill," p. 357). It is of course the overt concern of both novels where the torn hero is mirrored by an antihero who parodies his self-division. The ascetic action in all of these works is to allow for a purification of the rebellious self, to offer the possibility of opening the sleeping eye of the soul, to discover the image of God mirrored in the depths of the self.

When Hazel Motes turns from his particular rebellion against Jesus, the violent physical asceticism he adopts is entirely appropriate to *Wise Blood*. The pervasive antimaterialism of that novel makes his mortification of the body the inevitable expression of renunciation. Yet nowhere else in O'Connor's work do we find any justification for this denial of the senses. Indeed, when the motif appears again in Rayber of *The Violent Bear It Away* it is as a parody of young Tarwater's internal struggle. The schoolteacher is presented as engaged in "a rigid ascetic discipline" (p. 114), a suppression of sense and feeling designed to keep his mad vision of an apocalyptic universe at bay. In his physical mortifications, this antihero of O'Connor's second novel seems to gaze across at the hero of her first with the effect of ironic repudiation. For after *Wise Blood*, the ascetic impulse in her work takes an entirely different direction.

As we have seen, far from denying the body and the senses, the asceticism in the later fiction works consistently to affirm them, to release them from the false consciousness of her protagonists in order to experience reality. But reality, to the prophetic mind, is always double: "This world, no mere shadow of ideas in an upper sphere, is real, but not absolute; the world's reality is contingent upon compatibility with God."[28] For O'Connor's sacramentalism, it is the natural world that becomes the vehicle of the supernatural, and her characters' literal return to their senses becomes the means of opening their imaginations to receive it. This double motion in her fiction is part of a single process, and that process depends on mortification not of the body, but of the mind. As she observed, "violence is strangely capable of returning my characters to reality and preparing them to accept their moments of grace. Their heads are so hard that almost nothing else will do the work" (*Mystery and Manners*, p. 112).

It is entirely characteristic that where the biblical prophets spoke of the hardness of man's heart, O'Connor comments on the hardness of her characters' heads, for although the terms do not exclude one another, her emphasis reveals once again her deep mistrust of the mind. Certainly the recalcitrance of the head is evident enough in the intellectual figures, but it is equally operative in those characters whose pretensions may seem humbler but are no less arrogantly self-deluding. Thus the central pattern in the fiction after *Wise Blood* is the unexpected encounter of the senses with a physical reality which breaks through the presuppositions of the conscious mind and releases the long-suppressed imagination. Mr. Head—deliberately named—discovers Atlanta as a physical actuality rather than a moral paradigm before receiving the "action of mercy"; the grandmother touches The Misfit in recognizing him as one of her own; Tarwater is raped before undergoing his vision; Mrs. Turpin stares fixedly at the hogs before receiving her revelation; and it is the bull's violent embrace that leads to the unbearable opening of Mrs. May's eyes. Everywhere the raw contact with physical actuality, an affirmation of the senses, precipitates the onset of awareness of the divine.

The violence of this "return to the senses" is the result of her characters' stance of rebellion, their persistent if often unwitting revolt against God. Although she was aware that "our age is an age of searchers and discoverers" (*Mystery and Manners*, p. 159), in her fiction she literally could not imagine man deliberately and consciously seeking God. Thus the dominant cast of the religious event in her fiction is what Heschel calls "anthropotropic" rather than "theotropic": the "turning of a transcendent Being toward man" rather than the "turning of man toward a transcendent Being." Since the biblical prophetic experience is the classic example of anthropotropism, this central feature of O'Connor's religious imagination seems the projection of her own prophetic consciousness into the very form of her fiction, for despite her characters' stifled desire for God, what emerges most powerfully in her work is "a sense of being reached, being found, being sought after; a sense of being pursued."[29]

This "hound of heaven" motif[30] appears as early as *Wise Blood* in the "dark ragged figure" of Jesus that Haze's grandfather promises will "chase him over the waters of sin" (p. 22). But that image remains "in the back of his mind," the center of a fear and longing that in this novel receives no exterior embodiment. By the time of *The Violent Bear It Away*, however, the divine presence appears to haunt the landscape itself. Tarwater becomes aware of a threatening "silent country," to cross into which would be to lose forever "his own inclinations," and with his developing hunger, "a silence inside akin to the silence outside," the boy feels himself in a "grand trap" set by his "adversary" (pp. 160, 221, 162, 93).

The sense of anthropotropic pursuit reaches well back in Christian tradition beyond Francis Thompson's famous poem. It was, Evelyn Underhill remarks, "common to all the mediaeval mystics,"[31] and makes several notable appearances in Augustine's *Confessions*: "You are ever close upon the heels of those who flee from You, for You are at once God of Vengeance and Fount of Mercy."[32] It is this divinity that animates the fierce suns and glaring skies that appear with increasing frequency in O'Connor's stories, and it is this divinity that once memorably employs animal agency, as if O'Connor were deliberately recalling Thompson's poem. "Greenleaf" centers around a scrub bull invested with clear symbolic significance, and it is particularly notable in that it is the single O'Connor work, to my eye, in which the protagonist (and the bull's victim), Mrs. May, seems to harbor no longing, however suppressed, for the divine. Dreams, which are the agents of revelation in other stories, here promise only destruction, and although the language of love that O'Connor borrows from the mystics and the Song of Songs identifies Mrs. May as the bride of Christ, it is a role she fatally resists.[33] The bull thus turns from the "patient god come down to woo her" of his first appearance to the "wild tormented lover" (pp. 311, 333) of the story's climax, his two horns simultaneously embracing and killing her. As for Augustine, love and vengeance seem to be one, and the cost of Mrs. May's revelation measures the fullness of her denial: she is the only O'Connor character who pays for her vision with her life.

"Greenleaf" seems to mark an extreme limit in O'Connor's work. Such violent overpowering of the self by a God unknown and apparently undesired appears nowhere else in her fiction. Taken by itself, it might well suggest the theological doctrine of the irresistibility of grace, but the very next story she published, "A View of the Woods," shows its protagonist, Mr. Fortune, quite capable of resisting his saving vision and rushing onward to his own and his granddaughter's destruction. An attentive reading of even such a work as "The Enduring Chill," in which the final paragraph speaks of "the frail defense he had set up in his *mind* to protect him from what was coming" (p. 382; italics added) reveals that we are in the familiar territory of the divided will. The descent of the Holy Ghost is at the same time the release of Asbury's stifled imagination, the bird that has been "sitting huffy" in the cage of his ego and that has peeked out in his brief vision of the town's transformation at the story's start. It is, we note, Asbury's mind that protests, the false consciousness that is broken through when bird calls to bird, as it were, and imagination and grace become one to produce the story's final vision. The menacing motif of the pursuing God appears here in the "fierce bird" that has hovered on the boy's ceiling since childhood, but the use of bird imagery throughout the story reveals that although Asbury's mind attempts to deny it, this is a bird that he deeply desires to know.

As just these three stories suggest—and they were written, in this sequence, between 1956 and 1958—the operations of O'Connor's God are more frightening than any doctrine of the ways of grace would suggest precisely because they are past all human finding out. Why He should prove fatally irresistible to the unsuspecting Mrs. May yet be easily withstood by Mr. Fortune seems a conundrum not to be answered by appeals to free will (what freedom has Mrs. May in the matter?) but leads directly to the realm of terrifying mystery. The direct prophetic revelation, as Aquinas pointed out, "is governed by no laws of logic or method, it is not even subject to the recipient's volition; it may well be . . . clean contrary to it."[34] That God works in mysterious ways is the hoariest of pious clichés; in O'Connor's fiction it becomes frighteningly realized. He is, she had pointed out, "an unlimited God" (*Mystery and Manners*, p. 161), not to be confined within any human formulation of His workings. His ways are not, finally, our ways.

Yet if her God is unlimited, He has also "revealed himself specifically" (*Mystery and Manners*, p. 161); if He is at last inscrutable, He is not immediately so. Why anyone should be born hermaphroditic, for example, is unanswerable, but that *all* bodies are "temples of the Holy Ghost" has been disclosed to us. Similarly, we may recognize that Mrs. Turpin's revelation perfectly illustrates the text "The last shall be first" even if, as the story's allusion to Job suggests, it serves finally to deepen the mystery of that text rather than to explain it: why *should* the last be first? However, a closer look at Mrs. Turpin's vision, although it cannot dissolve the essential mysteriousness contained in it, does begin to yield part of an answer.

The "last" of this world who lead the procession—the "white-trash," the "niggers," the "freaks and lunatics"—have been throughout "Revelation" contrasted to Mrs. Turpin. Without attempting to make them humanly attractive, O'Connor has deftly suggested the deprivations of their lives—the poverty and illness of the "trash," the condescending racism suffered by the blacks, the physical and emotional pain of the "lunatic" Mary Grace. Against Mrs. Turpin, with her "good disposition" and her "little bit of everything," their lot in life is suffering. They stand with those many other secondary figures in O'Connor's fiction, with the boys of "A Circle in the Fire," the refugees of "The Displaced Person," the unnamed blacks of "The Artificial Nigger," with the carnival freak, Norton, and Sarah Ham, for all of whom misery is the given condition. Their existence has imposed on them the pain of an asceticism the protagonists of these stories do not know. What is startling is not the repeated implication of the Christian value of this suffering, but the suggestion that *only* suffering has value in God's eyes.

In "Revelation" Mrs. Turpin's vision shows *all* of the procession passing "through a field of living fire" (p. 508) that cleanses everyone not only of his sins, but also of his virtues. Those like herself, who had possessed "good order and common sense and respectable behavior," who had been blessed with a "God-given wit," discover that although these gifts are apparently their worldly responsibility, they have no final value in themselves. O'Connor noted that "the man in the violent situation reveals those qualities least dispensable in his personality, those qualities which are all he will have to take into eternity with him" (*Mystery and Manners*, p. 114), yet all that the visionary procession of "Revelation" clearly carries into eternity with it is the purifying action of the fire itself. Indeed, while the im-

225

agery of fire in O'Connor's fiction may be demonic, it is most often purgatorial ("Be saved in the Lord's fire or perish in your own!"), and what it signals is the infliction of a searing grace, the onset of a saving pain. As their woods burn, Mrs. Cope and her daughter of "A Circle in the Fire" discover "a new misery" they "had never felt before" (p. 193). Hazel Motes burns out his eyes with quicklime, and the "scorched eyes" that Tarwater earns lead directly to the cleansing configuration and vision at the climax of *The Violent Bear It Away*. As his great uncle had warned him, "Even the mercy of the Lord burns" (p. 20).

Such suffering is central to the prophetic consciousness. "The prophet is prepared for pain. One of the effects of his presence is to intensify the people's capacity for suffering, to rend the veil that lies between life and pain."[35] Yet O'Connor's native asceticism seems more radical still. It receives its most explicit statement at the end of "The Artificial Nigger." The little statue that rescues the Heads and releases the divine "action of mercy" is described as a "monument to another's victory," a victory that seems to spring directly from the "wild look of misery" the figure presents. The bond between suffering and triumph is clarified in the story's penultimate paragraph. Feeling again the flamelike "action of mercy," Mr. Head "understood that it grew out of agony, which is not denied to any man and which is given in strange ways to children. He understood it was all a man could carry into death to give his Maker and he suddenly burned with shame that he had so little of it to take with him. He stood appalled" (p. 269). The possibly deliberate syntactical ambiguity of the second sentence—does "it" there refer to "the action of mercy" or to "agony"?—makes the reciprocal dynamics of Mr. Head's perception apparent. It is suffering, and suffering alone, that makes available to man the burning grace of a purifying mercy, and the return of this merciful agony to its Source is the only gift of value man can offer God. As for Hopkins, the world is in a double sense "charged with the grandeur of God," yet for O'Connor it is not beauty that we must give back, but pain, the *imitatio Christi* of the crucified self.

This ascetic imperative in O'Connor is a part of that prophetic consciousness that "holds God and man in a single thought"; perhaps it helps explain why the true focus of her fiction is the relation-

ship of man with God rather than with his fellow man, what Kierkegaard called the religious as distinguished from the ethical sphere.
The two are not, of course, easily separable, and O'Connor repeatedly directs her prophetic outrage at that flouting of the divine Word
that reveals itself in moral failure. From the Christian perspective,
such failure can only result from the rampant egotism that expresses
itself as lack of love, from the grandmother's complacent self-con-
cern in "A Good Man Is Hard to Find" to Mrs. McIntyre's lack of
charity in "The Displaced Person," from Mrs. Turpin's self-serving
"good works" in "Revelation" to that most culpable offense, the parental indifference that leads to children's deaths in "The River" and
"The Lame Shall Enter First." Yet it would be facile to assume, by
the principle of reversal, that return to God automatically produces
the overflowing of "a golden heart" (*Mystery and Manners*, p. 192).

As a writer of fiction, Flannery O'Connor simply had no interest
in—no imagination for—"a socially desirable Christianity" (*The
Habit of Being*, p. 517). Indeed, the glimpses she gives of Christian
action hardly give assurance that religious commitment leads to
conventional forms of charity. Mrs. Greenleaf, wallowing in the
mud in the throes of her faith healing, pleads with Jesus to "stab
[her] in the heart." Tarwater returns to the dark city with a prophetic
message to which no one will listen. And Rufus Johnson prosely-
tizes young Norton to his lonely death. These are certainly activities
which involve religious man in the life of this world, yet they exist,
at best, on the fringes of the recognizably ethical. In *The Violent
Bear It Away*, O'Connor goes further still. There, Rayber's sense of
"a world transfigured," of a sacramental universe with its roots in
the divine, evokes in him a powerful impulse of love, a love so intense that he feels impelled to throw himself "to the ground in an
act of idiot praise." Yet, as he recognizes, this love is without ethical
dimension; it has no purpose in the world beyond itself. "It was not
the kind that could be used for the child's [Bishop's] improvement or
his own. It was love without reason, love for something future-
less, love that appeared to exist only to be itself, imperious and all-
demanding" (pp. 113–14). Stamped unmistakably with the imprint
of O'Connor's God, this "all-demanding" force has, as Rayber sees,
no recognizable earthly use whatever. Like the idiot child who is its

focus, such love is wholly gratuitous; beyond reason, all-consuming, it offers nothing to the humanist mind but the imperative to abandon itself.

It is characteristic that Rayber should be made to experience this overpowering love as pain, and nothing so clearly moves him toward the lost as his determination to escape from suffering. With Bishop's death he may have freed himself from his sacramental vision to achieve the supreme dignity his stoicism offers, the release into *apatheia*: "To feel nothing was peace" (p. 200). As Hazel Motes might have told him, "there's no peace for the redeemed" (*Wise Blood*, p. 140), and if Rayber's ideal of indifference is the most radical denial of suffering in O'Connor, that same drive frequently takes the form of affirmation of the pleasure principle. It is an urge that can assume a number of guises, from Thomas's attachment to his "comforts" to "General" Sash's overweening vanity, from the inflated fantasizing of the child of "A Temple of the Holy Ghost" to the moral gourmandism of Sheppard, who "had stuffed his own emptiness with good works like a glutton" ("The Lame Shall Enter First," p. 481). Such characters may know not what they do, but The Misfit, again, had articulated the choice for all of them: give up all for Jesus or "enjoy the few minutes you got left the best way you can" ("A Good Man Is Hard to Find," p. 132). Demanding everything, valuing only our diminishments, bringing not peace but a sword, O'Connor's Deity corresponds to no recognizable humanistic value. A Christian version of the fierce and awesome God of the prophets, He requires of man the total surrender of "his own inclinations" (*The Violent Bear It Away*, p. 221). Little wonder, then, that in the face of such a divinity her characters all run the other way: it is a fearful thing indeed to fall into the hands of the living God.[36]

IV

Concrete, passionate, and imaginative, poetic in its form, prophetic speech is nonetheless "a sharp sword," conveying a vision "designed to shock rather than edify."[37] Among other things, O'Connor's adoption of the prophetic stance enabled her to escape the writing of didactic fiction, of which she had a horror. From any humanistic standpoint, Christian or otherwise, the radical demands of the

Christianity embodied in her work can hardly seem enticing. She was aware of this herself; when *The Violent Bear It Away* was about to appear, she wrote a friend that she expected an unfavorable response "since there was nothing appealing in it."[38] Between the satirical perspective trained on her unaware protagonists and the apocalyptic view opened up to them, there is no possible compromise, no comfortable *via media*. Rebellion must therefore be the natural state of sinful man and not merely of the hypothetical modern man her essays and lectures seem so often concerned with. But a God who reveals Himself only in our pain, and who reveals Himself in order to demand all from us, will in any age be a stumbling block, and not only to nonbelievers.

Again and again the revolt of her protagonists takes the form of an exaltation of consciousness, of the mind, as the seat of their illusory self-sufficiency. The antiintellectual strain in her work, apparent as far back as "The Barber" and "The Turkey," receives its most extreme statement in *The Violent Bear It Away*. When she commented that "Rayber's thought has ceased to be dialogue—no voice answers him, no voice questions,"[39] she neglected to add that the same is true of Tarwater by the end of the novel. At the conclusion of their stories, these two figures are mirror images of one another: Rayber seems left with nothing but his reason, while Tarwater has burned his away altogether. That questioning, answering, plausible, empirical, skeptical, logical voice is of course identified with the devil, but it is that very identification of the discursive intellect with the demonic that is so deeply shocking in the novel. If grace completes nature rather than destroying it, as the central Catholic tradition holds, then nature here excludes the practical reason—a position well outside of orthodoxy.

Despite her real debt to Aquinas, O'Connor's affinities on this issue are not with the Thomistic tradition but with the antiintellectual strain in the church which appears, for instance, in the *Imitation of Christ* and in a number of the mystics. It is a strain that may be traced back to Augustine, who, while hardly to be characterized as an antirationalist, nevertheless deeply mistrusted the restlessness of the intellect. As Henri Marrou comments, "We cannot too strongly insist on the negative, or at least suspicious, attitude towards every kind of knowledge which is not very directly ordained to the supreme and only end of Man, to eternal salvation, to God. All this is so much vain, weak curiosity, the unhappy consequence of man's disordered desires. Here indeed we have one of the really essential notes of Augustinian thought . . . troubling the western conscience and challenging it to make a choice which is, in fact, fundamental."[40]

That choice is indeed fundamental everywhere in O'Connor, but the protagonists of the stories are in their comic complacency unaware that there is any choice to be made, while the heroes of the novels, obviously deeply rent, absurdly keep insisting that Jesus is nothing to *them*. The ascetic pressure of the action in her fiction, which strips, or fails to strip, the scales from their eyes, in either case brings them to a commitment which ends their self-divided state. The movement from the double to the single self is of course a classic religious phenomenon, and it is revealing to compare the traditional quality of that experience with what we find in O'Connor's work. William James's *The Varieties of Religious Experience* provides here an authoritative commentary. When he speaks of the central experience of the divided self—"There are two lives, the natural and the spiritual, and we must lose the one before we can participate in the other"—we are clearly in the general territory held by O'Connor's fiction. But when he goes on to describe the typical sense of "unification," we might be in another land altogether. "However it come," James writes, "it brings a characteristic sort of relief; and never such extreme relief as when it is cast into the religious mould. Happiness! Happiness! . . . Easily, permanently, and successfully, it often transforms the most intolerable misery into the profoundest and most enduring happiness. . . . the loss of all the worry, the sense that all is ultimately well with one, the peace, the harmony . . . the ecstasy of happiness."[41]

No reader of O'Connor will need to be told that James's language, drawn from many autobiographical accounts, is hardly appropriate to the awakenings of Tarwater or Hazel Motes, of Mrs. Turpin or Asbury Fox, of the grandmother or Mrs. May, of Mr. Head or O. E. Parker. Pain, shock, terror, awe—these terms from the other end of the emotional spectrum more nearly characterize those moments of unification in her work than the "peace," "relief," "harmony," "happiness," of James's account. Much of the difference, surely, derives from O'Connor's prophetic stance, from her portrayal of the anthropotropic rather than the theotropic experience, of figures whose discovery of the divine is both sudden and reluctant, a violent surprise. Those moments are always a kind of death, an annihilation of the known self, whether literal death is involved or not. The very use of the grotesque mode itself involved for her the intimations of those devastating revelations. "There is always an intensity about [the grotesque]," she claimed, "that creates a general discomfort, that brings with it a slight hint of death to the ego, a kind of memento mori that leaves us for an instant alone facing the ineffable."[42] The "death to the ego" is yet another expression of that deep asceticism which finds in those climactic experiences not the beginnings of peace but its end, not joy but pain. Indeed, the traditional term *unification* is itself misleading, for the emphasis in O'Connor falls, as we have seen, not on a bringing together, but on a splitting apart, not on harmony, but on sundering.

In their intensity and revolutionary effect, these climactic moments resemble more the awakening of the mystic than they do conversion in its usual sense. This is the opening of "the transcendental consciousness," not "religious conversion as ordinarily understood: the sudden and emotional acceptance of religious beliefs." It is an "unselfing" in which "the larger world-consciousness now press[es] in on the individual consciousness. Often it breaks in suddenly and becomes a great new revelation."[43] Yet this is also the prophetic sense of *inspiration*: "It is experienced as a divine act which takes place *not within* but *beyond*, as an event which happens in one's view rather than in one's heart. The prophet does not merely feel it; he faces it."[44] But although the awakening seems to come wholly from without, in O'Connor's work it comes from within also, for it entails the "emergence of intuitions from below the threshold," the "opening of the soul's eye."[45] The agony involved in these "unselfings," the violence of the transformations, are an index of the apocalyptic stakes, for a new vision demands a new man, a "transfigured universe" requires a creature transfigured to behold it. Only with the annihilation of the old consciousness does the new vision become possible.

O'Connor's deep strain of asceticism thus comes more and more in her fiction to work as a complement to her sacramentalism. If in *Wise Blood* it was the means of leaving behind a totally corrupt and impenetrable world, sunk in a matter incapable of revealing spirit, that same ascetic impulse gradually becomes the means of penetrating substance to reveal the vision of a universe both immanent and transcendent, in which here and hereafter, like interlocking arms, are both distinct realities that yet remain indissolubly linked, joined at the crosspiece of death. In this universe, both ends of the great polarities—body and soul, matter and spirit, this world and the next—are real. What is false is the self-aggrandizing consciousness, the overweening "mind" which in its illusory transcendence of the physical actualities of this world also creates an absurd competitor for the next, thus dissolving the creative tension between them, making both matter and spirit merely extensions of the self. Only pain is capable of piercing this pretension, the violent stripping away of complacency that can return man to his unaccommodated condition as the grotesque inhabitant of a world ruled by an all-demanding God—and this is the role of the prophet. As Martin Buber pointed out, "The prophets of Israel have never announced a God upon whom their hearers' striving for security reckoned. They have always aimed to shatter all security and to proclaim in the opened abyss of the final insecurity the unwished-for God who demands that His human creatures become real, they become human, and confounds all who imagine that they can take refuge in the certainty that the temple of God is in their midst."[46]

The prophetic world is thus necessarily one of sharp polarities, for those who are not with Him are willy-nilly in rebellion against Him. "It is the extreme situation that best reveals what we are essentially" (*Mystery and Manners*, p. 113), but O'Connor's extreme situations reveal not only what but where we are, for it is only at those moments that her characters are violently returned to the actuality of the sensible world and, perhaps, are offered a glimpse of the eschatological dimensions of their universe. Death is everywhere, either as the literal extreme of earthly life or as its metaphorical equivalent, the death of the self brought about by the transfiguration of consciousness. But so too, as her career proceeds, are the intimations of those other "last things," the frightening presences of the divine and the demonic that are the ultimate poles of her apocalyptic universe.

In this prophetic vision, there is no room for compromise: moderation is a delusion, and only extremists are in touch with reality.

And yet, and yet . . . there is something too grimly sober in ending a study of Flannery O'Connor on this note. What seems partly to have escaped is the incorrigible sense of comedy that animates and burnishes her creations everywhere, that cannot quite be contained by any thesis about the religious dimensions of her fiction. It overflows the borders, leaps beyond the ironic tones and satiric perceptions that may be ascribed to the prophetic stance, beyond even the caricaturing that accompanies the pressures of the ascetic action, to maintain a life of its own. The laughter that arises may often be "mean," may even sometimes seem to come from her "devil," but it is finally more catholic than that as it jumps from author to reader, from one fallen nature to another, to embrace both the holy fools and idiots and the posturing rebels. It flows over the entire procession revealed to Mrs. Turpin, bringing together at last the "battalions of freaks and lunatics shouting and clapping and leaping like frogs" with those preposterously normal types in their absurd dignity—a view of all humanity, of all "souls . . . rumbling toward heaven" ("Revelation," p. 508), as an inherently comic spectacle. In a final tension with the terror and awe of her extreme vision of reality, O'Connor's comedy is both the balm which makes that vision bearable and the sense against which it jars, returning as yet again to the grotesque as the heart of her work. For beyond questions of character or action, Flannery O'Connor's stories and novels are as realized forms the offspring of her aesthetics of incongruity. Evoking simultaneously laughter and fear, in the totality of their impact they are themselves grotesques.

Notes

Introduction

1. Henry James, preface to *The American*. See *The Art of the Novel* (New York: Scribners, 1934), p. 31.
2. Characteristically, O'Connor herself pointed to her Catholicism in noting the "extreme action" in her fiction to fellow writer John Hawkes: "I can't allow any of my characters, in a novel anyway, to stop in some halfway position. This doubtless comes of a Catholic education and a Catholic sense of history—everything works toward its true end or away from it, everything is ultimately saved or lost" (*The Habit of Being*, p. 350).
3. Carl G. Jung, *Psychology and Religion: West and East*, trans. R. F. C. Hull (New York: Pantheon, 1958), p. 22.
4. John Henry Cardinal Newman, *Apologia pro vita sua*, ed. C. F. Harrold (London: Longmans, Green, 1947), pp. 126, 179–80.
5. C. Ross Mullins, Jr., "Flannery O'Connor: An Interview," *Jubilee* 11 (June 1963): 35.

Chapter 1. Early Work and *Wise Blood*

1. The chapters of *Wise Blood* published under the titles "The Peeler," "The Heart of the Park," and "Enoch and the Gorilla" were *not* conceived as independent stories: all three when originally published in *Partisan Review* and *New World Writing* were clearly labeled portions of a novel-in-progress (see also *The Habit of Being*, pp. 4–6, 17). This seems worth insisting on, since Robert Giroux's inclusion of them in *The Complete Stories*, together with his misleading comment that O'Connor was recommended for a prize on the basis of "the stories she

235

later incorporated into her novel-in-progress, *Wise Blood*" (*The Complete Stories*, p. viii), seems to validate their pseudostatus as independent pieces and, worse, to encourage the false view of her first novel as assembled out of stitched-together shorter works. As recently as John R. May's *The Pruning Word* (Notre Dame, Ind.: University of Notre Dame Press, 1976), we find these three pieces being discussed as self-sufficient works among O'Connor's other "uncollected stories." Similarly, "You Can't Be Any Poorer than Dead" is an early version of the opening chapter of *The Violent Bear It Away* and was clearly so marked on its first publication (see also *The Habit of Being*, p. 77). All four of these pieces are of interest for studies of the geneses of O'Connor's two novels; they tell us nothing, however, about her development as a writer of short stories.

For other discussions of O'Connor's early stories, see my "The Road to *Wise Blood*," *Renascence* 21 (1969): 181–94; Stuart L. Burns, "Flannery O'Connor's Literary Apprenticeship," *Renascence* 22 (1969): 3–16; Carter W. Martin, "Flannery O'Connor's Early Fiction," *Southern Humanities Review* 7 (1973): 210–14; and May, *The Pruning Word*, pp. 21–49.

2. The seventh, "Woman on the Stairs," twice revised before being included in *A Good Man Is Hard to Find* under the title "A Stroke of Good Fortune," grew out of a discarded portion of *Wise Blood*.

3. See the Bible salesman of "Good Country People."

4. Unpublished manuscript, Flannery O'Connor Collection, Georgia College, Milledgeville.

5. I have quoted here from the published version, *Sewanee Review* 56 (1948): 268, as being (oddly) even more Faulknerian than the comparable passage in the thesis version. Cf. *The Complete Stories*, p. 60.

6. It is appropriate here to recall her lifelong interest in painting and drawing, particularly her early talent for cartooning, another visual art that comically distorts and simplifies to reveal "essences."

7. See especially Stanley Edgar Hyman, *Flannery O'Connor* (Minneapolis: University of Minnesota Press, 1966), p. 43; Leon V. Driskell and Joan T. Brittain, *The Eternal Crossroads: The Art of Flannery O'Connor* (Lexington: University of Kentucky Press, 1971), pp. 14–16; Miles Orvell, *Invisible Parade: The Fiction of Flannery O'Connor* (Philadelphia: Temple University Press, 1972), pp. 51–52, 73.

8. "A Short Story Symposium," *Esprit* 3 (Winter 1959): 10.

9. Respectively, Robert Fitzgerald, introduction to *Everything That Rises Must Converge* (New York: Farrar, Straus and Giroux, 1965), p. xix; Lewis A. Lawson, "Flannery O'Connor and the Grotesque: *Wise Blood*,"

originally published in *Renascence* 17 (1965), conveniently reprinted in *Flannery O'Connor*, ed. Robert Reiter (St. Louis: B. Herder, 1968), p. 59; Caroline Gordon, "Flannery O'Connor's *Wise Blood*," *Critique* 2 (1958): 6.

10. Orvell, *Invisible Parade*, pp. 35–39, discusses affinities and differences between Poe and O'Connor generally; and Marion Montgomery, "Vision and the Eye for Detail in Poe and O'Connor," *Flannery O'Connor Bulletin* 6 (1977): 36–46, (despite finding a "hint of a parallel" between "William Wilson" and *Wise Blood*, as I do below) is mainly concerned to argue O'Connor's superiority to Poe. Neither makes a case for Poe's influence on O'Connor.

11. "Hulga" Hopewell's detachable wooden leg in "Good Country People" may owe something to this story of Poe's.

12. Cited in *The Added Dimension: The Art and Mind of Flannery O'Connor*, ed. Melvin J. Friedman and Lewis A. Lawson (New York: Fordham University Press, 1966), p. 251.

13. *The Complete Tales and Poems of Edgar Allan Poe* (New York: Random House, 1938), pp. 626, 630, 632, 641. Italics in original.

14. Fitzgerald, introduction to *Everything That Rises Must Converge*, p. xxvi.

15. Victor R. Yanitelli, "Types of Existentialism," *Thought* 24 (1949): 495.

16. James Collins, "The Fashionableness of Kierkegaard," *Thought* 21 (1947): 211.

17. Marjorie Greene, "Kierkegaard: The Philosophy" and "L'Homme est une passion inutile: Sartre and Heidegger," *Kenyon Review* 9 (1947): 53, 57, 168, 66–67.

18. Yanitelli, "Types of Existentialism," pp. 497–99, 501.

19. I am of course not arguing here that O'Connor read any specific writings at this time but merely that, through whatever sources, she was (as Fitzgerald suggests) clearly aware of the characteristic postures, ideas, language, and imagery associated with existentialism.

20. Fitzgerald, introduction to *Everything That Rises Must Converge*, p. xxvi. As he acknowledges, this point was first suggested by Brainard Cheney in "Flannery O'Connor's Campaign for Her Country," *Sewanee Review* 72 (1964), reprinted in *Flannery O'Connor*, ed. Reiter, pp. 1–4.

21. W. H. Auden, "Religion and the Intellectuals," *Partisan Review* 17 (1950): 124.

22. Unpublished manuscript, O'Connor Collection.

23. Jacques Maritain, "From Existential Existentialism to Academic Existentialism," *Sewanee Review* 56 (1948): 211, 210, 224. "The Train" occupies pp. 261–71 of this issue.

24. Jacques Maritain, *The Dream of Descartes*, trans. Mabelle L. Andison (New York Philosophical Library, 1944). The quotations are from pp. 66, 179, 180–82.
25. Maritain, *Dream of Descartes*, p. 181.
26. David H. Hirsch, "The Pit and the Apocalypse," *Sewanee Review* 76 (1968):652.
27. Søren Kierkegaard, *The Sickness unto Death*, trans. Walter Lowrie (Princeton, N.J.: Princeton University Press, 1941), p. 25.
28. The appearance of the double motif in *Wise Blood* has of course been noted before, but its centrality for the novel and the precise functions of Haze's reflectors have not been shown. See, for instance, Stuart L. Burns, "The Evolution of *Wise Blood*," *Modern Fiction Studies* 16 (1970):159; Gilbert H. Muller, *Nightmares and Visions: Flannery O'Connor and the Catholic Grotesque* (Athens: University of Georgia Press, 1972), p. 29.
29. The generally ritualistic quality of Enoch's behavior has often been observed, but the sources of O'Connor's parodies have been rather vague to her critics. See, for instance, Hyman, *Flannery O'Connor*, pp. 9–10; Kathleen Feeley, *Flannery O'Connor: Voice of the Peacock* (New Brunswick, N.J.: Rutgers University Press, 1972), p. 65; Burns, "Evolution of *Wise Blood*," p. 152; Martha Stephens, *The Question of Flannery O'Connor* (Baton Rouge: Louisiana State University Press, 1973), pp. 56–57.
30. After this passage was first written, James L. Green's explanation, "Enoch Emery and His Biblical Namesakes in *Wise Blood*," appeared to deal more fully with the matter. See *Studies in Short Fiction* 10 (1973):417–19.
31. Compare passages from *Wise Blood* and the Bible:

> [The washstand] was built in three parts and stood on bird legs six inches high. The legs had clawed feet that were each one gripped around a small cannon ball. The lowest part was a tabernacle-like cabinet which was meant to contain a slop jar. . . . Directly over this place for the treasure, there was a gray marble slab and coming up from behind it was a wooden trelliswork of hearts, scrolls and flowers, extending into a hunched eagle wing on either side, and containing in the middle, just at the level of Enoch's face when he stood in front of it, a small oval mirror. The wooden frame continued again over the mirror and ended in a crowned, horned headpiece, showing that the artist had not lost faith in his work.
>
> As far as Enoch was concerned, this piece had always been the center of the room and the one that most connected him with what he didn't know. . . . he

had dreamed of unlocking the cabinet and getting in it and then proceeding to certain rites and mysteries. [Wise Blood, pp. 131–32]

> And let them make me a sanctuary; that I may dwell among them. . . . And they shall make an ark of shittim wood. . . . And thou shalt make a mercy seat of pure gold. . . . And thou shalt make two cherubims of gold, of beaten work shalt thou make them, in the two ends of the mercy seat. . . . And the cherubims shall stretch forth their wings on high, covering the mercy seat with their wings. . . . Thou shalt also make a table of shittim wood. . . . And thou shalt make for it four rings of gold, and put the rings in the four corners that are on the four feet thereof. . . . And thou shalt put the mercy seat upon the ark of the testimony in the most holy place. . . . And thou shalt make an altar of shittim wood. . . . And thou shalt make the horns of it upon the four corners thereof. [Exodus 25–27]

Enoch's clean-up, one recalls, is followed by a gilding of the washstand, again following the orders of his blood.

32. O'Connor seems to be making a rather elaborate play on 1 Corinthians 15 in the final scenes with Enoch. A waitress asks him, "Did you swallow a seed?" and Enoch prophesies to her, "You may not see me again . . . the way I am" (p. 194). He intercepts Gonga at a theater called the Victory, located on 57th Street. The language suggests Paul's famous account of bodily resurrection under the figure of the grain of wheat, with its well-known climax, "Death is swallowed up in victory." Verse 57 (57th Street?) is quite relevant to Enoch's experience: "But thanks be to God, which giveth us the victory through our Lord Jesus Christ." Like everything else in the Enoch story, the biblical original is paradoxically inverted in his transformation into Gonga.

33. See Green, "Enoch Emery" pp. 417–19.

34. For other approaches to these parallels, see Jonathan Baumbach, *The Landscape of Nightmare* (New York: New York University Press, 1965), pp. 90–95; Josephine Hendin, *The World of Flannery O'Connor* (Bloomington: Indiana University Press, 1970), pp. 44–45; Driskell and Brittain, *Eternal Crossroads*, pp. 48–57; Orvell, *Invisible Parade*, pp. 86–89; Preston M. Browning, Jr., *Flannery O'Connor* (Carbondale: Southern Illinois University Press, 1974), p. 30.

35. Haze's final actions have been attributed to everything from his receiving a divine revelation to his seeing a "total blankness" that confirms his denials of Jesus. For views representative of this spectrum, see Dorothy Walters, *Flannery O'Connor* (New York: Twayne, 1973), pp. 56–57; Feeley, *Flannery O'Connor*, p. 64; Robert M. Rechnitz, "Passionate Pilgrim: Flannery O'Connor's *Wise Blood*," *Georgia Review* 19 (1965):

315; Hendin, *World of Flannery O'Connor*, pp. 54–55; Browning, *Flannery O'Connor*, pp. 36–37.

36. Yanitelli, "Types of Existentialism," p. 501.

37. Søren Kierkegaard, *The Concept of Dread*, trans. Walter Lowrie (Princeton, N.J.: Princeton University Press, 1944), p. 92.

38. The language of such critics often makes the assumptions behind their procedures clear: "With no institution to channel its violence, in Miss O'Connor's view, [Haze's] call can only destroy him" (Hyman, *Flannery O'Connor*, p. 15); "from her vantage point the entire world did look grotesque, since her audience did not recognize the normative value of faith" (Lawson, "Flannery O'Connor and the Grotesque," p. 67); "Surely the author must have felt the inadequacy of Haze's salvation" (Browning, *Flannery O'Connor*, p. 38). Both the views that divorce the author from her protagonist and those that ally the two depend heavily on the construction of a Flannery O'Connor from *outside* the novel.

39. The term is not, in its precise historical meaning, quite accurate; thus the quotation marks. The problem is that no traditional category conveys exactly the radical dualism of *Wise Blood*, and although I find, for instance, no sense of an *active* evil force operative in the material world of the novel, *Manichean* perhaps comes closer than any other recognizable term to expressing the vision at work here. (A possible alternative is "Gnostic," again with qualifying quotation marks.)

    David Eggenschwiler, *The Christian Humanism of Flannery O'Connor* (Detroit: Wayne State University Press, 1972), sees that Hazel Motes is a "Manichean," which leads him to this conclusion: "Miss O'Connor is . . . criticizing Haze's attitudes, not because they are extreme or violent, but because they are morbid and Manichean, a contrast to the Christian-humanistic position that she assumes throughout her work" (p. 103). Eggenschwiler does not observe that, far from suggesting Christian humanism, the very landscape of *Wise Blood* endorses the protagonist's "Manicheanism."

40. Compare *Wise Blood*, p. 37 and *The Complete Stories*, p. 63.

41. Comment on *The Phenomenon of Man*, *American Scholar* 30 (1961): 618.

42. In addition to early reviewers, who sometimes made both complaints, see, for instance, Walter Sullivan, "Flannery O'Connor, Sin, and Grace: *Everything That Rises Must Converge*," *Hollins Critic* 2 (September 1965): 2; Robert Drake, *Flannery O'Connor: A Critical Essay* (Grand Rapids, Mich.: William B. Eerdmans, 1966), p. 22; Stephens, *Question of Flannery O'Connor*, pp. 43–82, esp. pp. 43–44, 50–54, 64.

43. Stephens, *Question of Flannery O'Connor*, pp. 43–82 is the most re-

cent to make this implicit demand. Orvell, *Invisible Parade*, pp. 91–93 provides a defense of the mode of the novel by arguing that *Wise Blood* presents an "image of Christian reality."

44. Melvin J. Friedman in *Added Dimension*, ed. Friedman and Lawson, p. 24.

45. Baumbach, *Landscape of Nightmare*, p. 99. Baumbach's reading first appeared in *Georgia Review* 17 (1963).

46. Sullivan, "Flannery O'Connor, Sin, and Grace," pp. 2–3.

47. See O'Connor's own comment on a reported conversation between J. F. Powers and Dwight MacDonald (*The Habit of Being*, p. 400): "I can't understand why either of them should find the mummy hard to understand. I thought it dangerously obvious."

   The source of the mummy may well be Allen Tate's "More Sonnets at Christmas, I" where Jesus appears as "mummy Christ, head crammed between his knees" to the speaker. Sonnet 3 in the series requests a "faith not personal" and uses the phrase "Unstalked by Christ." Tate's collected *Poems 1922–1947* (New York: Swallow Press) appeared in 1948, just as O'Connor was fully launching into work on *Wise Blood*.

Chapter 2. The Duality of Images

1. Unpublished manuscript, O'Connor Collection.

2. *Numinous* (from L. *numen*, divinity), Rudolf Otto's coinage, has the virtue of being familiar. See *The Idea of the Holy*, trans. John W. Harvey (New York: Oxford University Press, 1958), esp. pp. 1–40. However, it is applied here in an extended sense to any images which suggest the presence of the more than natural, that is, the demonic as well as the divine. Unfortunately there seems to be no comparably well known term to designate the reductive tendency in O'Connor's imagery. *Hylic* (from Gr. *hyle*, matter, substance) is perhaps the best available, especially since it was used by the Gnostics to refer to men whose lives were overwhelmed by matter.

3. The reductive tendency in O'Connor's work is, it seems to me, the major insight of Josephine Hendin's study. However, in her willful ignoring of the larger contexts of the fiction, Hendin takes the part for the whole. See Hendin, *World of Flannery O'Connor*, esp. pp. 19–29.

4. Fitzgerald, introduction to *Everything That Rises Must Converge*, p. xi.

5. Those suns have often been noted. Their significance has been treated most fully in Stuart L. Burns's "'Torn by the Lord's Eye': Flannery O'Connor's Use of Sun Imagery," *Twentieth Century Literature* 13 (1967): 154–66.

6. Fitzgerald, introduction to *Everything That Rises Must Converge*, p. xxxii. See also Stephens, *Question of Flannery O'Connor*, pp. 153–54.
7. Many of O'Connor's critics have of course followed up her own comments on her sacramentalism, but almost always to flatten the radical tensions of her fiction into a serene orthodoxy. An early treatment is that of Carter W. Martin, *The True Country: Themes in the Fiction of Flannery O'Connor* (Nashville: Vanderbilt University Press, 1969), pp. 10–27. The fullest exposition of this view can be found in Feeley, *Flannery O'Connor*. For a different treatment of the relationship between the sacramental and the grotesque in O'Connor, see Muller, *Nightmares and Visions*, esp. pp. 99–114.
8. Wolfgang Kayser, *The Grotesque in Art and Literature*, trans. Ulrich Weisstein (New York: McGraw-Hill, 1966), p. 184. The quotations from Kayser below can be found on pp. 185 and 184 respectively.
9. Mullins, "Flannery O'Connor," p. 33.
10. *Flannery O'Connor*, pp. 25–26.
11. Hendin notes this literalistic tendency in O'Connor but views it as simply reductive. See Hendin, *World of Flannery O'Connor*, esp. pp. 27–28.
12. Aside from the draft of *The Violent Bear It Away* that contains the germ of the story, the O'Connor Collection has four manuscripts pertaining to "The Artificial Nigger": (1) a full typescript carbon of 31 pages; (2) a single-page typescript of the opening; (3) a single-page typescript of the ending; (4) four pages of consecutive typescript which move from Mr. Head's betrayal of Nelson to their boarding of the train for home. The condition of the paper suggests that numbers 2 and 3 may come from the same manuscript, the rest of which has been lost.

    See also O'Connor's remark to a correspondent (*The Habit of Being*, p. 78): "I wrote that story a good many times, having a lot of trouble with the end."
13. For a full reproduction of this version of the episode, see May, *Pruning Word*, pp. 160–61. The other manuscript (number 4 above) has: "Neither he nor Nelson ever knew how they were actually reconciled and neither would have acknowledged that it was the plaster figure that did it, if they had."
14. "The Artificial Nigger" has frequently been explicated, but not from the point of view of O'Connor's manipulation of dual perspectives. Among the best of the earlier readings are those by Eggenschwiler, *Christian Humanism of Flannery O'Connor*, pp. 85–91; Feeley, *Flannery O'Connor*, pp. 120–24; Orvell, *Invisible Parade*, pp. 152–60.
15. Unpublished manuscript, O'Connor Collection.
16. Previous commentators on the Dantean imagery in the story assume

that O'Connor, like Mr. Head, thinks that the city is truly the devil's domain. Yet Mr. Head in this respect is like a number of other O'Connor protagonists—Mrs. Cope of "A Circle in the Fire," for instance, or Thomas of "The Comforts of Home," or Tarwater on his visit to the city in *The Violent Bear It Away*—who think they find evil anywhere but in themselves, but are always brought back to discover its locus within. For the view of the inferno of "The Artificial Nigger" as exterior, see particularly Peter L. Hays, "Dante, Tobit, and 'The Artificial Nigger,'" *Studies in Short Fiction* 5 (1968):263–68, and Gilbert H. Muller, "The City of Woe: Flannery O'Connor's Dantean Vision," *Georgia Review* 23 (1969):206–13.

17. Orvell, *Invisible Parade*, p. 152, notes that the movement from "misery" to "grace" in the story is "unusual" in O'Connor. In fact, the double action is peculiar to this tale.

18. Cf. Turner F. Byrd, "Ironic Dimension in Flannery O'Connor's 'The Artificial Nigger,'" *Mississippi Quarterly* 21 (1968):243–51. As his title suggests, Byrd believes that the Heads are merely confirmed in their bigotry and provincialism and thus that the end of the story is ironic.

19. See O'Connor's comment that "in fiction . . . the hardest thing for the writer to indicate is the presence of the anagogical which to my mind is the only thing that can cause the personality to change. Perhaps even here it changes within what it has been made" (*The Habit of Being*, p. 503).

20. Unpublished manuscript, O'Connor Collection.

Chapter 3. The Double

1. Albert J. Guerard, "Concepts of the Double" in *Stories of the Double*, ed. Albert J. Guerard (Philadelphia: J. B. Lippincott, 1967), p. 3. For other general studies of the double configuration, see Claire Rosenfield, "The Shadow Within: The Conscious and Unconscious Use of the Double," originally published in *Daedalus* 92 (1963), reprinted in *Stories of the Double*, ed. Guerard, pp. 311–31; Ralph Tymms, *Doubles in Literary Psychology* (Cambridge: Bowes and Bowes, 1949); Robert Rogers, *A Psychoanalytic Study of the Double in Literature* (Detroit: Wayne State University Press, 1970); C. F. Keppler, *The Literature of the Second Self* (Tucson: University of Arizona Press, 1972).

2. Sigmund Freud, *Collected Papers*, vol. 4 (New York: Basic Books, 1959), p. 332. Freud here is actually following the suggestion of critic Ludwig Jekels.

3. O'Connor's use of double figures in her novels has been recognized, but

the persistence of the pattern in her stories—which thus makes it a fundamental feature of her fiction as a whole—has not been observed. At times, however, the appearance of the *Doppelgänger* in individual stories has been noted. See, for instance, Irving Malin, *New American Gothic* (Carbondale: Southern Illinois University Press, 1962), pp. 143–51 (the novels and "The Artificial Nigger"); Hendin, *World of Flannery O'Connor*, pp. 108–11, 119, 124, 127 ("A View of the Woods" and "Revelation"); Browning, *Flannery O'Connor*, pp. 63–65, 112–14 ("The Artificial Nigger" and "A View of the Woods").

4. In his essay of this title; see Otto Rank, *Beyond Psychology* (New York: Dover, 1958), pp. 62–101.

5. For earlier discussions of "A View of the Woods" that partially anticipate the present argument, see Hendin, *World of Flannery O'Connor*, pp. 108–11; Eggenschwiler, *Christian Humanism of Flannery O'Connor*, pp. 68–70; and, especially, Browning, *Flannery O'Connor*, pp. 109–18.

6. "Good Country People" has been frequently discussed, but the presence of the double motif and the reflective relationship among the characters has not been fully recognized. Orvell (*Invisible Parade*, p. 141) and Browning (*Flannery O'Connor*, pp. 46–47) do note the echoes of Mrs. Freeman in the Bible salesman. Browning (*Flannery O'Connor*, p. 50) also points out that Joy remains the girl's real identity, but he does not see how close that brings her to her mother.

7. Such an apparently open invitation has not of course been refused: for earlier psychological readings which differ from the present one, see Hendin, *World of Flannery O'Connor*, pp. 115–18 and Muller, *Nightmares and Visions*, pp. 88–89. No one has recognized the centrality of the double motif in this story—unless one excepts Hendin's tentative speculation that Sarah Ham is the double of Thomas's mother.

However, against my suspicion of parody here should be set O'Connor's apparently genuine disclaimer when a correspondent gave the story its first psychological interpretation (*The Habit of Being*, p. 375). The most she was willing to grant was that "if the Oedipus business is visible in it, it is so because it is in nature, not because I worked with that in mind."

8. Carl Gustav Jung, *The Archetypes and the Collective Unconscious*, trans. R. F. C. Hull (New York: Pantheon, 1959), pp. 26–29. Given my arguments here and in Chapter 5, it is perhaps worth noting that O'Connor's personal library contained two works by Jung and several about him, and that in her book reviews and letters she more than once displayed her familiarity with his theories. Around the time of the com-

position of "The Comforts of Home" (1960), she commented to a Jung enthusiast, "I admire him and . . . have been interested in [his work] for some time" (*The Habit of Being*, p. 382).

9. Jung, *Archetypes and the Collective Unconscious*, p. 31.

10. Carl Gustav Jung, *Two Essays on Analytical Psychology*, trans. R. F. C. Hull (New York: Meridian, 1956), pp. 207–8.

11. Cf. Carl Gustav Jung, *Symbols of Transformation*, trans. R. F. C. Hull (New York: Pantheon, 1956), pp. 283–84: "An infantile disposition . . . is always characterized by a predominance of the parental imago. . . . he is so identified with his parents through his close ties with them that he behaves like his father or his mother."

12. This point has also been made in Joseph R. Millichap, "The Pauline 'Old Man' in Flannery O'Connor's 'The Comforts of Home,'" *Studies in Short Fiction* 11 (1974): 96–99.

13. Unpublished manuscript, O'Connor Collection.

14. This crucial point, first noted by Joyce Carol Oates over a decade ago, has been neglected by O'Connor's critics. See Oates, *New Heaven, New Earth* (New York: Vanguard Press, 1974), pp. 143–76. Further ramifications will be developed in Chapter 6 below.

15. Cf. Rogers, *Psychological Study*, pp. 60–61: "Because decomposition always reflects psychic conflict, one would expect doubles to be portrayed as characters highly antagonistic to each other. Contrary to expectation, overt dramatic conflict between doubles proves to be the exception rather than the rule. . . . in almost all cases some feeling of closeness and sympathy will be manifested by the doubles at some point in the story."

16. The determination to turn O'Connor into a cheerful writer seems especially strong among her Christian commentators. On Joy Hopewell, for instance, see Eggenschwiler (*Christian Humanism of Flannery O'Connor*, p. 57): "Her old self has been burned away, and she might be forced into a free choice that may be a new beginning. Perhaps it might even lead to her accepting her own body, etc."; or Feeley (*Flannery O'Connor*, pp. 23–27), who repeatedly vitiates her intelligent discussion of "Good Country People" by speculations on the "new life" ("the sacred may become manifest in her") that the girl may discover after the story's ending.

17. The passage from Matthew is referred to in unpublished manuscripts, O'Connor Collection.

18. Unpublished manuscript, O'Connor Collection. Cf. *The Habit of Being*, p. 328: "I have now to sit down and write a graduate student in Cleve-

land who wants to know why my stories are grotesque; are they grotesque because I am showing the frustration of grace? It's very hard to
tell these innocents that they are grotesque because that is the nature of
my talent."

19. Ernest Becker, *The Denial of Death* (New York: Free Press, 1973), p.
225.

20. Quoted by Feeley, *Flannery O'Connor*, p. 165.

Chapter 4. The Aesthetics of Incongruity

1. The recurrence of the family situation in O'Connor's writings has of
course often been pointed out. See, for instance, Hyman, *Flannery
O'Connor*, pp. 30–32; Hendin, *World of Flannery O'Connor*, esp. pp.
97–130; Stephens, *Question of Flannery O'Connor*, pp. 144–86, esp.
pp. 149–53; Alfred Kazin, *Bright Book of Life* (Boston: Atlantic, Little,
Brown, 1973), pp. 54–59. Claire Katz, "Flannery O'Connor's Rage of Vision," *American Literature* 46 (1974–75): 54–67, gives the family conflict an intelligent psychoanalytic reading.

2. With characteristic insight, Kazin (*Bright Book of Life*, pp. 59–60) puts
his finger on O'Connor's critique of the will to power, but he goes on to
the dubious conclusion that she therefore saw all action as futile and
grotesque.

3. Unpublished manuscript, O'Connor Collection.

4. Quoted by Margaret Inman Meaders in "Flannery O'Connor: 'Literary
Witch,'" *Colorado Quarterly* 10 (1961–62): 385.

5. Unpublished manuscript, O'Connor Collection.

6. Meaders, "Flannery O'Connor," p. 382.

7. John Hawkes, "Flannery O'Connor's Devil," originally published in
Sewanee Review 70 (1962), conveniently reprinted in Reiter, *Flannery
O'Connor*, pp. 25–37.

8. Wylie Sypher, "The Meanings of Comedy," in *Comedy* (New York: Doubleday, 1956), p. 222.

9. Eric Bentley, *The Life of the Drama* (New York: Atheneum, 1970), pp.
237, 311.

10. Eric Bentley, "The Psychology of Farce," in *Let's Get a Divorce! and
Other Plays* (New York: Hill and Wang, 1957), p. ix.

11. Bentley, *Life of the Drama*, p. 201.

12. Peter Brooks, *The Melodramatic Imagination* (New Haven, Conn.: Yale
University Press, 1976), pp. 14–20, 54, 36, 21.

13. Ibid., p. 21.

14. The language is again from Brooks (ibid., p. 54).

15. Richard Chase, *The American Novel and Its Tradition* (New York: Doubleday, 1957) p. 39.
16. Unpublished manuscript, O'Connor Collection.
17. Blaise Pascal, *Pensées*, trans. W. F. Trotter (New York: Dutton, 1958), p. 137.
18. *The Complete Stories* (p. 132) silently "corrects" The Misfit's dialect in this passage, substituting *thrown* for *thown* and *throw* for *thow*. Thus I have followed in this quotation the spelling as found in *A Good Man Is Hard to Find and Other Stories* (New York: Harcourt, Brace and World, 1955), p. 28.
19. Indeed, two critics see this division in the action as final: as one of them puts it, "the story breaks in two." See William S. Doxey, "A Dissenting Opinion of Flannery O'Connor's 'A Good Man Is Hard to Find,'" *Studies in Short Fiction* 10 (1973): 199–204; and Stephens, *Question of Flannery O'Connor*, pp. 18–36. Doxey argues that the point of view shifts from the grandmother to The Misfit and Stephens that there is a sudden shift in tone which then runs "out of control." But there is no shift in point of view—we never see through The Misfit's eyes in this story—and Stephens's failure to discern tone in the first half of the story (especially since her entire case rests on it) is dismaying. I shall deal further with problems of tone below.
20. Although The Misfit's philosophy has often been discussed and is not here directly my concern, I cannot resist suggesting another source for it. It has long been recognized that his views are in some sense existentialist, and he has been plausibly related to figures in Dostoyevski and Kafka and to Camus's Meursault, but no one seems to have noticed how close his preoccupations (and sometimes language) are to those of *The Myth of Sisyphus*. His central vision of a universe in which nothing fits sounds suspiciously like a homespun version of Camus's Absurd, that divorce "between an action and the world that transcends it . . . the Absurd is not in man . . . nor in the world, but in their presence together" (Albert Camus, *The Myth of Sisyphus and Other Essays*, trans. Justin O'Brien [New York: Random House, 1959], pp. 22–23). Compare The Misfit's view of the world as the extension of the prison, his desire to know, and his final either/or absolutism with the following passages:

> The only conception of freedom I can have is that of the prisoner. . . . Now if the absurd cancels all my chances of eternal freedom, it restores and magnifies, on the other hand, my freedom of action. [p. 42]

> I don't know whether this world has a meaning which transcends it. But I know that I do not know that meaning and that it is impossible for me just now

> to know it. . . . And these two certainties—my appetite for the absolute and for unity and the impossibility of reducing this world to a rational and reasonable principle—I also know that I cannot reconcile them. [p. 38]

> There is God or time, that cross or this sword. This world has a higher meaning that transcends its worries, or nothing is true but those worries . . . I . . . want all or nothing. [p. 64]

The English translation of Camus's work did not appear in book form until after "A Good Man Is Hard to Find" was written, but translations of various parts of the essay and articles on Camus had been appearing in American journals since the mid-1940s.

21. The insistence on her role rather than her particular individuality (which would be fixed by naming her) suggests that O'Connor may be playing with the type of Mary in her portrayal. The grandmother insists that she is a "lady"—the term by which The Misfit also regularly addresses her—and dresses the part, but the repetition of that term throughout and the emblematic array of colors in her attire (blue and white dress and hat, both purple and white violets affixed) raise one's suspicions. It would be characteristic of O'Connor's irony that only with the destruction of her pretensions to being a "lady" would she become for a brief moment a woman and thus a type of the true Lady. On this level her final gesture to The Misfit would be an *imitatio Virginis* whereby the grandmother suggests the Grand Mother—Our Lady of Sorrows, the Hope of Criminals, the Mother of Mercy.

22. In arguing against Stephens's theory of a radical tonal shift in the story, May (*Pruning Word*, p. 62) cites many of these same elements.

23. Katherine Fugina, Faye Rivard, and Margaret Sieh, "An Interview with Flannery O'Connor," *Censer*, Fall 1960, p. 53.

24. The symbolic displacement here—analogous to, but the reverse of, Mary Grace's attack on Mrs. Turpin rather than her own mother in "Revelation"—is further suggested by Bailey's parting words as he goes off to the woods: "I'll be back in a minute, Mamma, wait on me!" I advance this reading in full awareness of O'Connor's "shock" when it was suggested to her that the second half of the story was actually Bailey's dream whereby, through The Misfit, he vicariously murdered all his family (*The Habit of Being*, pp. 436–37). Nothing, it seems to me, could be less dreamlike than the second part of "A Good Man Is Hard to Find."

25. Quoted by Sister M. Bernetta Quinn in "Flannery O'Connor, A Realist of Distances," in Friedman and Lawson, *Added Dimension*, p. 167. To another correspondent she revealed how important this discovery was to her personally: "I have found a lucky find for me in St. Thomas's sec-

tions of the *Summa* and the *De veritate* on prophecy" (*The Habit of Being*, p. 367).

26. Thomas Aquinas, *Truth* [*De veritate*], trans. Robert W. Mulligan, 3 vols. (Chicago: Regnery, 1952–54), 2:129–31.

27. Victor White, *God and the Unconscious* (New York: Meridian, 1952) p. 127.

28. Compare Joy-Hulga Hopewell's secret pride in the uniqueness of her hidden self (see Chapter 3).

29. Unpublished manuscript, O'Connor Collection.

30. In an unpublished version of a lecture on the problems of the Catholic novelist (now in the O'Connor Collection), she had this to say about Mauriac's famous directive: "Now this is fine advice, of course, but it is certainly not sufficient. It takes us a lifetime just to begin making ourselves holy, just to decide, for that matter, that it's the thing to do; and in addition to that, we see plenty of awful novels issuing from sources that, relatively speaking, are amply pure."

    For a more detached (but no less dismissive) consideration of Mauriac's remark, see *The Habit of Being*, p. 143.

31. Here, as so often when O'Connor cites Aquinas (particularly on the subject of art), she seems to have encountered his thinking through the work of Jacques Maritain rather than directly from a Thomist text. For the present citation, for instance, see Maritain, *Art and Scholasticism*, trans. J. F. Scanlan (London: Sheed and Ward, 1930), pp. 15–16, 47–48, and *Creative Intuition in Art and Poetry* (New York: Meridian, 1955), p. 36. However, see also note 26 above and *The Habit of Being*, pp. 93, 439.

32. See Hawkes, "Flannery O'Connor's Devil." It is easy to sympathize with James O. Tate's complaint (in "Faith and Fiction: Flannery O'Connor and the Problem of Belief," *Flannery O'Connor Bulletin* 5 [1976]:107) that all the "devil-mongering" which followed Hawkes's article has had a "befogging" effect on O'Connor criticism. Yet, given O'Connor's own statements outside of the fiction, to say nothing of her creations within it, the issue seems difficult to avoid. The problem is surely not that she is unconsciously attracted to the demonic, but that she quite deliberately exploits those feelings, urges, responses (call them what you will) within herself that, in her theological terms, can only be characterized as evil. If it is silly to argue that O'Connor is of the devil's party, much less without knowing it, it seems to me also a diminution of her achievement—and a falsification of the actual experience of her fiction—to argue that she somehow wrote out of a pure piety. To put the issue in its simplest form: the writer who claimed that her characters

ere *all* in some sense herself" (Thomas F. Gossett, "Flannery O'Con-
r on Her Fiction," *Southwest Review* 59 [1974]: 35; italics added) presumably was not excepting such figures as Rufus Johnson, The Misfit,
and Manley Pointer.

For some other treatments of this question, see Hendin, *World of
Flannery O'Connor*, pp. 18–20; Walters, *Flannery O'Connor*, esp. pp.
39–41; Browning, *Flannery O'Connor*, pp. 11–15, 128–30.

Chapter 5. *The Violent Bear It Away*

1. "Thematically the two novels are much alike, though it seems to me
   that everything in the first one has been expanded and brought out in
   the open in the second." Quoted by Paul Levine in Charles Alva Hoyt,
   ed., *Minor American Novelists* (Carbondale: Southern Illinois University Press, 1970), p. 111.
2. Nathanael West, "Some Notes on Miss L," reprinted in Jay Martin, ed.,
   Nathanael West: A Collection of Critical Essays (Englewood Cliffs,
   N.J.: Prentice-Hall, 1971), p. 66.
3. According to James Tate's unpublished "An O'Connor Remembrance,"
   O'Connor Collection.
4. Unpublished manuscript, O'Connor Collection.
5. These patterns have frequently been discussed. See, for instance, Hyman, *Flannery O'Connor*, pp. 21–23; Clinton W. Trowbridge, "The
   Symbolic Vision of Flannery O'Connor: Patterns of Imagery in *The Violent Bear It Away*," *Sewanee Review* 76 (1968): 298–318; Martin, *True
   Country*, pp. 141–42; John R. May, *Toward a New Earth: Apocalypse in
   the American Novel* (Notre Dame, Ind.: Notre Dame University Press,
   1972), pp. 126–44.
6. Not surprisingly, O'Connor viewed Jung's theories as "dangerous to religion" because they "use belief in the practical service of psychotherapy"
   (manuscript of a book review, O'Connor Collection; see also *The Habit
   of Being*, p. 362). Yet the very closeness she saw as a danger is precisely
   what makes Jung useful in exploring her dramatization of the development of the self in this novel. It will be pointed out below where the two
   clearly part company.
7. Jung, *Psychology and Religion*, p. 181.
8. Throughout this section my discussion of what for convenience's sake I
   am calling the heroic myths is indebted to Joseph Campbell's well-
   known synthesis in *The Hero with a Thousand Faces* (New York:
   Meridian, 1956). Stuart L. Burns, "Flannery O'Connor's *The Violent*

Bear It Away: Apotheosis in Failure," *Sewanee Review* 76 (1968): 319–36, also evokes Campbell and rites of passage generally, but Burns is not concerned to explore specifically how O'Connor uses mythic analogues.

9. See Campbell, *The Hero with a Thousand Faces*, pp. 49–58, esp. pp. 51–52.

10. Cf. Hyman, *Flannery O'Connor*, p. 35: "All his positions are counter-positions."

11. Jung, *Psychology and Religion*, p. 181.

12. Ibid., pp. 181–82.

13. O'Connor seems to have the Antichrist tradition explicitly in mind in her insistence on Rayber's right ear, which is not only deaf but has had a wedge shot out of it by old Tarwater. Compare the beast of Revelation 13, traditionally associated with Antichrist, whose head is wounded and miraculously healed, and the legend of Antichrist as a human monster deaf in his right ear (see W. Bousset, *The Antichrist Legend*, trans. A. H. Keane [London: Hutchinson, 1896], pp. 156–57). These echoes would suggest that Rayber himself is one of the beasts Tarwater must confront on his heroic journey.

14. P. 174. Compare Hawthorne's description of Holgrave in *The House of the Seven Gables*: "With the insight on which he prided himself, he fancied that he could look through Phoebe, and all around her, and could read her off like a page of a child's story book." The nearness of the echo here suggests how close the perceptions of these two writers sometimes are, particularly in their common conviction that the probing of the presumably detached intellect is always sinister.

15. The "unbelieving searchers have their effect even upon those of us who do believe," O'Connor remarked. "What Christian novelist could compare his concern to Camus'?" (*Mystery and Manners*, p. 160). I have noted above her apparent response to Camus's earlier work; here, Rayber's summary of his position seems to echo the final chapter of *The Rebel*, "Moderation and Excess," in which Camus argues the necessity of moderation, a humanism "born of rebellion" which avoids all absolutes and extremes. Not only the thought but the language of such a passage as the following seems to be parodied in the portrayal of the schoolteacher: "I alone, in one sense, support the common dignity that I cannot allow either myself or others to debase. This individualism is in no sense pleasure; it is perpetual struggle, and, sometimes, unparalleled joy when it reaches the heights of proud compassion" (*The Rebel*, trans. Anthony Bower [New York: Random House, 1956], p. 297).

16. Cf. Mark 9:44, in which hell is described as a place of torment "where their worm dieth not, and the fire is not quenched."

17. P. 123. As Campbell points out (*The Hero with a Thousand Faces*, pp. 91–92) the entrance of the worshipper into a temple is symbolically equivalent to the disappearance into the jaws of the whale.

18. See Revelation 15:2 for the "sea of glass mingled with fire." At one point, irritated by Rayber, Tarwater looks "as if he were vainly searching for a way to get out of the boat and walk off," and when he does make his getaway he swims "smashing the glassy lake as if he would like to make it sting and bleed" (pp. 171, 175).

19. Cf. John 4:13–14, where Christ tells the woman of Samaria at the well, "Whosoever drinketh of this water shall thirst again. But whosoever drinketh of the water that I shall give him shall never thirst; but the water that I shall give him shall be in him a well of water springing up into everlasting life." The suggestion that Tarwater's suppressed longing for the divine is a "well of water" is made throughout the novel. For instance, note his ironic choice of terms in describing the baptism: "They were just some words that *run* out of my mouth and *spilled* in the water" (p. 209; italics added).

20. Cf. Stephens, *Question of Flannery O'Connor*, pp. 137–38, who finds this crucial episode not only "melodramatic" but "artificial," apparently because she views the stranger as "not simply a diabolic figure, but the devil himself come down to complete the job of Tarwater's subjugation." Stephens is uneasy throughout with the presentation of the boy's "voice" as demonic.

21. Compare O'Connor's use of cigarettes as a mock Host in the less sinister "communion" of "The Enduring Chill" (pp. 378–80).

22. The problem of freedom in *The Violent Bear It Away* has been argued since the book's publication, and virtually every critic of the novel has had his say on it. A useful recent discussion is Browning's (*Flannery O'Connor*, pp. 75–98), not only for its own perceptions but for its summary of earlier critical arguments.

23. For other discussions of language and action in the novel see Orvell, *Invisible Parade*, pp. 110–11, 116; May, *Toward a New Earth*, pp. 134–37; and Sister Jeremy, C.S.J., "*The Violent Bear It Away*: A Linguistic Education," originally published in *Renascence* 17 (1964), conveniently reprinted in Reiter, *Flannery O'Connor*, pp. 103–10.

24. See Campbell, *The Hero with a Thousand Faces*, pp. 126–49.

25. Jung, *Psychology and Religion*, pp. 182–83.

26. Ibid., pp. 182–83, 186. However, Jung does mention cases where the predominating symbols are "ternary" rather than "quarternary," and his ob-

servations on these exceptions seem relevant to Tarwater: "I have found
that they were distinguished by something that can only be called a 'medieval psychology'. This does not imply any backwardness and is not
meant as a value judgment, but only as denoting a special problem. That
is to say, in all these cases there is so much unconsciousness, and such a
large degree of primitivity to match it, that a spiritualization appears
necessary as a compensation. The saving symbol is then a triad in which
the fourth is lacking because it has to be unconditionally rejected" (p.
191). The passage might be clearer, but Jung's comments do seem to
support the argument that the forces of Tarwater's "unconsciousness"
do overwhelm and unconditionally reject the rational side of the self.
27. See, for instance, Martin, *True Country*, p. 129; Driskell and Brittain,
Eternal Crossroads, pp. 81–103, esp. p. 83; May, *Toward a New Earth*, p.
144; Stephens, *Question of Flannery O'Connor*, p. 141. Orvell (*Invisible Parade*, p. 118) argues that at the end the *tone* moves from comedy
to the "solemnity of the festival epic," but structurally he seems to find
the novel broadly comic.
28. Northrop Frye, *Anatomy of Criticism* (Princeton, N.J.: Princeton University Press, 1957), p. 212.
29. Some of the ambivalence in O'Connor's use of the two mythic strains is
caught by Frye's recent observation on the motif of descent to the lower
world: "Though purely demonic in Christianity, [it] is in romance often
a world where great reward, of wisdom or wealth, may wait the ex-
plorer" (*The Secular Scripture* [Cambridge, Mass.: Harvard University
Press, 1976], p. 98).
30. Mullins, "Flannery O'Connor," p. 34.

Chapter 6. The Prophetic Imagination

1. O'Connor has had, of course, a number of other theological labels fixed
to her as well. She has been called Augustinian and Jansenistic, Teil-
hardian and Protestant, ecumenical and humanistic, heterodox, mystical, reductionist, and so on. Often these designations seem to proceed
from no very thorough investigation of her work. Some of the more
stimulating considerations of the religious sense in the fiction seem to
me those of Hyman, *Flannery O'Connor*, pp. 37–39; Eggenschwiler,
Christian Humanism, esp. pp. 9–30; Orvell, *Invisible Parade*, pp.
17–23; Oates, *New Heaven, New Earth*, pp. 141–76; and Robert Milder, "The Protestantism of Flannery O'Connor," *Southern Review* 11
(1975): 802–19.
   In the argument below, all theological labels that appear should be un-

derstood as being enclosed in quotation marks. There are two reasons for this. One is that these designations are less precise than is sometimes pretended: to what extent Augustine's writings are Manichean, say, or Aquinas's Augustinian is still a matter of disagreement among theologians. The second—and more important—reason is that O'Connor's fiction seems to me to escape the confines of any single label, and while I do want to suggest where her deepest affinities on central matters lie, I have no desire to appear to place any particular theological seal on her work as a whole.

2. To James Tate, cited in "An O'Connor Remembrance," O'Connor Collection. See, however, such apparently contradictory testimony as *The Habit of Being*, pp. 93, 439.

3. Unpublished manuscript, O'Connor Collection.

4. Saint Augustine, *The Confessions*, trans. F. J. Sheed (New York: Sheed and Ward, 1943), pp. 173–74.

5. Fitzgerald, introduction to *Everything That Rises Must Converge*, p. xxxii.

6. Walter Mitchell and the Carisbrooke Dominicans, trans., *Christian Asceticism and Modern Man* (London: Philosophical Library, 1955), p. 11.

7. Ibid., pp. 112, 25, 53.

8. The quotations are from pp. 367, 376, 378, and 382. The following passage from Martin C. D'Arcy's *The Mind and Heart of Love* (New York: Henry Holt, 1947) may have stuck in O'Connor's mind when she came to write "The Enduring Chill": "In Christianity the truth is free from subjective fancyings; it comes down from above and exercises the severest control of symbol and image and fantasy; it can be as cold as ice and as inflexible as the historical fact on which it rests, and it beats down upon the soul with all the alien power of an existent truth which is not a dream" (p. 151).

9. Mitchell and Carisbrooke Dominicans, trans., *Christian Asceticism*, p. 27.

10. Evelyn Underhill, *Mysticism* (New York: Meridian, 1955), p. 199.

11. Mullins, "Flannery O'Connor," p. 35.

12. Unpublished manuscript, O'Connor Collection.

13. Unpublished manuscript, O'Connor Collection.

14. As is, I hope, clear, I am using such terms as *faith*, *belief*, and *knowledge*, in their common and subjective senses—the senses in which these matters arise for O'Connor's characters—rather than entering into the theological controversies surrounding these terms. Thus for my purposes here, Saint Paul with his well-known designation of faith as "the

evidence of things not seen" (Hebrews 11:1) has seemed sufficient guide. Knowledge then becomes, in this context, the evidence of things sensibly apprehended. The need for the word *sensibly* will, I trust, become evident as my discussion proceeds.

15. White, *God and the Unconscious*, pp. 127, 145. My discussion in this paragraph is indebted to White's entire chapter "Revelation and the Unconscious," pp. 125–57.

16. Margaret Smith, *The Way of the Mystics* (London: Sheldon Press, 1976), p. 81.

17. Cf. John L. McKenzie, *The Roman Catholic Church* (New York: Holt, Rinehart and Winston, 1969), p. 187: "The official Roman Catholic Church is not sympathetic to mysticism and never has been. . . . The mystics have something in common with the Israelite prophets; they often criticized the institutional church and came under the suspicion of the authorities."

18. In addition to Underhill's standard work (*Mysticism*), her library contained books by and about Saints John of the Cross, Teresa of Avila, Catherine of Genoa, Catherine of Siena, and Therese of Lisieux; Meister Eckhart; and such general titles as *The Medieval Mystics of England, Mystics of Our Times*, and *The Physical Phenomena of Mysticism*.

19. Quoted in Underhill, *Mysticism*, p. 265.

20. The quotations are from Herbert Thurston, *The Physical Phenomena of Mysticism* (London: Burns, Oates, 1952), p. 346; and Underhill, *Mysticism*, p. 265.

21. Abraham J. Heschel, *The Prophets* (New York: Harper and Row, 1962), pp. xviii, 24, 21; Heschel's italics.

22. Ibid., p. 22.

23. Ibid., pp. 16, 408.

24. Cf. J. Philip Hyatt, *Prophetic Religion* (New York: Abingdon Press, 1947), p. 162: "They [the prophets] viewed sin as being primarily *rebellion* against God" (italics in original).

25. Saint Augustine, *The City of God*, 14. 28. I have followed Henri Marrou's translation (in *Saint Augustine and His Influence through the Ages* [New York: Harper and Row, 1957]).

26. John Burnaby, *Amor dei: A Study of the Religion of St. Augustine* (London: Hodder and Stoughton, 1938), p. 261.

27. Jung, *Psychology and Religion*, p. 315.

28. Heschel, *Prophets*, p. 10.

29. Ibid., pp. 439–40.

30. The presence of this motif has of course been noted before. See, for in-

stance, Drake, *Flannery O'Connor*, esp. pp. 17, 34; Louise Y. Gossett, *Violence in Recent Southern Fiction* (Durham, N.C.: Duke University Press, 1965), p. 76; Walters, *Flannery O'Connor*, pp. 24, 90; Browning, *Flannery O'Connor*, pp. 12, 87.

31. Underhill, *Mysticism*, p. 135.
32. Saint Augustine, *Confessions*, p. 65. See also pp. 70, 123.
33. I have discussed this aspect of the story at greater length in "The Mythic Dimensions of Flannery O'Connor's 'Greenleaf,'" *Studies in Short Fiction* 5 (1968): 317–30. For the mystics' use of the language and imagery of love, see Underhill, *Mysticism*, pp. 136–40, 196, 291–93, 343–45, 356.
34. Quoted in White, *God and the Unconscious*, p. 126.
35. Heschel, *Prophets*, p. 179.
36. Something of the tenor of O'Connor's work is captured by the observation of John L. McKenzie in *The Two-Edged Sword* (Milwaukee: Bruce, 1956), p. 188: "When one has read the history of the Hebrews, one reflects that the impact of God upon human life is indeed a violent impact. . . . Christians who forget that Jesus said that He came to bring not peace but a sword are sometimes mildly scandalized at the tone of much Old Testament history and prophecy; they are innocent souls who have little idea of the manner in which men receive God."
37. Heschel, *Prophets*, p. 7.
38. Cited in T. Gossett, "Flannery O'Connor on Her Fiction," p. 40.
39. Quoted in Feeley, *Flannery O'Connor*, p. 165.
40. Marrou, *St. Augustine*, p. 73.
41. William James, *The Varieties of Religious Experience* (New York: Random House, n.d.), pp. 163, 172, 242, 249.
42. Unpublished manuscript, O'Connor Collection.
43. Underhill, *Mysticism*, pp. 176–77.
44. Heschel, *Prophets*, p. 433.
45. Underhill, *Mysticism*, p. 177.
46. Martin Buber, *Eclipse of God* (New York: Harper and Row, 1957), p. 73.

Bibliography

Readers who wish a more complete listing of writings on O'Connor are referred to Robert E. Golden's annotated bibliography in Robert E. Golden and Mary C. Sullivan, *Flannery O'Connor and Caroline Gordon: A Reference Guide* (Boston: G. K. Hall, 1977). Although Golden's listings go up to 1976, he does not claim completeness after 1973; for the ensuing years the most reliable guides are the annual bibliographies of *PMLA*.

The asterisks below designate works that were in O'Connor's personal library, now a part of the Flannery O'Connor Collection at Georgia College, Milledgeville.

Aquinas, Thomas.* *Truth* [*De veritate*]. Translated by Robert W. Mulligan. Chicago: Regnery, 1952–54.

Asals, Frederick. "The Mythic Dimensions of Flannery O'Connor's 'Greenleaf.'" *Studies in Short Fiction* 5 (1968): 317–30.

———. "The Road to *Wise Blood*." *Renascence* 21 (1969): 181–94.

Auden, W. H. "Religion and the Intellectuals." *Partisan Review* 17 (1950): 120–28.

Augustine.* *The Confessions*. Translated by F. J. Sheed. New York: Sheed and Ward, 1943.

Baumbach, Jonathan. *The Landscape of Nightmare*. New York: New York University Press, 1965.

Becker, Ernest. *The Denial of Death*. New York: Free Press, 1973.

Bentley, Eric, ed. *Let's Get a Divorce! and Other Plays*. New York: Hill and Wang, 1957.

———. *The Life of the Drama*. New York: Atheneum, 1970.

Bousset, W. *The Antichrist Legend*. Translated by A. H. Keane. London: Hutchinson, 1896.

Brooks, Peter. *The Melodramatic Imagination*. New Haven, Conn.: Yale University Press, 1976.

Browning, Preston M., Jr. *Flannery O'Connor*. Carbondale: Southern Illinois University Press, 1974.

Buber, Martin.* *Eclipse of God*. New York: Harper and Row, 1957.

Burnaby, John. *Amor dei: A Study of the Religion of St. Augustine*. London: Hodder and Stoughton, 1938.

Burns, Stuart L. "The Evolution of *Wise Blood*." *Modern Fiction Studies* 16 (1970): 147–62.

———. "Flannery O'Connor's Literary Apprenticeship." *Renascence* 22 (1969): 3–16.

———. "Flannery O'Connor's *The Violent Bear It Away*: Apotheosis in Failure." *Sewanee Review* 76 (1968): 319–36.

———. " 'Torn by the Lord's Eye': Flannery O'Connor's Use of Sun Imagery." *Twentieth Century Literature* 13 (1967): 154–66.

Byrd, Turner F. "Ironic Dimension in Flannery O'Connor's 'The Artificial Nigger.'" *Mississippi Quarterly* 21 (1968): 243–51.

Campbell, Joseph. *The Hero with a Thousand Faces*. New York: Meridian, 1956.

Camus, Albert. *The Myth of Sisyphus and Other Essays*. Translated by Justin O'Brien. New York: Random House, 1959.

———. *The Rebel*. Translated by Anthony Bower. New York: Random House, 1956.

Chase, Richard.* *The American Novel and Its Tradition*. New York: Doubleday, 1957.

Cheney, Brainard. "Flannery O'Connor's Campaign for Her Country." *Sewanee Review* 72 (1964). Reprinted in *Flannery O'Connor*, edited by Robert Reiter. St. Louis: B. Herder, 1968.

Collins, James. "The Fashionableness of Kierkegaard." *Thought* 21 (1947): 211–15.

D'Arcy, Martin C.* *The Mind and Heart of Love*. New York: Henry Holt, 1947.

Doxey, William S. "A Dissenting Opinion of Flannery O'Connor's 'A Good Man Is Hard to Find.'" *Studies in Short Fiction* 10 (1973): 199–204.

Drake, Robert. *Flannery O'Connor: A Critical Essay*. Grand Rapids, Mich.: William B. Eerdmans, 1966.

Driskell, Leon V., and Brittain, Joan T. *The Eternal Crossroads: The Art of Flannery O'Connor*. Lexington: University of Kentucky Press, 1971.

Eggenschwiler, David. *The Christian Humanism of Flannery O'Connor*. Detroit: Wayne State University Press, 1972.

Esprit 8 (Winter 1964). [O'Connor memorial issue.]

Feeley, Kathleen. *Flannery O'Connor: Voice of the Peacock*. New Brunswick, N.J.: Rutgers University Press, 1972.

Fitzgerald, Robert. Introduction to *Everything That Rises Must Converge*, by Flannery O'Connor. New York: Farrar, Straus and Giroux, 1965.

Freud, Sigmund. *Collected Papers*. Vol. 4. New York: Basic Books, 1959.

Friedman, Melvin J., and Lawson, Lewis A., eds. *The Added Dimension: The Art and Mind of Flannery O'Connor*. New York: Fordham University Press, 1966.

Frye, Northrop. *Anatomy of Criticism*. Princeton, N.J.: Princeton University Press, 1957.

———. *The Secular Scripture*. Cambridge, Mass.: Harvard University Press, 1976.

Fugina, Katherine; Rivard, Faye; and Sieh, Margaret. "An Interview with Flannery O'Connor." *Censer*, Fall 1960, pp. 53–56.

Gordon, Caroline. "Flannery O'Connor's *Wise Blood*." *Critique* 2 (1958): 3–10.

Gossett, Louise Y. *Violence in Recent Southern Fiction*. Durham, N.C.: Duke University Press, 1965.

Gossett, Thomas F. "Flannery O'Connor on Her Fiction." *Southwest Review* 59 (1974): 34–42.

Green, James L. "Enoch Emery and His Biblical Namesakes in *Wise Blood*." *Studies in Short Fiction* 10 (1973): 417–19.

Greene, Marjorie. "Kierkegaard: The Philosophy." *Kenyon Review* 9 (1947): 48–69.

———. "L'Homme est une passion inutile: Sartre and Heidegger." *Kenyon Review* 9 (1947): 168–85.

Guerard, Albert J., ed. *Stories of the Double*. Philadelphia: J. B. Lippincott, 1967.

Hawkes, John. "Flannery O'Connor's Devil." *Sewanee Review* 70 (1962). Reprinted in *Flannery O'Connor*, edited by Robert Reiter. St. Louis: B. Herder, 1968.

Hays, Peter L. "Dante, Tobit, and 'The Artificial Nigger.'" *Studies in Short Fiction* 5 (1968): 263–68.

Hendin, Josephine. *The World of Flannery O'Connor*. Bloomington: Indiana University Press, 1970.

Heschel, Abraham J. *The Prophets*. New York: Harper and Row, 1962.

Hirsch, David H. "The Pit and the Apocalypse." *Sewanee Review* 76 (1968): 632–52.

Hoyt, Charles Alva, ed. *Minor American Novelists*. Carbondale: Southern Illinois University Press, 1970.

Hyatt, J. Philip. *Prophetic Religion*. New York: Abingdon Press, 1947.

Hyman, Stanley Edgar. *Flannery O'Connor*. Minneapolis: University of Minnesota Press, 1966.

James, Henry. *The Art of the Novel*. New York: Scribners, 1934.

James, William.* *The Varieties of Religious Experience*. New York: Random House, n.d.

Jeremy, Sister, C.S.J. "*The Violent Bear It Away:* A Linguistic Education." *Renascence* 17 (1964). Reprinted in *Flannery O'Connor*, edited by Robert Reiter. St. Louis: B. Herder, 1968.

Jung, Carl Gustav. *The Archetypes and the Collective Unconscious*. Translated by R. F. C. Hull. New York: Pantheon, 1959.

―――. *Psychology and Religion: West and East*. Translated by R. F. C. Hull. New York: Pantheon, 1958.

―――. *Symbols of Transformation*. Translated by R. F. C. Hull. New York: Pantheon, 1956.

―――. *Two Essays in Analytical Psychology*. Translated by R. F. C. Hull. New York: Meridian, 1956.

Katz, Claire. "Flannery O'Connor's Rage of Vision." *American Literature* 46 (1974–75): 54–67.

Kayser, Wolfgang. *The Grotesque in Art and Literature*. Translated by Ulrich Weisstein. New York: McGraw-Hill, 1966.

Kazin, Alfred. *Bright Book of Life*. Boston: Atlantic, Little, Brown, 1973.

Keppler, C. F. *The Literature of the Second Self*. Tucson: University of Arizona Press, 1972.

Kierkegaard, Søren. *The Concept of Dread*. Translated by Walter Lowrie. Princeton, N.J.: Princeton University Press, 1944.

―――. *The Sickness unto Death*. Translated by Walter Lowrie. Princeton, N.J.: Princeton University Press, 1941.

Lawson, Lewis A. "Flannery O'Connor and the Grotesque: *Wise Blood*." *Renascence* 17 (1965). Reprinted in *Flannery O'Connor*, edited by Robert Reiter. St. Louis: B. Herder, 1968.

Malin, Irving. *New American Gothic*. Carbondale: Southern Illinois University Press, 1962.

Maritain, Jacques.* *Art and Scholasticism*. Translated by J. F. Scanlan. London: Sheed and Ward, 1930.

―――. *Creative Intuition in Art and Poetry*. New York: Meridian, 1955.

―――. *The Dream of Descartes*. Translated by Mabelle L. Andison. New York: Philosophical Library, 1944.

―――. "From Existential Existentialism to Academic Existentialism." *Sewanee Review* 56 (1948): 210–29.

Marrou, Henri. *St. Augustine and His Influence through the Ages*. New York: Harper and Row, 1957.

Martin, Carter W. "Flannery O'Connor's Early Fiction." *Southern Humanities Review* 7 (1973): 210–14.

———. *The True Country: Themes in the Fiction of Flannery O'Connor.* Nashville: Vanderbilt University Press, 1969.

Martin, Jay, ed. *Nathanael West: A Collection of Critical Essays.* Englewood Cliffs, N.J.: Prentice-Hall, 1971.

May, John R. *The Pruning Word: The Parables of Flannery O'Connor.* Notre Dame, Ind.: University of Notre Dame Press, 1976.

———. *Toward a New Earth: Apocalypse in the American Novel.* Notre Dame, Ind.: University of Notre Dame Press, 1972.

McKenzie, John L. *The Roman Catholic Church.* New York: Holt, Rinehart and Winston, 1969.

———.* *The Two-Edged Sword.* Milwaukee: Bruce, 1956.

Meaders, Margaret Inman. "Flannery O'Connor: 'Literary Witch.'" *Colorado Quarterly* 10 (1961–62): 377–86.

Milder, Robert. "The Protestantism of Flannery O'Connor." *Southern Review* 11 (1975): 802–19.

Milledgeville, Ga. Georgia College. Flannery O'Connor Collection.

Millichap, Joseph R. "The Pauline 'Old Man' in Flannery O'Connor's 'The Comforts of Home.'" *Studies in Short Fiction* 11 (1974): 96–99.

Mitchell, Walter, and the Carisbrooke Dominicans, trans.* *Christian Asceticism and Modern Man.* London: Philosophical Library, 1955.

Montgomery, Marion. "Vision and the Eye for Detail in Poe and O'Connor." *Flannery O'Connor Bulletin* 6 (1977): 36–46.

Muller, Gilbert H. "The City of Woe: Flannery O'Connor's Dantean Vision." *Georgia Review* 23 (1969): 206–13.

———. *Nightmares and Visions: Flannery O'Connor and the Catholic Grotesque.* Athens: University of Georgia Press, 1972.

Mullins, C. Ross, Jr. "Flannery O'Connor: An Interview." *Jubilee* 11 (June 1963): 33–35.

Newman, John Henry Cardinal.* *Apologia pro vita sua.* Edited by C. F. Harrold. London: Longmans, Green, 1947.

Oates, Joyce Carol. *New Heaven, New Earth.* New York: Vanguard Press, 1974.

O'Connor, Flannery. Comment on *The Phenomenon of Man. American Scholar* 30 (1961): 618.

———. *The Complete Stories.* New York: Farrar, Straus and Giroux, 1971.

———. *Everything That Rises Must Converge.* New York: Farrar, Straus and Giroux, 1965.

———. *A Good Man Is Hard to Find and Other Stories.* New York: Harcourt, Brace and World, 1955.

――――. *The Habit of Being*. Edited by Sally Fitzgerald. New York: Farrar, Straus and Giroux, 1979.

――――. *Mystery and Manners*. Edited by Sally Fitzgerald and Robert Fitzgerald. New York: Farrar, Straus and Giroux, 1969.

――――. Comment in "A Short Story Symposium." *Esprit* 3 (Winter 1979): 10.

――――. "The Train." *Sewanee Review* 56 (1948): 261–71.

――――. *The Violent Bear It Away*. New York: Farrar, Straus and Cudahy, 1960.

――――. *Wise Blood*. New York: Farrar, Straus and Cudahy, 1962.

Orvell, Miles. *Invisible Parade: The Fiction of Flannery O'Connor*. Philadelphia: Temple University Press, 1972.

Otto, Rudolf. *The Idea of the Holy*. Translated by John W. Harvey. New York: Oxford University Press, 1958.

Pascal, Blaise.* *Pensées*. Translated by W. F. Trotter. New York: Dutton, 1958.

Poe, Edgar Allan. *The Complete Tales and Poems*. New York: Random House, 1938.

Quinn, Sister M. Bernetta. "Flannery O'Connor, A Realist of Distances." In *The Added Dimension: The Art and Mind of Flannery O'Connor*, edited by Melvin J. Friedman and Lewis A. Lawson. New York: Fordham University Press, 1966.

Rank, Otto. *Beyond Psychology*. New York: Dover, 1958.

Rechnitz, Robert M. "Passionate Pilgrim: Flannery O'Connor's *Wise Blood*." *Georgia Review* 19 (1965): 310–16.

Reiter, Robert, ed. *Flannery O'Connor*. St. Louis: B. Herder, 1968.

Rogers, Robert. *A Psychological Study of the Double in Literature*. Detroit: Wayne State University Press, 1970.

Rosenfield, Claire. "The Shadow Within: The Conscious and Unconscious Use of the Double." *Daedalus* 92 (1963). Reprinted in *Stories of the Double*, edited by Albert J. Guerard. Philadelphia: J. B. Lippincott, 1967.

Smith, Margaret. *The Way of the Mystics*. London: Sheldon Press, 1976.

Stephens, Martha. *The Question of Flannery O'Connor*. Baton Rouge: Louisiana State University Press, 1973.

Sullivan, Walter. "Flannery O'Connor, Sin, and Grace: *Everything That Rises Must Converge*." *Hollins Critic* 2 (September 1965): 1–8, 10.

Sypher, Wylie, ed. *Comedy*. New York: Doubleday, 1956.

Tate, Allen. *Poems 1922–1947*. New York: Swallow Press, 1948.

Tate, James O. "Faith and Fiction: Flannery O'Connor and the Problem of Belief." *Flannery O'Connor Bulletin* 5 (1976): 105–11.

Thurston, Herbert.* *The Physical Phenomena of Mysticism*. London: Burns, Oates, 1952.

Trowbridge, Clinton W. "The Symbolic Vision of Flannery O'Connor: Patterns of Imagery in *The Violent Bear It Away.*" *Sewanee Review* 76 (1968): 298–318.

Tymms, Ralph. *Doubles in Literary Psychology.* Cambridge:Bowes and Bowes, 1949.

Underhill, Evelyn.* *Mysticism.* New York:Meridian, 1955.

Walters, Dorothy. *Flannery O'Connor.* New York:Twayne, 1973.

White, Victor.* *God and the Unconscious.* New York:Meridian, 1952.

Yanitelli, Victor R. "Types of Existentialism." *Thought* 24 (1949):495–508.

Index